RIVIERA LIGURE

ITALY BIKE HOTELS

LIGURIA BIKE HOTELS

www.liguriabikehotels.it · info@liguriabikehotels.it

Hotel Florenz
Finale Ligure · Tel. 019/695667
www.florenzhotel.com

Hotel Maria Nella
Bardineto · Tel. 019/7907017
www.marianella.net

Hotel Medusa
Finale Ligure · Tel. 019/692545
www.medusahotel.it

Nyala Suite Hotel
Sanremo · Tel. 0184/667668
www.nyalahotel.com

Hotel Villa Ida
Laigueglia · Tel. 0182/690042
www.villaida.it

Hotel Zurigo
Varazze · Tel. 019/932618
www.hotelzurigo.it

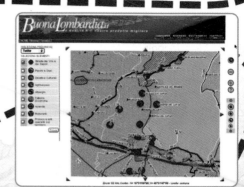

Italy by Bike

105 Tours from the Alps to Sicily

TOURING CLUB OF ITALY

Touring Club Italiano
President and Chairman: *Roberto Ruozi*
General Manager: *Guido Venturini*

Touring Editore
Managing Director: *Guido Venturini*
General Manager: *Alfieri Lorenzon*
Editorial Manager: *Michele D'Innella*

International Department
Fabio Pittella
fabio.pittella@touringclub.it

Senior Editor: *Ornella Pavone*
Texts and pictures: *Enrico Caracciolo*
Maps: *Studio Aguilar, Milano*
Translation: *Edicomma, Milano*
          Anthony Rocco
Cover picture: *Darjl Benson/Zefa*

Advertising Manager: *Claudio Bettinelli*
Local Advertising: *Progetto*
www.progettosrl.it - info@progettosrl.it

Printing: *Grafiche Mazzucchelli, Settimo Milanese (MI)*
Binding: *Legatoria Torriani, Cologno Monzese (MI)*

Distribution:
USA/CAN - Publishing Group West
UK/Ireland - Portfolio Book
NL - Nilsson e Lamm

Touring Club Italiano, corso Italia 10, 20122 Milano
www.touringclub.it

© 2004 Touring Editore - Milano
Code: K7A00
ISBN 88 365 2937 2
Printed in February 2004

Summary

A guide for every
cycle tourist

Cycle tourism is no longer a fad for some lone traveler seeking solitary adventures along the trails of the globe. Many have discovered that a bicycle is the perfect vehicle for people who consider journeys an experience inspired by slow movement. The full immersion in Nature, the opportunity to live the territory without being shut inside a compartment and, last but not least, the silent engine humming inside your legs.

A cycling holiday is virtually a journey that takes you back in time to childhood. It's an opportunity to have fun all day long in the open air and feel the experience that modern-day traveling is genetically changing. A cycling holiday, or even a mere outing, has the power of hugely expanding time-space dimensions and enhancing your spiritual side.

There's no need to be a mile-hungry super-athlete to go on a cycling holiday: it just boils down to understanding the importance of active holidays, or what English-speaking people call outdoor living. Cycle tourism has picked up a frantic pace over the past ten years. Spearheading this phenomenon were the travelers in search of dreams and adventure, the inventors of a system of travel which, by using such a simple vehicle as a bicycle, offers a vivid awareness of the territory and of the road too, which is no longer considered a mere blacktop to clock up kilometers on.

The Old Continent has roads and locations that seem especially made for cycle tourists. Most of all, you can easily find made-to-measure facilities and cycling lanes to experience a cycling holiday.

What about good old Italy? Italy doesn't seem to be the ideal country for bicycle riders. It has longstanding traditions in this sport, but they mainly regard racing epics. Bicycles, as a means of transportation, became particularly important in the immediate post-war years of World War II to the Economic Boom, in areas where Mother Nature had not given birth to mountains. But the curled-up shape of our Peninsula presents heights that are not always simple. For incidental reasons of space, Italy will never have a road system such as in the Netherlands, where cycling lanes are found virtually everywhere. However, its network of routes offers cycle tourists golden opportunities. This guide intends to provide readers with an understanding of the territory, and is not restricted only to the rideable itineraries in areas where cyclists don't have to challenge the force of gravity.

The guide illustrates 105 itineraries, crossing all the regions of Italy, and split up into three levels of difficulty: easy, average, hard.

The easy itineraries (46) are routes accessible to everyone, from families with children along to the recreational riders. The average ones (41) do not require special training, just legs willing to pedal and not averse to changing gradients.

A small section is dedicated to the hard itineraries (18) that require good basic practice and are therefore designed for cycle tourists who are accustomed to using a bicycle rather often and are willing to spare some effort to reach really enchanting places.

The guide illustrates the itineraries covered either on asphalt or unsurfaced roads, as well as most of the mixed routes, for a total distance of 4,540 kilometers.

Almost all itineraries have a circular layout, with starting point and destination based at the same location, while 24 have a linear pattern, which means returning to the starting point by integrated transport (14 by train, 7 by ship or ferry, 2 by bus, 1 by car).

39 itineraries run through protected territories, while the others discover areas crossed by quiet roads and, when possible, you can have the chance of reaching the starting point by train.

These are all daily routes, except for three journeys that have to be covered in stages: the Murradweg cycling track in Austria, the Tirreno-Adriatico across Tuscany, Umbria and Marche, and the mountain bike trip on the Asiago Plateau.

The guide is a useful traveling tool that offers a detailed description of each itinerary's route, plus a map of the itinerary and a range of information and useful contacts regarding that particular area.

THE TWO BORDER CROSSINGS

Of these 105 itineraries, 2 cross the border but are easily reached. One is the wonderful **ride in Austria along the River Mur**, from the sources near the Alti Tauri up to the borderline with Slovenia, crossing the breadth and length of Styria. The other border crossing runs in **Switzerland**, an unforgettable trip to the eternal ices of the Grigioni, switching from a bicycle ride to a train trip on the spectacular Bernina Express.

Cycle tourism:
choosing the bicycle

The ideal bicycle is the one that best fits the type of terrain and holiday or journey you're about to embark on. There are four most common types of bikes: road bike, mountain bike, all-terrain and city bike.

REGULAR BICYCLE CHECKS

Bicycle checks can be made personally, while some operations are better left to your trusted mechanic. Bicycles must be fully checked on a yearly basis. These are the parts to control:

Bolts
Check the conditions and tightness of every bolt and give a good tightening to the loose ones.

Gear and brake cables
Check the smoothness inside the housings; it worsens as time goes by; you should change worn out housings and cables.

Tires
Change them whenever the tread is worn and the rubber shows the first lateral cracks.

Rims
Control the balancing: by spinning them, check that the distance between rim and brake pad remains constant (without jerks). Leave the balancing to expert hands.

Brake shoes
Check that the brake shoes are centered to the rim. Replace them before they're too worn out.

Hubs
They may be worn or loose: keep the wheel lifted off the ground and try

Road bike
By definition a sports vehicle, the one racers use, designed for riders who adore the competitive edge on routes running entirely on smooth roads.
Technical features: frame in aluminum, steel, carbon, titanium, and lately also in magnesium. 28-inch wheels with thin slick tires. The components generally include a gear shift with two front gears and an 8-10 speed rear cog set. The handlebar folder is bent to allow an aerodynamic position.
This vehicle suits cyclists who are thrilled by the technical features of routes, meaning trajectories, climbs, descents and every detail that enhances the qualities of this kind of bicycle. The road bike is a technical vehicle that is refined, light and resistant, sensitive to the road, all in all, a "precision watch" and a cult object.

Mountain bike
Designed for off-road cycling on rugged terrain, the "fat-wheeled" bicycle offers an extensive range of gears that allows you to challenge even steep-sloped roads and trails.
Technical features: frame in steel, aluminum, titanium or mixed materials, a compact and compressed geometry, a "hardtail" system (in front of the suspension fork), or full suspension, also involving the rear triangle (designed for very winding, especially downhill routes). 26-inch wheels with knobby tires capable of assuring good grip

even on the bumpiest of terrains. 21 to 27-speed gear shift with triple front gear and the chance to use reduction gears: with a full revolution of the pedal, the wheel covers less than a revolution.

Ideal vehicle on mule tracks, pathways and tracks with devious surface and rocks, dirt and considerable slopes too.

By replacing the broad-profiled knobbies with slicks, your mountain bike turns into a good two-wheeler for on-road touring.

The all-terrain or hybrid

Hailed as the queen bicycle by cycle tourists, a perfect blend between mountain bike and road bike. Reliable and tough, with mechanics and almost all components usually seen on mountain bikes.

Technical features: the steel or aluminum frame is less compressed, the position on the saddle less aggressive and more relaxed than on a mountain bike. The gear shift includes a triple front gear with a 7-9 speed freewheel. As far as the wheels and the handlebar are concerned, there are no specific rules: it can either mount 28 or 26-inch wheels, depending on its on or off-road use, and can have either straight-across flat handlebars as on the mountain bike or cruiser bars curving back toward the rider as on a road bike.

The all-terrain does not achieve the performances of a road bike (light and smooth) or of a mountain bike (maximum performance on bumpy stretches), but is definitely the most versatile bicycle that does well either on paved or dirt roads. Excellent vehicle for daily outings and long-term trips, the all-terrain is more touring and less "urban" than the city bike, generally assembled with medium-low series components.

City bike

Also known as "Dutch" bike. Technically speaking, this bike does not feature refined qualities, although it may sport a very elegant look. The gear shift is unnecessary, so it may be used for "serious" cycle tourism on level, not too lengthy roads.

The more up-right seated position on the bike seems very comfortable, but is not suitable for lengthy rides on the saddle: the more outstretched position is physiologically more balanced, distributing part of the weight on the shoulders and arms, without burdening the lumbar region only.

to move the rim sideways. Should you feel even a slight "wobble", it would be wise to pay a visit to your mechanic.

Headset
Stand astride the bike with feet on the ground, keep the front wheel braked; shift the handlebar with your arms repeatedly back and forth. If you feel a slight wobble or snap inside the steerer tube, the best thing to do is tighten it.

Bottom bracket
Core of the bicycle around which the pedal axle revolves. Try moving the pedals sideways (not with a rotary motion): if you should feel a slight wobble, fix it as soon as you can.

READY FOR NORMAL FIXES

Your emergency bag should always carry:
- a kit for flats, with patches, glue, glass paper
- 1 inner tube
- levers to take off the tires
- pump
- 8", 10" and 15" spanners (for pedals)
- pincers
- small crosshead screwdriver
- gear shift and brake cables.

ACCESSORIES

Lights
There are various brands of front and tail lights sold today, which fit easily on the bicycle and work with batteries. Very effective are the flashing tail lights.

Cyclecomputer
You can buy at a fairly competitive price a cyclecomputer with the following functions: partial distance, total distance, current speed, average/maximum speed, clock and actual riding time.

Mudguards
When cycling on wet roads, they're a very handy accessory. The best solution are plastic mudguards, easily mountable; no bolts or screws required.

Bar ends
Required for flat bars found on mountain bikes, as they allow you to change the position of your hands.

Racks
Required to attach loaded bags. The best types are made in aluminum. For long journeys, besides the rear-mounted racks, you can also mount them at the front (best choice are the low ones like the low rider to the fork). The bicycle frame must be arranged with eyelets and mounting holes for the attachment.

Bags
Two at the back and one on the handlebar to carry personal belongings. Two at the front for long journeys. You fix them to the racks and the heavier objects are placed at the bottom. If not waterproof, it would be wise to store the load in plastic bags.

Choosing clothes

When cycling, even for touring purposes, technical apparel is required, especially when the cyclist's health is concerned.

For short outings on city bikes, there's no need to don technical garments. A different case altogether when the outings involve physical exercise. Here below is a list of apparel every cycle tourist should always keep ready in the closet.

Helmet. This is a very important feature: let's hope you never need it, but if you should, not having it on could mean fatal consequences. Just a touch of inattention is needed and falling down at 10 km per hour may prove to be very dangerous. Helmets sold nowadays have reached excellent fitting standards, and are well ventilated and extremely light.

Gloves. They safeguard your hands against likely irritation from the constant contact with the handlebar, and are an important protection against grazes in case of falls.

Eyewear. Light and shatterproof. Cycling means continuous exposure to atmospheric agents: sun rays, and especially headwinds. They are a good protection against those perky insects.

Shorts. Fitted with synthetic chamois to protect the perineum, which is the most strained area, they guarantee proper freedom of movement. Cold weather doesn't help muscles, so apart from the summer period, a good basic rule is to cover your legs with long pants.

Undershirt. A mesh undershirt will do nicely. It prevents the outward part to absorb sweat, thus avoiding possible chill attacks.

Jersey. Made in light and synthetic fabric that dries up quickly in case of rain or heavy perspiration.

Windcheaters. A breathable wind repeller such as Windtex or Windstopper is required. There are thin, lightweight and microporous middle layers inside other fabrics that allow body perspiration to escape and also to block wind.

Waterproof jacket. A light waterproof jacket will do, not too bulky, easily carryable in a pocket. Excellent but fairly expensive are the Gore-Tex products, a membrane that blocks water and is breathable.

Good cycling tips

Embarking on a cycle journey or a holiday means sporting a good physical shape. You don't need to practice as cycling professionals do. In our case, practice basically means getting used to staying on a saddle. So it would just take some cycling during the weekends, switching from short to just a little longer outings.

Practicing means developing staying power, in other words, the ability to deliver a cadence that is more prolonged than powerful. The thrust must be agile, shifting to low gears that allow what is called "spinning" or "pedaling in circles", whilst crushing the pedals produces the "mashing" effect.

These rules also apply in order to properly pedal during a journey or a daily outing. In fact, cycling implies far-sighted administration of one's energy which, of course, eventually runs out. Therefore, your momentum must be constant, avoiding sudden spurts and sprints.

Your mental approach is basic too, meaning that, at times, it's more a matter of mind than body. Adjusting to environmental conditions is one of the cycle tourist's most precious qualities.

Uphill, the rookie cycle tourist makes a series of mistakes that can be avoided, like cycling hard and fast to "shorten" fatigue. This is just an illusion that saps the energy out beforehand.

Even despair at the bottom of a long uphill climb frequently occurs. Another foe awaiting you, probably the worst for cyclists, is wind, invisible, yet extremely impacting and difficult to battle against, especially mentally.

Under these circumstances, you must display strength, which doesn't mean flaunting strong muscles, but facing the extremely hostile conditions with peace of mind. Engage the

SHOES AND PEDALS

The best system features a mechanism that clips the shoe into the pedal, guaranteeing a "spinning" thrust that optimizes performance.

Clipping and unclipping is simple and functional: only a light pressure on the pedal to clip is required and a small sideways movement of the foot to unclip. In case of falls, the shoe automatically clips itself off the pedal.

proper gear, the one that gives you an agile and spinning thrust (even though muscles must be sometimes used when riding uphill) and pedal at a steady pace. The secret of a cycle tourist is serenity. Overanxious people will never become good cycle tourists.

How to feed the cyclist's "engine"

Cycling is basically an aerobic activity that entails an extended drain of energy, so it's vital to provide your engine with the right amount and quality of fuel. The cyclist's engine burns up, in different stages, sugars, proteins and fat that must always be reloaded after a day's cycling.

A particularly important feature when riding is nutrition. One basic principle must be followed in this sense: when riding, never wait for thirst or hunger to attack; by the time the first symptoms engulf you, it's too late. Absorbing liquids when salts and sugars in your body have already dropped below danger levels is pointless; your muscles will never manage to metabolize the conversion in fresh energy since they are already stressed and fatigued by a grueling replenishing action.

So Rule No. 1 says: intake liquids regularly once every 15-20 minutes, and absorb easily digestible energy solids in small quantities, but frequently, once every 40 or 50 minutes.

In any case, one thing to consider is the fact that salts must be reintegrated in the closing stage and especially after riding, while sugars must be quickly assimilated, trying not to overdo things as you may easily get the boomerang effect with hypoglycemic attacks that "cut" your legs.

Nutrition when riding is very important and prevents the ill-famed "crack-ups" or hunger crises that appear most of the times unexpectedly and cause a sense of emptiness with legs turning to mush, which is virtually impossible to fight. The experience is rather nasty. Cyclists have a way of saying it that goes straight to the point: "hitting the bonk" or "hitting the wall".

FILLING YOUR WATER FLASK

Nowadays it's easy to find replacement drinks to recover mineral salts, and energy drinks too. They are all good remedies, although no energy bombs are needed for cycle tourists. Highly recommended is the famous "weak tea" enriched with honey. Your jersey pockets should never be empty: a fruit always at hand, apple or banana, is the proper solution. As for energy bars, we recommend the dried fruit and cereal-based brands.

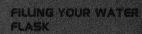

Cycling
with children

Short outings or long trips: everything's possible with kids along too. The magic word is: Organisation. Rely basically on two essentials: plan a vacation, trying to work out the ideal balance between children's needs and your expectations; extend time without making big plans and manage your energy well. Don't burn up all of your strength on the riding side, because the uphill part of the job comes after the pedaling, when you have to take care of the kid-captains during the final part of the day.

You don't need to be an athlete, just opt for active holidays. The philosophy of family cycle journeys is based on a "take it easy" approach, which becomes "the" rule especially when children come along.

The main requirement, in this particular case, is safety when choosing routes and vehicles: your best choice would be by-roads and quiet roads, better yet if ridable. Not so easy to find throughout Italy, whereas in many European countries, cycling trips can be planned on cycle lanes.

As far as means and tools of transport are concerned, there are three solutions: baby's seat, trailer and trailer-bike. The **baby's seat** is fitted at the back of the frame (sometimes at the front) and the more interesting models include a shock absorption system as well as an adjustable backrest. Safety belts and helmets should always be a must have. The seat is ideal for short stretches and can be used when the child is able to sit comfortably (from 1 or 2 years old onwards).

For outings and/or journeys, the **trailer** is an extraordinary device: it is fitted to the frame and does not impact at all on bicycle manoeuvrability. It's extremely comfortable for the passenger, who considers it a kind of traveling home; it's usually equipped with waterproof canopy and is quite roomy to load the child's gear. Ideal for children from 8 months to 4 years old. Just one snag: the best models are expensive but can be rented in some European countries.

Third and last possibility, the **trailer-bike**, which is fitted to the frame, a kind of semi-bicycle with one wheel (rear), which allows children to pedal too: it's the natural evolution from the trailer to the very first bike to travel with Mum and Dad.

WEB SITE FOR THOSE WHO WISH TO CYCLE WITH CHILDREN

http://www.fiab-onlus.it/andare/bambini.htm

The web site of the Amici della Bicicletta Federation offers many good tips, stories, suggestions and very useful links. Check it out.

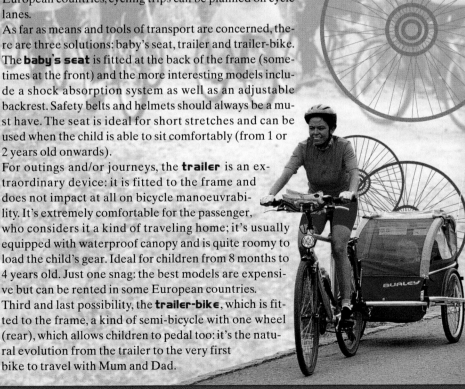

Understanding the guide

The guide presents 105 cycle tourism itineraries. One hundred routes, split up by region, can be covered in a day; two, *Plateau of the 7 Towns - Asiago - Stage trip by mountain bike* and *Tuscany/Umbria/Marche - From the Tyrrhenian to the Adriatic*, are real journeys crossing a rather vast territory requiring several days' cycling. Lastly, two itineraries on the other side of the Alps, *Austria /Styria - The Mur cycle lane* and *Switzerland /The Poschiavo Valley - The Bernina Express*, recommended for its proximity to the Italian border and for the amenity of the cycling track.

General map of Italy
Pages 14 and 15 illustrate the areas covered by the 105 itineraries described in the guide.

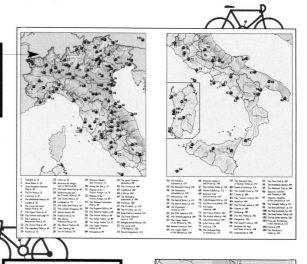

- 🔴 Starting point and destination
- 🔴 Stage point
- Information office
- Railway station
- Castle
- Tower
- Church
- Museum
- Monastery, abbey
- Farm
- Manor, palace, park
- Refuge
- Panorama
- Spring
- Relics, ruins
- Cave
- Beach
- Mechanic
- Wine-tasting cellars

Legend
Along the route of every itinerary, special signs allow cyclists to recognize the most interesting locations on the route.

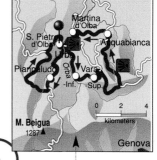

Layout of itinerary
The road map of each specific area illustrates the route of that specific itinerary, enriched with special symbols with legend appearing on the left.

Technical info

Route

35 Km: Assisi - Costa di Trek - Armenzano - San Giovanni - Collepino - Spello - via degli Ulivi - Assisi. Almost entirely on asphalt road with some dirt stretches. It would be preferable to use a mountain bike to easily cross the more challenging stretches and ride better on the dirt roads.

Difficulty

An itinerary with an average difficulty level; some stretches and the final stretch before Assisi. You don't need specific training, but the itinerary is barred to people who are not used to cycling at all.

Cycling period

All year round, although it may be chilly in the winter months.

Map

Atlante stradale d'Italia, Central volume, 1:200,000, TCI.

Technical assistance

• Testi Cicli, via Trasimeno Ovest 287/289, equipped for cycle touring, home delivery and collection service of rented bikes, cycling road books, guides and tour leaders.

• Battistelli Carlo, via XX settembre 88, Foligno; t. 0742344059. Sale and assistance.

Tourist information

• Azienda Promozione Turistica, piazza del Comune; Assisi, t. 075812534.

Technical info

• For each itinerary, the box provides information on *Route, Difficulty, Cycling period, Map.*
• Useful addresses and telephone numbers appear under the headings: *Technical assistance, Bicycle rental, Tourist information.*
• In Italy, road distances are in kilometers (Km).
Remember: 1 Km = 0.6214 miles.
• To call Italy from abroad, the international code is +39 + phone number.
For example: +39029090443.

Points of Interest

For the more practiced cyclists, or even by car, we suggest a further stretch up to Triora to visit the **Ethnographical and Witchcraft Museum** *(corso Italia 1, t. 018494487). The*

Points of interest

This section describes the artistic, cultural, "culinary or environmental" spots that are worth a detour or a stop along the route.

Symbols

For each itinerary, special symbols describe:

Route pattern:

 Circular, with start and destination based in the same location.

 Linear, with start and destination in different locations. In this case, next to the name of the itinerary appears the best way to get back to the base:

 Bicycle + Train

 Bicycle + Coach

 Bicycle + Ferry boat

Road-bed features:

 Asphalt

 Mixed

 Bumpy

Level of difficulty:

 Easy, for all the family

 Average, for the regular cyclists

 Hard, for the skilled cyclists

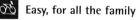
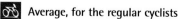

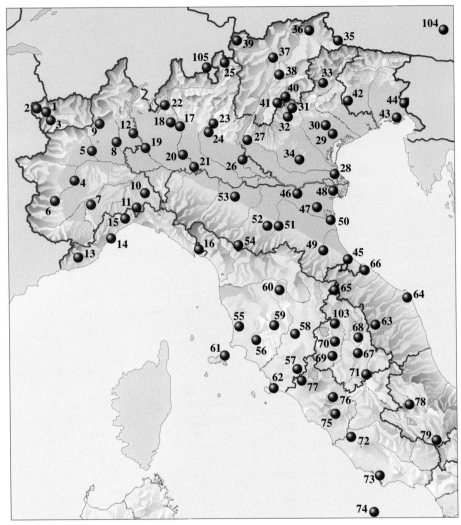

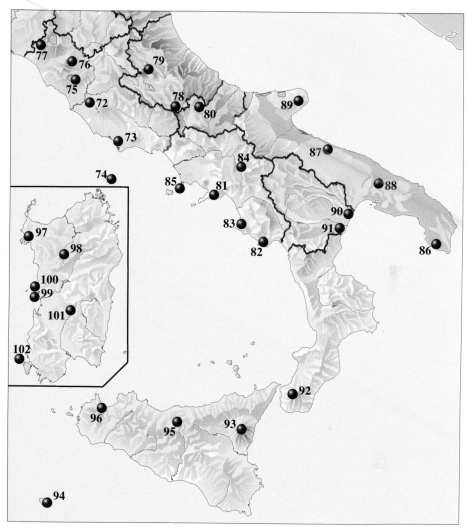

Valle d'Aosta

 Valdigne   **20 Km**

Down in the wine-scented valley

The name Valdigne indicates an area situated in the north-western part of Valle d'Aosta, which stretches from the basin of La Salle and Morgex to Pré-Saint-Didier, reaching Courmayeur, at the foot of the Mont Blanc massif, and Thuile, in the valley heralding the Piccolo San Bernardo pass.

You start your tour from **La Salle**, situated at an altitude of 1,000 m on the sunny south side, famed for its magnificent examples of well-kept rural Alpine architecture. After crossing

the S.S. 26 main road, ride up towards the hamlet of Chabodey. Continue along a short stretch of asphalt road running under the freeway and, shortly afterwards, take the uphill climb on an unsurfaced road on your right. Turn quickly

right, following a wooden road sign pointing to the hamlet of Tirivel.

From Tirivel, continue your tour towards Morgex (923 m above sea level), lying at the bottom of the basin and surrounded by lush vineyards with white grapes that

Technical info

Route
Approximately 20 Km
(14 Km asphalt,
6 Km unsurfaced):
La Salle - Pont de La Salle - Chabodey - Tirivel - Morgex - Pré-Saint-Didier - Dailley - Villair di Morgex - La Salle.

Difficulty
This is an easy ride, no difficulties and ideal for "family" cycle outings.

Cycling period
From spring through fall.

Map
Monte Bianco e Gran Paradiso, 1:50,000 Kompass.

Technical assistance
• Cicli Benato,

via Lostan 106, Arvier; t. 016599131.
• M.B. Aventure, haml. of Villair 15, La Salle; t. 3472417667.
www.mbaventure.it
Guided tours and cycle tourist information on Valdigne.

Tourist information
• APT Valdigne Mont Blanc, piazzale Monte Bianco 13, Courmayeur; t. 0165842060.
apt.montebianco@psw.it
• Pro Loco La Salle, via Col Serena 13, La Salle; t. 0165861190.

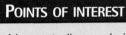

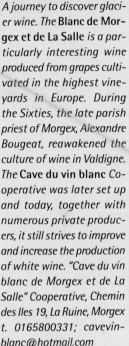

A journey to discover glacier wine. The **Blanc de Morgex et de La Salle** *is a particularly interesting wine produced from grapes cultivated in the highest vineyards in Europe. During the Sixties, the late parish priest of Morgex, Alexandre Bougeat, reawakened the culture of wine in Valdigne. The* **Cave du vin blanc** *Cooperative was later set up and today, together with numerous private producers, it still strives to improve and increase the production of white wine. "Cave du vin blanc de Morgex et de La Salle" Cooperative, Chemin des Iles 19, La Ruine, Morgex t. 0165800331; cavevinblanc@hotmail.com*

produce the famous "Blanc de Morgex et de La Salle", the "highest" cultivated DOC of Italy.

Once at Morgex, reach the bridge over the Dora Baltea, then turn left towards the industrial area and ride upwards and along the hydrographical right side of the Dora. The short stretch of asphalt then switches to unsurfaced road. After crossing a narrow gully, you reach Pré-Saint-Didier (1,000 m above sea level), a small town at the heart of the Valdigne, where you can stop and enjoy one of the most stunning sceneries of the Mont Blanc chain.

At Prè-Saint-Didier, keep right, following the signs pointing to the railroad station, then cross the Dora Baltea. At this stage, ride along one of the most pleasant and fascinating roads of the valley that curls through the aforementioned vineyards.

After passing the "Arc en Ciel" camping site, turn left towards the village of Dailley, then turn quickly right and take the downhill road to Villair di Morgex. Cross the village keeping left, then at this point, climb up along a Romanesque-style cobbled road that crosses vineyards.

During the grape harvest, you can arrange to gather grapes with consortium owners.

The final stretch of the itinerary is a smooth ride up to

La Salle, starting point and destination. After crossing the built-up area, ride down the asphalt road until you reach the main road.

ABOVE, stop near the Dora Baltea. PAGE OPPOSITE, a "casaro" (cheesemaker) at La Salle.

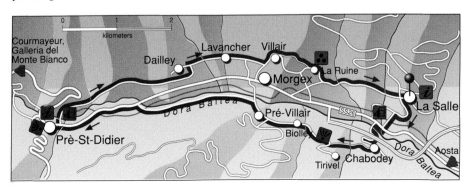

Mont Blanc 30 Km
The loop of Col Chavanne

Here's a great idea for thrill-seeking bikers on mountain roads and tracks at the foot of the Mont Blanc, in full harmony with the wilderness of the high peaks.

The starting point is **La Thuile** (1,441 m), where your ride begins by following the road signs leading to the Colle del Piccolo San Bernardo, on the asphalt main road (S.S. 26) taking you to the pass. Shortly after a slow ride, you reach the built-up area of Pont Serrand (approximately 1,600 m), and after crossing a bridge over the Dora di Verney, turn right along a new asphalt road up on a steep climb crossing the

"alpeggio" (mountain pasture) of Orgere (1,884 m). This first stretch requires quite an effort and rises somewhat reaching the "alpeggio" of Porassey (1,860 m above sea level), where it switches to dirt road. At this point, the route winds down an old military road, which steadily, but surely, climbs up the deep narrow valley of Chavanne, entering high mountain territory. After a few kilometers, the road continues in the valley line up to the Chavanne chalets, while the itinerary turns right uphill on the unsurfaced road that starts the ascent to the Col Chavanne. The track climbs gently upwards, with hairpin

bends, up to the summit of the valley line, reaching the Col Chavanne at 2,603 m. The ridge is breathtaking, with a spectacular view that opens out towards the majestic mountain chain, with the Piramid de Calcaire and Mont Blanc in the foreground. After taking a breather, start riding back down in the Veny Valley. The first part of the downhill

Technical info

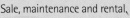

Route
Approximately 30 Km:
La Thuile - Pont Serrand –
Col Chavanne - Veny
Valley - Courmayeur.
Mainly dirt roads.
Bicycle + Bus
From Courmayeur, go
back to La Thuile by bus:
timetables and information
available at the IAT Office
in La Thuile.
Difficulty
No particular technical qualities
required, but the route is rather
challenging due to the 1,200 m
rise, which needs good basic

physical conditions.
You must have a good
mountain bike.
You can also ride the distance
together with guides
(MTB instructors)
from MB Aventure.
Cycling period
From July through
September.
Map
Monte Bianco e Gran Paradiso,
1:50,000, Kompass.
Technical assistance
Only Sky,
Planibel complex,
La Thuile;

t. 0165885307.
Sale, maintenance and rental,
Tourist information
• IAT - Tourist Office,
via Collomb,
La Thuile;
t. 0165884179.
www.lathuile.it
• IAT Courmayeur,
piazzale Monte Bianco 13,
Courmayeur;
t. 0165842060.
apt.montebianco@psw.it
• Associazione Operatori
Turistici del Monte Bianco;
t. 0165842370.
courmayeurincoming@libero.it

POINTS OF INTEREST

The great adventure of the **Grand Tour of Valdigne**, *a three-day wandering trip by mountain bike through the Veny and Ferret valleys. You sleep in mountain refuges and all the logistics is handled by MB Aventure haml. of Villair 15, 11015 La Salle, t. 3472417667; www.mba venture.it, m.pettavino@ tiscali.it, MTB Instructors' Center and specialized operator, offering baggage transport service from one refuge to another. You can also plan your tour accompanied by an expert guide, and receive all the information material you need.*

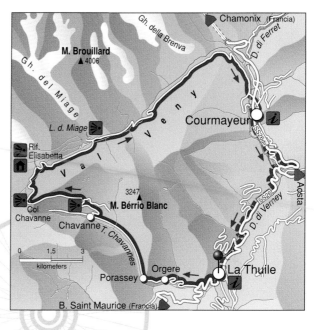

stretch is not rideable, so get off and start pushing your bicycle: a bumpy exposed track drops down to the valley. After several hundred meters, you can get back on your bike and just enjoy the smooth ride down along the path towards the deep narrow valley of Lex Blanche, where the Dora di Verney originates.

Once you reach the deep narrow valley of Lex Blanche, follow the path on your right running smoothly along the Dora, up to the lower "alpeggio" of Lex Blanche. Now gaze to the left and you'll see the Elisabetta ref-

Right, the dirt track of the Col Chavanne. Page opposite, descending the Veny Valley.

uge (2,200 m), an ideal refreshment spot. The road now runs broader and smoother into the heart of the valley. After the downhill stretch, continue on a gently descending road. On your left, you should take the short detour to Lake Miage: leave your bike near the chalet (refreshment bar), getting there on foot after just a few minutes' walk. Hop back onto

your bike and ride down the exciting downhill stretch running a stone's throw from the eternal ices of the Brenva and the raging waters of the Dora di Verney. The last downhill part takes you in no time to **Courmayeur**.

The skilled cyclists can ride up to the starting point (15 km, 420 m rise) on the fairly busy asphalt road, not an ideal path for bicycles.

Gran Paradiso National Park: from   25 Km
Villeneuve to the gates of the National Park

Starting from early spring through late fall, you can follow an itinerary crossing the Rhemes Valley and the Valsavarenche. Most of the route curls along the perimeter of the National Park, and in spring you can quite often spot the ibex and chamois leaping down to the valley to nibble on the early buds.

You start your ride from **Villeneuve**, an old village situated on the S.S. 26 main road from Aosta to Courmayeur. The starting point is located in the parking area of the sports grounds. From the parking lot, take the uphill asphalt stretch until you reach the built-up area of Champlong (995 m above sea level), then ride for 4 km with a roughly 300 m rise: the

climb is tough and must be covered with great calm. Once you get out of the built-up area, leave the asphalt road, continuing on your right along an uphill dirt road: after about a very steep

300 m stretch, take the first road on your right, which is initially dirt, then turns level. Now ride along a pleasant road with the right edge constantly overhanging the River Savara. Along this route, right at the beginning, a natural window opens up and offers a magnificent view on the Mont Blanc chain. This road ends after 3.8 km in the built-up area of Chevrere at 1,106 m. At this point, follow the asphalt road, crossing the bridge over the Savara torrent, brushing the Gran Paradiso National Park. The asphalt stretch enters the road that drops gently along the Valsavarenche, and after 3 km, after passing a bend on

ABOVE, a house in Villeneuve.
PAGE OPPOSITE, cycling across the Rhêmes Valley.

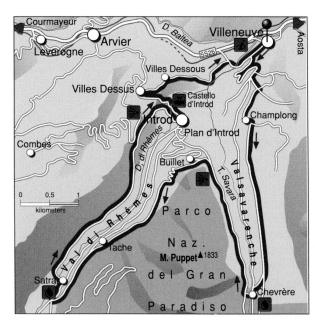

POINTS OF INTEREST

The adventure park of Villeneuve running through pine, poplar and chestnut woods, is the first tree walkway open for public use In Valle d'Aosta and one of the first in Italy. Across a series of daring passages, venture from one tree to another with the maximum safety, tied to a steel cable through a double longe line and a harness.
Different programs for children under and/or over 14 years of age. The Dora Baltea rapids are quite an interesting experience too. Rafting Adventure, Chavanne, Villeneuve, t. 016595082; www.raftin gaventure.com

your left, at Buillet, before entering the village, you come across a building on your right. Just opposite starts an asphalt ascent. Climb for 1.2 km up to a small verdant patch with a house whose door shows the year of construction: "1923". Now take the scenic level road that enters the second of the valleys, the Rhemes Valley. Towards the end of the road (3.5 km), you can spot the steeple of the church of Rhemes Saint Georges. After reaching the asphalt road (S.R. 24) of the valley, turn right and left immediately after. The road drops for 450 m, and by turning left again, you cross the bridge over the Dora di Rhemes. Immediately on your right, leave the asphalt road and take a pleasant cart road – a

path that sharply drops and reaches Norat, the farming area that dominates the built-up area of Introd (884 m above sea level), with its towering castle. After a stop at the imposing Orrido bridge (a deep canyon), get ready for the final downhill asphalt stretch of the tour to **Villeneuve**, crossing the hamlets of Villes Dessus and Villes Dessous.

Technical info

Route
Approximately 25 Km:
Villeneuve - Champlong - Valsavarenche - Rhemes Valley - Introd - Villes Dessus - Ville Dessous – Villeneuve: 25 km on a mixed asphalt-dirt route (9.2 km).
Difficulty
The route can be easily covered also by people with not too much training in their legs. The only "nasty" exception is the first 4 km stretch (plus 300 m of dirt track) climbing sharply from Villeneuve to Champlong. Some effort is required for the climb from Buillet (1.2 km) too.

Cycling period
From May to October.
Map
• *Monte Bianco e Gran Paradiso*, 1:50,000, Kompass
• *Monte Bianco e Gran Paradiso*, 1:50,000, FMB.
Technical assistance
• Cicli Benato, via Lostan 106, Arvier; t. 016599131. www.ciclibenato.com
• Gal Sport, via Paravera 6A, Aosta; t. 0165236134.
• Lucchini, c.so Battaglione Aosta 49/51, Aosta; t. 0165262306
Useful information
• APT Grand Paradis -

Villeneuve, Champagne 18; t. 016595055.
• Cooperativa Habitat, via E. Aubert 48, Aosta; t. 0165363851. www.ambientenatura.com Ecotourism, ecoeducation. Guided tours, trekking on foot and horseback, skiing weeks and outings in the Gran Paradiso National Park.
• MB Aventure, haml. of Villair 15, La Salle; t. 3472417667. www.mbaventure.it National MTB Center, run by expert instructors and guides.

Piedmont

The Po Park   35 Km
From Racconigi to Le Vallere

The ride along the Turin side of the Po Park unfolds the river which, at this stage of its journey towards the sea, picks up a less raging and slower flow typical of a lowland waterway. From an environmental point of view, the Po becomes more interesting owing to the presence of wet areas such as mortlakes and meanders, ideal natural habitats for many species of fauna. The course of the river winds along a mixed route of cycling lanes and country roads.

You start your ride from **Racconigi**, where it would be worthwhile to pay a visit to the castle, the former summer residence of the Savoia, surrounded by a wonderful park. From the castle, continue your ride towards Murello-Pinerolo and follow the road signs for the Stork and Anatidae Center of the LIPU (via Stramiano 30, t. 017283457), which is easily recognizable by the stork nests on the roof of the building, the Stramiano farm. After this pleasant and educational visit, proceed along the XIX century Migliabruna farms, riding through the extensive cultivated lands stretching between the Maira and the Po.

After approximately 3 km, you arrive near the Po, with the road bending right towards Carmagnola (about 3 km), where we suggest to stop and pay a visit to the Ecomuseum of the Hemp (via Crissolo 20) and to the Vigna farm - Municipal Museum of Natural History (at the main offices of the Po Park Visit Center).

From Carmagnola, continue

POINTS OF INTEREST

Near the XVIII century **Le Vallere farm,** *you'll find a multimedia info spot on the Po, equipped with congress hall, and an exhibition room for periodical displays. You can also book guided tours to visit the most interesting spots in the Park. The farm also houses the Regional Center for Documentation and Research on Protected Areas.*

PAGE OPPOSITE, spring blooming in a plain wood along the Po.

your tour towards the crooks of the river up to the Gerbasso wood, an interesting example of renaturalization of a country area along the river. The mortlake of San Michele is marshland with a rich population of birdlife.

Now cross the busy S.S. 20 main road of the Tenda hill and ride through fields, mortlakes, the Pochettino and Fortepasso farms near the Po Morto Oasis. After a short detour, reach the old village of Cornalese. From the Fortepasso farm, go straight ahead passing a canal. The road now switches to asphalt and skirts a lake up to the S.P. 122 provincial road, which you take turning left, and after 600 m, turning right and reaching the hamlet of La Gorra. Follow the road signs along the cycle lane, passing through the hamlets of Tetti Sapini and La Rotta. After the Molinello equipped area (where environmental reclamation projects are ongoing), you reach the gates of **Moncalieri** with the Le Vallere equipped area. You can get back to the starting point by train in just less than half an hour.

Technical info

Route
35 Km: Racconigi - Migliabruna farms- Carmagnola - Lanca di San Michele - Gerbasso wood - Po Morto Oasis - La Gorra - Tetti Sapini - La Rotta - Moncalieri.
Along pathways and cyclable dirt roads.

Difficulty
Easy route running entirely along flat country, no special training required.

Cycling period
All year round; take due care during the hotter and wetter periods of summer and in the chilly winter days.

Bicycle + Train
The Moncalieri-Racconigi stretch (25 minutes) runs along the Turin-Genoa line. From Moncalieri reach the center of Turin by train or on a cycling lane up to the Turin Lingotto railroad station.

Map
Sentieri della Collina Torinese - map n. 1, 1:15,000 Moncalieri, Turin, Pecetto, Pino Torinese, San Mauro Torinese, published by the Province of Turin.

Technical assistance
• Bosco Luca,
via Fiume 4, Racconigi;
t. 017284602.
• Cicli Caporali,
via Torino 47, Carmagnola;
t. 0119723010.
• Cicli SF,
viale Barbaroux 20, Carmagnola;
t. 0119723012.
• Terzano Pierino,
via Torino 170, Carmagnola;
t. 0119720370.
• Giobike,
strada Carignano 6, Moncalieri;
t. 0116407413.

Bicycle rental
Agriturismo Cascina Montebarco, via Poirino 650, haml. of Casanova, Carmagnola; t. 0119795051.

Tourist information
• Parco Fluviale del Po – Turin side, Cascina Le Vallere, corso Trento 98, Moncalieri; t. 011642831.
www. parks.it/parco.po.to/
• Centro Visite Parco Po, c/o Casina Vigna, via San Francesco di Sales, Carmagnola; t. 0119724390.
www.storianaturale.org
• Itineraria (guided bicycle tours), via Principi d'Acaja 28, Turin; t. 0114347954.
• Bici & Dintorni, via Andorno 35 b, Turin; t. 011888981.
www.biciedintorni.org

Canavese   55 Km
From Chivasso to Ivrea

Nice ride along the cycle road of the Canavese, at the heart of the Ivrea snout, amid villages, castles and peaceful natural oases.

From the railroad station of **Chivasso**, pass the railroad bridge and continue your ride keeping right. At the end of the road (Post Office), cross the S.S. 26 main road cycling up to the Capuchin Church. At this stage, follow the road signs pointing to Mazzè along the perimeter of the former Lancia (cycling lane). At the Bethlehem Church, turn right for Torassi, and at the two following crossroads, keep left. After passing through the expressway and the A4 freeway, you reach an intersection, then turn right and, immediately after, turn left through the Mandria farm, where you keep right for Mazzè. At Tonengo di Mazzè, ride towards Rondissone, then left for Casale di Tonengo up to Mazzè. Continue your ride towards Caluso and the Mazzè castle after a climb to the topmost part of the town. After the castle, turn right, then left taking a descent, then right again on an uphill stretch.

After riding down towards Vische, pass the church and follow the signs for the Pratoferro farms. At the next crossroads, turn left for the Cafasso farms, then go left again

Technical info

Route
55 Km: Chivasso - Mandria - Mazzè - Vische – Lake Candia - Vische - Crotte - Realizio - Canton Moretti - Ivrea. On by-roads with dirt stretches. The entire route has been indicated with blue arrows for cyclists.
Difficulty
None in particular. If you take the whole day out, it could become an outing for all the family.
Cycling period
All-year round.
Take note: from Cerone the cycle lane should go right, but due to heavy floods, it's no longer accessible. Ask for information on the spot. Should the route not be accessible, follow the description up to Canton Moretti.

Bicycle + Train
The return trip is by train, which, from Ivrea to Chivasso, takes roughly 30 minutes. The route covers the railroad lines of Chivasso, Candia and Ivrea.
Map
• *Ciclostrada della Dora Baltea e Itinerari Cicloturistici dell'Anfiteatro Morenico d'Ivrea*, 1:110.000, Province of Turin and ATL Canavese e Valli di Lanzo.
• *Il Canavese da Ivrea a Chivasso*, map of the tracks and refuges (including indication of the cycle road), 1:50.000, IGC Turin (t. 011534850).
Technical assistance and bicycle rental
• Cora,
via Momo 6, Chivasso

(100 m from the railroad station); t. 0119109669.
• Bici Sport,
corso Nigra 46, Ivrea
(50 m from the railroad station); t. 012540348.
Tourist information
• ATL Canavese e Valli di Lanzo,
corso Vercelli 1, Ivrea;
t. 0125618131.
www.canavese-vallilanzo.it
• Amici della Bici - Legambiente,
c/o Centro Gandhi,
via Arduino 75, Ivrea;
t. 012544202.
• Bici & Dintorni,
via Andorno 35 b, Turin;
t. 011888981.
www.biciedintorni.org

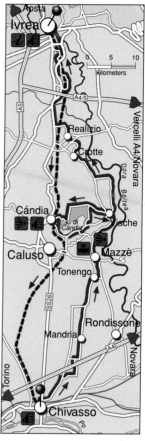

for the Rossi farms. Near the dirt road, turn right, passing through a wet area with plain woods and reed beds that are part of the Provincial Nature Park of Lake Candia.

At the following crossroads, keep left along the dirt road

POINTS OF INTEREST

A stop half way through the day at the **Provincial Nature Park of Lake Candia** *(main offices: via Vittoria 12, Turin; t. 0118612584, www. parks.it/ parco.lago. candia/), an ideal spot to snack. You can rent rowing boats (Lido restaurant, t. 0119834528; Zaghi, t. 011 9831026) and explore the lake expanse, enjoying the sights on the western Alpine arc (Mount Rosa and Gran Paradiso). In the nature oasis, many birds winter, including the grebe. A very interesting feature of the Park is its 425 species of flora (half of them typical of lake and marshy environments).*

up to the Società Canottieri, then turn left again on asphalt roads. At a crossroads, proceed on your left-hand side towards Vische. After the La Barcaccia restaurant, continue left along the dirt road for the Pratoferro farms, and once you reach the crossroads with a big poplar, turn right towards Vische.

Before reaching the church, turn left for the Luisina farm. At the following crossroads, go straight ahead, then on the right-hand side of the cemetery. At the crossroads go straight passing the canal, then turn left. After a few farms, keep left of the two crossroads. Now skirt round the Luisina farm, and take the main road on your right for Crotte. At the church, go right on the dirt road, then left and pass a canal on your left again. After crossing the main road, you enter Realizio; now turn right then left, passing though Santa Maria.

ABOVE, a stop on the bank of Lake Candia. PAGE OPPOSITE, along the Canavese cycle road.

Go left for Cerone where you keep left (see heading "Cycling period"). At the church, turn right, then, past the railroad, on your right again towards Ivrea on busy roads, and after passing the Chiusella torrent, turn right towards San Bernardo d'Ivrea, right again, then left, and right again for Canton Moretti. After the level crossing, take the left-hand side for the dirt road along the tracks, and by following the road signs on the cycle lanes, you finally reach **Ivrea**.

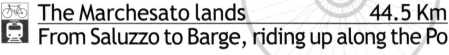

The Marchesato lands 44.5 Km
From Saluzzo to Barge, riding up along the Po

You start from the city shaded by the Monviso, a small capital where you can sense the strong XIX century mark of the porticoed streets. The warm Piedmontese cafés invite you to a refined refreshment before hopping back on your saddle.

You start your ride from **Saluzzo** taking the S.P. 260 Martiniana provincial road (at the crossroads, coming out of the city, ignore the spur road on your right for Revello). After passing the bridge over the Bronda torrent, ride towards the Po River Park, which you reach after approximately 5 km.

Now climb up the valley with long tree-lined roads and a charming countryside with the river bed on your right. The provincial road passes some up and downhill stretches, and after skirting the centers of Martiniana Po and Gambasca, it enters the S.P. 26 provincial road on the outskirts of Sanfront. After reaching the crossroads with the "stop", turn left towards Paesana. Take due care of traffic along this stretch of road. The road increases its inclination and climbs up the valley, offering a view of the rocky pyramid of the Monviso. After passing the hamlets of Robella, Bollani

and Morena, you reach the gates of Paesana. Now turn right, in front of the church, right again, then cut the built-up area lengthways, riding over the bridge that crosses the Po. After reaching the other bank, continue your ride towards Barge. The road now rises steadily to La Colletta di Barge, which you reach after a sharp hairpin bend. At the end of the climb, you'll find a refreshment spot (Colletta eating house) that heralds the descent towards Mondarello and Barge (approximately 8 km from Paesana). The Infernotto torrent splits into two hamlets the town of

Technical info

Route
44.5 Km: Saluzzo - Martiniana Po - Gambasca - Sanfront - Paesana - La Colletta - Barge - San Martino - Saluzzo.
You can reach Saluzzo from Turin by taking the A6 freeway for Savona up to the Marene toll, and then by taking the S.S. 662 main road.

Difficulty
No particular difficulty along this itinerary, since the uphill climb to La Colletta doesn't offer too challenging slopes. Same thing for the climb up to the Colletto along the possible alternative.

Cycling period
All year round. You might find traffic along the Po stretch, especially during holidays.

Bicycle + train
The Saluzzo railroad station is situated along the Savigliano-Cuneo-Mondovì line, directly linked to the main Turin-Savona.

Map
Atlante stradale d'Italia, Northern volume, 1:200,000, TCI.

Technical assistance
• Chiara,
corso Roma 4, Saluzzo;
t. 017544732.
• La Bici,
via Savigliano 53, Saluzzo;

t. 0175248160.
• Bonetti Cicli,
via Roma 36, Manta;
t. 017585453.

Tourist information
• Ente Turismo del Saluzzese,
via Griselda 8, Saluzzo;
t. 0175240352.
www.terredelmarchesato.it
• Parco del Po Cuneese,
via Griselda 8, Saluzzo;
t. 017546505.
www.parks.it/parco.po.cn
• Associazione ciclistica
"lj 'npaotà", via Deportati Ebrei 5, Saluzzo; t. 017541252,
017542632, 0175477665.
www.ijnpaota.org

POINTS OF INTEREST

A visit to the **Manta castle**, *a small XIII century fort, owned since 1984 by the FAI, which has seen to its restoration and enhancement. The painting cycle inside recalls the "courtly" atmosphere of the Piedmontese Renaissance. Visits every day (except for the second half of December, January and working Mondays) 10 a.m.-1 p.m. and 2- 5 p.m. (from February to September until 6 p.m.). Information: t. 017587822.*

Barge, where you can stop, if you haven't done so at La Colletta. Now exit Barge, following the road signs for Saluzzo, and take the S.P. 29 provincial road, demarcation line between the hilly area and the lowlands. At the roundabout sign of San Martino, turn right, and after approximately 2 km, leave the main road and follow on your left via Saluzzo Antica. The old "Pedemontana" then becomes via Barge Vecchia and crosses orchards of peach trees and kiwis. Now ride in a stretch of small country areas such as Tetti Fraile, approaching a big plane tree that acts as a traffic island. At this point, turn right and enter via Traversa Lungo Po (you can't continue on the old road due to an inaccessible ford).

ABOVE, the old town center of Saluzzo.

Once back on the S.P. 26 provincial road, cross the Po to close the circle at **Saluzzo**.

ALTERNATIVE

For the trained cyclists, the tour can be completed by another shorter, although equally challenging circle which, from Saluzzo, takes you to the Bronda Valley passing through Manta, Verzuolo, Venasca and the Colletto pass (uphill climb of 5 km, 4.1% average gradient).

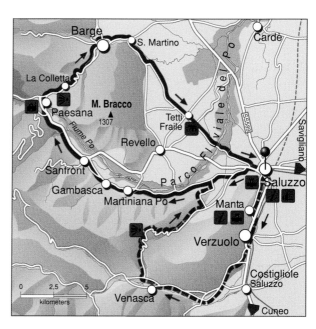

Langhe
The Barolo path at La Morra

14 Km

Full immersion in the soothing hilly environment of the Langhe, cycling across an enchanting landscape, where the hand of man and nature have shaped wine-scented geometries.

You start your ride opposite the Municipal Wine-Producers' Cooperative of **La Morra**, proceeding along the pathway leading to the medieval walls known as Bastioni. Once you get to the bottom of the town, follow the road signs for Cerequio-Fontanazza. At the crossroads between Fontanazza and Cerequio, keep right and after a stretch along a ridge, drop down amid vineyards reaching Cerequio. After crossing this small hamlet, the dirt road follows the contour line passing under the houses of the Fontanazza. Now continue, firstly on an uphill climb, then downhill towards Pelorosso, where

you turn left on a downhill stretch towards the bottom of the valley.

After crossing the houses of the small village of Torriglione (on your left), ride through the vineyards of the Rocche dell'Annunziata. The path then passes the Gallinotto stream and briefly rises towards the Rocchette and Annunziata, passing through the Giachini and Bricco Rocca vineyards. Now take the provincial road, skirting the Church of the Annunziata, with its Baroque façade and Romanesque steeple, and the cellars of the former convent of the Benedictine friars of Marcenasco, which today houses the Ratti Museum of Alba wines.

Shortly afterwards, leave the provincial road, riding on a mainly level road up to Monfalletto. Near a huge cedar of Lebanon, the dirt road turns left and then connects itself to the road running around the Bricco di San Biagio hill and reaching the center of the hamlet of Santa Maria.

The track then proceeds along a hilly slope almost at the bottom of the valley, crossed by the Porretta streamlet, and soon after-

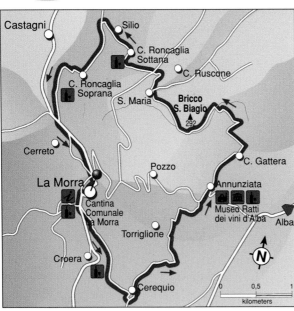

ABOVE, view on La Morra.
PAGE OPPOSITE, wine tasting of Barolo at the Ballarin farm.

POINTS OF INTEREST

A visit to the La Morra Municipal Wine-Producers' Cooperative *(via Carlo Alberto 2, t. 0173509204), where you can buy some excellent Barolo, or a stop at the local wineries. Addresses and telephone numbers are found on the map distributed by the Cooperative. In August, "Marcialonga" in La Morra, a 3 km wine-food trip, with four mouth-watering stops, closing the feast and dances in the barnyard.*

wards, it starts climbing up to the slope of the hill, reaching the hamlet of Tetti Santa Maria.

At this stage, continue your ride on the provincial road, up to the square dominated by the Church of the Madon-na di Plaustra, where you take the track that leads to the hamlet of Silio with the vineyard bearing the same name.

Approaching Silio, the road turns left on an upward stretch towards La Morra. In the Roncaglie vineyard, at Roncaglia, turn right on a steep climb, reaching the plateau of Madonna di Loreto with its chapel. The final stretch of the route enters the built-up area of **La Morra** skirting the sports ground.

Technical info

Route

14 Km: La Morra - Cerequio - Pelorosso - Torriglione - Rocchette - Annunziata - Monfalletto - Tetti Santa Maria - Silio - Roncaglia Soprana - La Morra: almost entirely on dirt road. La Morra is 18 km away from Alba.

Difficulty

The route, as far as altitude is concerned, is fairly varied; since it runs mainly on dirt roads, a mountain bike would be necessary. With the proper peace of mind, the route can be challenged also by cyclists with little practice in their legs. There are few short steep stretches that can also be covered on foot.

Cycling period

All year round. Our suggestion is not to ride after strong rain when the road bed on some tracks may get muddy.

Map

• *La Morra, le vigne del Barolo e il loro Sentiero*, 1:12,000, Cantina Comunale and Pro Loco, La Morra.

• *Carta dei Sentieri e dei Rifugi Asti-Alba-Aqui Terme*, sheet 19, 1:50,000, IGC.

Bicycle rental

Cascina Ballarin, haml. of Annunziata 115, La Morra; for guests only;
t. 017350365.

Technical assistance

• Cicli Gagliardini, via Ospedale 7, Alba; t. 0173440726.

• Idea Bici Dogliani, via Cappa 59, Dogliani; t. 017371129.

Tourist information

• Atl Ente Turismo Langhe Monferrato e Roero, piazza Medford 3, Alba; t. 017335833. www.langheroero.it

• Municipality of La Morra, piazza Municipio 1, La Morra; t. 017550105; www.la-morra.it

The Lame del Sesia Nature Park   15 Km
Between Greggio and Isolone di Oldenico

A peaceful ride across the fluvial settings of the Lame del Sesia Nature Park, which encloses an 8 km stretch of the river that originates in the snows of Mount Rosa (a total of 138 km). The Park was created by the Piedmont Region in 1978 to enhance and protect the important strip of Isolone di Oldenico, surrounded by the rapid streams of the river. Near Greggio, special mention must be made of the Malinverni quillwort (Isoëtes malinverniana), an aquatic plant and the only example of endemic vegetation of the Po Plain growing in few other areas in Piedmont and in the Pavese.

From the Park seat at **Albano Vercellese**, ride straight towards Via XX Settembre. Pass the castle and take the first dirt road

on the right directed to the Sesia bank. Immersed in such a spectacular environment, proceed southwards following the riverside up to the Isolone di Oldenico Nature Reserve, one of the most important nesting sites for herons in the Po Plain.

If you're lucky and with good binoculars at hand, you may spot egrets, grey herons, cattle egrets, black-crowned night herons, sacred ibis, cormorants and the rare spoonbills. Nearby flow the waters of the Sesia and the Cervo.

At this stage, turn backwards on the same route, and after roughly 5 km, stop at the crossroads for the Park seat. Instead of turning left (towards the seat), turn right approaching a parking area. Now take the dirt road in the woods running along the fitness route.

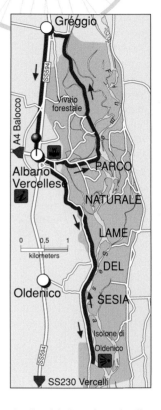

POINTS OF INTEREST

*The **fitness route** is a very enjoyable path you can follow on foot inside the Park. Pay a visit, on the Novara bank, to the Benedictine **Abbey of Saints Nazario and Celso** in the small town of San Nazzaro Sesia. Another interesting place to see is the **Rice Museum**, housed in the town's former school.*

At the third station, the fitness route turns right, while the itinerary continues straight ahead towards the Sesia bank in the area of the confluence of the Cavour Canal drainage. Ride back along an old embankment on the left, until you reach an observation hut, and after approximately 2 km, the town of Greggio.

To return to **Albano Vercellese**, take the S.S. 594 main road stretching southwards and reaching the town after roughly 2.5 km.

Technical info

Route

15 Km: Albano Vercellese - right bank of the Sesia - Isolone di Oldenico Nature Reserve - parking area in the Park - right bank of the Sesia (northwards) - Greggio - Albano Vercellese: on asphalt and well-beaten unsurfaced roads.

Difficulty

None. The route is ideal even for "family" bicycle outings.

Cycling period

All year round. Avoid the hottest periods (June-August) and the days following torrential rain.

Map

• *Carta della provincia di Vercelli*, 1:150,000, Litografia Artistica Cartografica Firenze.
• A good detailed map of the Park is available at the Park seat.

Bicycle rental

At the Albano Vercellese Park seat. No problems during week days. On Saturdays and Sundays, book in advance, as offices may be closed. Rental of mountain bikes also at the Cascine Colombare farm holidays at Casaleggio Novara; t. 0321839206.

Tourist information

• Parco Naturale Lame del Sesia, via XX Settembre 12, Albano Vercellese; t. 016173112. www.parks.it/parco.lame.sesia/
• Ufficio Turismo San Nazzaro Sesia, via Barbavara 1, San Nazzaro Sesia; t. 0161253273.
• Atl. Novara, Baluardo Q. Sella 40, Novara; t. 0321394059. www.turismonovara.it
• Amici della Bici, c/o C.d.Q. San Martino, via Parazzi 5/a, Novara; t. 0321455090. amici.della.bici.novara@msoft.it

Finally, turn left for the Park seat, which ends this easy cycling route.

ALTERNATIVE

You can get to the protected area from Vercelli by following the Novara bank of the Sesia. This cycling route, however, lacks road signs (project still in the pipeline). The route starts from the bridge crossing the Sesia (S.S. 11), just outside the centre of Vercelli, and runs upstream along the bank for 15 km, leaving Villata and San Nazzaro Sesia on the right, up to the tombs of the Cavour Canal.

RIGHT, small bridge along the pathway in the park.
PAGE OPPOSITE, Abbey of Saints Nazario and Celso.

The Zegna Oasis 60 Km
The "Panoramica" and the Cervo Valley

The "scenic" ride par excellence is the ride that crosses the Zegna Oasis. Every self-respecting cyclist knows far too well that the best panoramic views are won after challenging the force of gravity; this is a view that's really worth your feat.

You start from **Andorno Micca** taking the S.P. 105 provincial road leading to Mosso Santa Maria. You have to immediately challenge changing gradients that herald the degree of the whole ride, crossing the hamlet of Locato and then descending the Strona stream. Now pass near San Giuseppe di Casto, reaching the secluded small chapel of Sant'Antonio Marcone, from where you proceed left towards Mosso on the S.P. 105 provincial road.

After passing the hamlets of Nelva and Corte, nearing a crossroads, keep left, ignoring the road running to Pianezze. Shortly after, go downhill to the Camandona dam, then continue uphill. After reaching Cerale, the road runs straight towards Pianezze, while the itinerary continues left (turn in front of a small church). After passing the road bridge of Pistolesa, you reach Mosso Santa Maria. From the church

square, take the road to Trivero, challenging yet another climb, riding uphill to the Viebolche crossroads, where you turn left.

The climb gets tougher approaching the first hamlets of Trivero. At Lora, start riding along the "Panoramica" Zegna. Once you've crossed the roundabout sign at the Zegna Center, get ready for the steep gradient where you have to get to grips with a grueling uphill climb.

The vegetation and the magnificent view over the Biella valleys, the Po plain and Monferrato accompany your ride, which becomes smoother when approaching the contour line of 1,000 m, while breathtaking sceneries open out towards the north on the upper Valsassera and the Valsesia mountains. A sight that is a must is the view on Mount Rosa from the Margosio pass.

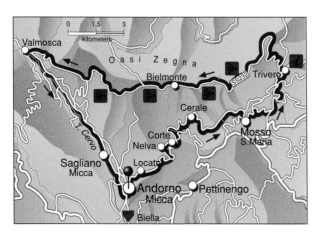

Technical info

Route:
60 Km: Andorno Micca - Locato - Nelva - Corte - Cerale - Mosso Santa Maria - Trivero - Bielmonte - Valmosca - Cervo Valley - Sagliano Micca - Andorno Micca. On asphalt roads. You can easily reach the starting point from Biella.

Difficulty
This stretch requires trained legs, given the total rise in excess of 1,200 m and to the uphill 11 km climb from Lora di Trivero to Bielmonte (average gradient over 7%). We suggest a good touring bike or a road bike equipped with 39 x 25 or 26 uphill gear. Take due care on the downhill stretch. Furthermore, you need to wear a shoulder cape wind repeller for the long ride downhill.

Cycling period
From late spring to fall. The "Panoramica" may be busy during the holidays. In the weekends, we suggest starting the ride early in the morning, before the "four wheelers" appear.

Map
Atlante stradale d'Italia, Northern volume, 1:200,000, TCI.

Technical assistance
• Motocicli Pasin, haml. of Falcero 115, Valle Mosso; t. 015706158.
• Cicli Bertinetti, via Trento 31, Biella; t. 015405285.

Tourist information
• Zegna Oasis, Trivero; t. 01575911. Free phone number 800012022. www.oasizegna.com
• Pro Loco of Trivero, Tourist Board, Zegna Center; t. 015351128.
• Bucaneve Hotel, Bielmonte; t. 015744184. www.bucaneve.it

POINTS OF INTEREST

The Zegna Oasis is real heaven for bikers. Besides the spectacular routes, worth mentioning are the programs for children, families and grown-ups fond of mountain bike touring, arranged by **Mtb Adventure**. *From the weekend to the theme week, there are various offers, alternated by mountain courses (environment, traditions, flora, fauna), orienteering courses and ecocompatible activities. The program can be requested by contacting the Zegna Oasis National MTB School (t. 015542254 and 3357878738), which works side by side with the hotel Bucaneve of Bielmonte.*

Once you've reached the Luvera pass, brace yourself for yet another steep climb, and after a few tunnels, you reach Bielmonte, the highest peak with its 1,483 m. Continue your ride along

ABOVE, road signs in the park
PAGE OPPOSITE, stop at Bocchetto Sessera.

the "Panoramica" towards the Sessera pass, where you start your smooth and well-deserved ride down the road, taking due care however of the thrilling trajectories.

Wonderful panoramas over the Cervo Valley disclose the entry on the valley road, which is precisely at Valmosca, near Rosazza, considered a model holiday village as early as the end of the XVIII century.

The S.P. 100 provincial road penetrates into the narrow valley between rocky mountainsides; you can ride easily along and when you reach Sagliano Micca, in a fully urban area, take the last 4 km reaching **Andorno Micca**.

The Tortona hills
On the roads of Fausto Coppi

57 Km

Welcome to the roads of the "Campionissimo!". The Tortona hills dominate the Scrivia Valley and offer very interesting cycling routes.

You start from **Castellania** riding towards the crossroads to Costa Vescovato; keep right, taking the S.P. 130 provincial road. Proceed along a downhill road crossing Costa Vescovato and Montale Celli and reaching the bottom of the valley cut by the Ossona torrent. Now ride along the level provincial road and follow the signs indicating Cer-

RIGHT, entrance to Casa Coppi at Castellania.

Technical info

Route
57 Km: Castellania - Costa Vescovato – bridge over the Ossona - Cerreto Grue - Avolasca - Mount Rosso - Baiarda - Garbagna - Agliani - Poggio Maggiore - Vargo - Sardigliano - Sant'Agata - Carezzano Superiore - Castellania. On asphalt roads. You can easily reach Castellania from the Scrivia Valley through Tortona or Villalvernia.

Difficulty
The itinerary is rather tough (about 1,200 m rise), with harsh roads plus some really steep stretches with gradients over 15%. You need a good physical shape: if you're well trained, you can challenge the ride with a road bike equipped with uphill gears (39 x 26 or 27). The not too trained cyclists should ride the distance with a good touring bike equipped with triple gear ratio.

Cycling period
The winter season is out of the question.

Map
• *Atlante stradale d'Italia*, Northern volume, 1:200,000, TCI.
• *Terre di Fausto Coppi*, 1:110,000, Consorzio Turistico Terre di Fausto.

Technical assistance
• Le Bici, via E. Raggio 1, Novi Ligure;
t. 01432995, 014372623.
www.hobbymoto.it
• La Bici, strada del Vapore 17, Arquata Scrivia;
t. 0143667594.
www.labici.it

Tourist information
• Consorzio Turistico Appennino Ligure Terre di Fausto
via A. Saffi 55, Novi Ligure;
t. 0143744537.
• Comunità Montana Alta Val Lemme Alto Ovadese, piazza Repubblica 2, Bosio;
t. 0143684220.

Casa Coppi *at Castellania, a "sanctuary" for all bicycle lovers, which brings to memory the heroic feats of the "Great Heron". His home-museum hosts more than 100 pages of newspapers that unfold the victories of Fausto Coppi. The house was inaugurated on January 2, 2000, the day of the 40th anniversary of the untimely departure of the "Campionissimo!". Visits: Saturday 2.30-6.30 p.m., Sunday and holidays 10.30 a.m.-6.30 p.m. Information: Terre di Fausto Tourist Consortium, t. 0143744907 or 3358235773.*

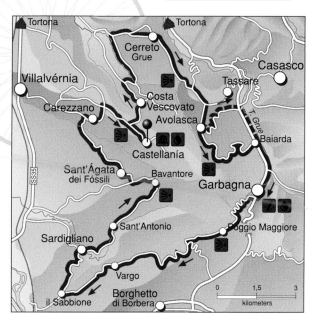

reto Grue. After crossing the bridge over the Ossona torrent, get ready for the tough stretch climbing up towards Cerreto for about 1.5 km.

Now proceed downhill to reach the S.P. 125 provincial road, riding on your right on rolling landscape up to Avolasca (6 km). Cross the town, disregarding the detour for Garbagna, and go straight on to the S.P. 136 provincial road that climbs quite steeply up on Mount Rosso (2 km): this is the toughest uphill ride of the tour, which you can avoid (see alternative below). Now ride on a downhill stretch reaching Garbagna, passing through the hamlets of Casa Borella, Oliva and Baiarda. At the crossroads, turn right. After crossing the old town center of Garbagna, take the S.P. 120 provincial road and, immediately after (100 m), turn right on the provincial road leading you to Sorli. Soon afterwards, keep left on the road to Agliani and Bagnara, after crossing a bridge that heralds a steep climb with hairpin bends. Once you reach the S.P. 135 provincial road, turn left passing through the hamlets of Poggio Maggiore and Cervari up to Sorli, where you cross the hill and start riding down towards the Church of San Martino.

Ride towards Albarasca and the Vargo castle until you reach the bottom of the valley at Sabbione. At the crossroads, take a right turn entering the S.P. 142 provincial road to Sardigliano. At the two subsequent crossroads, turn right towards Cuquello along the S.P. 141 provincial road that requires good responsiveness on the uphill stretch. Just after passing the small chapel of Sant'Antonio Abate (XIV century), the route curls towards Malvino, Bavantorino, Bavantore and Sant'Agata dei Fossili (roughly 9 km from Sabbione). Now take a steep descent, and after the hamlet of Torre Sterpi and the bridge over the Castellania torrent, keep right and prepare yourself for the challenging climb (approximately 2 km, 125 m rise) up to Carezzano Superiore, where you turn right towards the Bric delle Streghe and **Castellania** (3 km).

ALTERNATIVE

From Avolasca, ride down the Scura Valley up to Grue, where you turn right reaching Baiarda and getting back on the itinerary.

The Capanne di Marcarolo Park   22 Km
Piota Valley

The Capanne di Marcarolo Nature Park is a terrace in Piedmont that opens onto Liguria and the Mediterranean. Its extraordinary solitude gives it that wild aspect and extreme importance from an environmental point of view.

You start your trip from the **Cirimilla** square where you begin riding on the dirt road which, initially on an uphill stretch, then with a rolling route, climbs up the Piota Valley amid chestnut woods. After 2.1 km, and after skirting an electricity substation and the Manuale Inferiore farm, you reach the vicinity of a junction with an ENEL substation. Now take the central road that climbs up towards the Rocche Nere, a panoramic spot named after the rocks dominating it. At this stage, get ready for an easy uphill ride, entering the territory of the Capanne di Marcarolo Park.

After 1.5 km, you reach the crossroads with the G2 route (on your left) and a building of the municipal waterworks. Now proceed along the G1 riding along the dirt road

Technical info

Route
22 Km: Cirimilla - Piota Valley - Cascina Fuia - Cascina Cornaggia - Capanne di Marcarolo - Cascina Cornagetta - Cascina Maggie - Mond'Ovile (Upper and Lower) - Cascina Manuale (Upper and Lower) - Cirimilla.
On dirt roads. You can reach the starting point by taking the A26 Sempione-Genova Voltri, Ovada exit, continuation to Lerma and the Cirimilla equipped area.

Difficulty
This itinerary doesn't require special technique and effort. In any case, you have to challenge quite a few uphill stretches that need some training. A mountain bike is preferred since most of the itinerary runs along dirt roads.

Cycling period
From spring to fall.

Map
Il Parco Naturale Capanne di Marcarolo, 1:25,000, Studio Cartografico Italiano - Genoa.

Technical assistance
• Hobby Bici,
via Roma 3, Gavi.
Including guide and bicycle rental service; t. 0143642612.
• Cicli Guizzardi,
corso Martiri Libertà 30, Ovada; t. 014386021.

Bicycle rental
Hobby Bici (see left).
Circolo Ippico Le Miniere, strada Cirimilla, Masino, Lerma;
t. 0143877801.

Tourist information
• Parco Naturale Capanne di Marcarolo,
via Umberto I 32/A, Bosio;
t. 0143684777.
www.parcocapanne.it
(open from Monday to Friday 8.30-12.30 a.m. and 2-3.30 p.m.).
• IAT Alexala,
via Savona 26, Alessandria;
t. 0131288095.

POINTS OF INTEREST

The Park owes the characteristics of its environment to the meeting of three different geographical areas: the Mediterranean, the Po and the Apennines. The botanic gardens of Prato Rondanino *play host to 50 species of* Sempervivum *coming from all over Europe, plus several endangered mountain plants such as the* Eryngium alpinum. *For information, please contact the Park's main offices.*

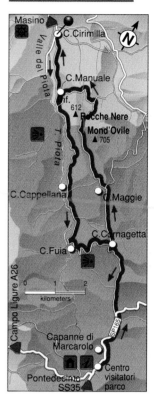

which, with its up and downhill stretches, continues to follow the Piota Valley. Cross the slopes of the Bric Boscobello and brush the Cappellana and Palazzo farms (on your right).

After crossing the ford (easy job) over the Ciechi streamlet, the gradient increases. Climb up to the Fuia farm and continue your ride uphill, enjoying an increasingly spectacular view over the Piota Valley, reaching the junction with the G2 route near the Cornagetta farm (to be precise, it's situated on the G2 and is not visible). After riding for 8.5 km from the starting point, after the Cornaggia farm, go back riding in the woods, continuing with no particular effort, alternating uphill and downhill stretches until you reach the

asphalt road of the S.P. 165 provincial road near I Foi, 1 km away from the Visitors' Center of the Park situated at Capanne di Marcarolo. This is where the journey back begins, riding again towards I Foi. Ride for 3.9 km up to the crossroads, where you keep right and take the G2 route to the Cornagetta farm.

On a mainly downhill stretch of 1.1 km, approach a hairpin bend, where, on your right, the dirt road leading to the Lombardo farm starts. Disregard that. Soon after, on your right again, near the remains of the Maggie farm, starts the F1 route leading you to Lake Inferiore della Lavagnina. The itinerary continues along the G2 shaded by cluster pines for about 1 km up to Mond'Ovile Superiore (on your left starts a dirt road towards the G1 route).

On a downhill stretch, the itinerary continues towards the Mond'Ovile Inferiore plateau, where you ignore the detour on your right and take the downhill track,

crossing a chestnut and oak wood down to the bottom of the Piota Valley.

At the G1 route junction, turn right, proceeding mainly downhill, until you reach the **Cirimilla** square.

RIGHT, chestnut wood in the Benedicta forest.
PAGE OPPOSITE, scenic view of the Piota Valley.

The Ticino Park
Along the cyclists' river

30 Km

The Ticino Park offers many cycling routes running along the protected area. Owing to its environmental features, it is considered an authentic paradise for cycle touring enthusiasts.

The itinerary starts from **Oleggio**; after passing the ring road, ride up to the small Church of San Giovanni, then continue towards Mulino Vecchio di Bellinzago, which you reach after crossing the Regina Elena Canal. Now take the cycling lane running southwards, along the Molinaria irrigation ditch

(XIV century), which used to supply water to eight flour and rice mills, up to Lido Margherita, passing through the Molinetto area. On this stretch, the cycling lane offers spectacular views over the river. At Lido Margherita (about 10 km from Oleggio), you find a refreshment spot. Pass near the intake of the Naviglio di Langosco and on your left, near the Vedro wood, a nature reserve accessible only with guided visits. At this point, approach the Galdina farm, in a panoramic spot on the mortlake of Cameri.

From the small bridge that heralds the uphill stretch to the farm, you can continue on foot in the mortlake of Cameri, where you find a bird observation hut.

After covering about 3 km

from Lido Margherita, you reach the XVI century Villa Picchetta, an important landholding and residential estate once owned by the Order of the Jesuits. At this stage, the cycling lane enters a beautiful plain wood with trees even 30 m tall.

The road runs under the railroad and crosses the S.S. 341 main road before passing near the Cava Dogana and then reaching the Vecchia Dogana that marked the border between the Kingdom of Sardinia and the Lombard-Veneto Kingdom. Here you find another refreshment spot (3 km from Villa Picchetta). Now continue your ride on the bridges that pass over the Naviglio

ABOVE, the Ticino in the Molinetto area. PAGE OPPOSITE, along the bank near the cycling lane.

The **Ethnographical Town Museum** *of Oleggio (vicolo della Chiesa 3, t. 032191324 and 032191429; open on Saturday from 3 to 6 p.m.; from Tuesday to Friday on demand): real art and traditions of the life of these centers before the advent of the industrial civilization; an interesting section is the one dedicated to vine processing and wine production.*

along the road to Galliate. Just after leaving the Naviglio Longosco behind, turn left towards Torre Mandelli and **San Martino** (roughly 12 km from the Vecchia Dogana). From here onwards, you can continue by bike after passing the Boffalora bridge, and riding up the river, until you reach Oleggio along the Naviglio Grande embankment crossing Boffalora, Turbigo and the Oleggio bridge (31 km). Or you can reach Trecate taking the S.S. 11 main road (3 km) and catching the train to Oleggio (via Novara, approximately 30 minutes).

Longosco, the Molinara irrigation ditch and the Cavour Canal, passing near the XVI century Villa Fortuna (on your right).

After skirting the Ticinazzo Canal and the "Sette Fontane" equipped area, named after a resurgence with seven spouts, the route continues

Technical info

Route
30 Km: Oleggio - Mulino Vecchio di Bellinzago - Lido Margherita - Cascina Galdina - Villa Picchetta - Vecchia Dogana - Villa Fortuna - Sette Fontane equipped area - Torre Mandelli - San Martino - Boffalora bridge - Trecate. Most of the route runs along a protected cycle lane.
Difficulty
None. A nice pleasant outing for everyone.
Cycling period
All year round; with some exceptions during heavy rain periods.
Bicycle + Train
You can reach the area by train from Milan and Turin. Oleggio is situated along the Novara-Domodossola line, while Trecate lies along the

Turin-Vercelli-Novara-Milan line.
Map
Carta dei Sentieri Ciclopedonali, 1:17,000, Orizzonte. Distributed with other maps at the Park offices at Oleggio, Ponte Vecchio di Magenta and at Mulino Vecchio of Bellinzago.
Bicycle rental
Orizzonte, C/o Cicli "Battistella" Pontevecchio di Magenta; t. 0267391283.
Technical assistance
• Milani,
via Novara 80, Oleggio;
t. 0321992208.
• Borsari Sergio,
via Gramsci 17, Galliate;
t. 0321866783.
• Tamarin,
via Giovanni XXIII 3,
Boffalora Sopra Ticino;
t. 029756299.

• Giarda Gaudenzia,
via Novara 73, Magenta;
t. 0297299821.
• Miglio Ezio,
via Libertà 95,
Bellinzago Novarese;
t. 032198424.
Tourist information
• Ente di gestione del Parco naturale della Valle del Ticino, Villa Picchetta, Cameri;
t. 0321517706.
www.parks.it/parco.ticino.
piemontese/
www.parcodelticino.pmn.it/
• Consorzio Parco Lombardo della Valle del Ticino,
via Isonzo, haml. of Ponte Vecchio di Magenta;
t. 02972101.
www.parks.it/parco.ticino.
lombardo/
www.parcoticino.it

Liguria

🚲 The Argentina Valley 67 Km
The loop of Mount Ceppo

The Argentina Valley is a magnificent lung named after the silver torrent that runs from the Maritime Alps to the Riviera dei Fiori and the blue sea of Arma di Taggia.

The itinerary starts from **Taggia**. The slightly sloped road runs up the Argentina tor-

rent, but only after passing under the imposing viaduct that sustains the Autostrada dei Fiori does the journey start, a journey into Liguria marked by woods and silence. The S.S. 548 main road narrows itself, and after approximately 7 km, reaches what was once the large landed estate of Badalucco, scene of the bloody battle between Romans and Ligurians in 181 B.C. Today it is a peaceful village that looks out onto the old bridge of Santa Lucia with its two imposing stone arches which, since 1555, have witnessed the slow flow of the "silver" torrent.

From Badalucco, the road rises gently, and in the 15 km before Molini di Triora, the environment gradually transforms itself: the hill sides covered by olive groves are replaced by mountainsides blanketed by chestnut groves. After 14.3 km, turn right reaching, after a few hundred metres, Molini di Triora, where the Argentina

torrent and its tributaries were once the engine of those 23 mills that gave the name to this stone village. At this stage, turn backwards, taking a downhill stretch to the crossroads, where you turn right. Moneghetti is where the real uphill climbs starts. Ride immersed in the parkland, with the wheels of your bike brushing enormous ferns. The bridge over the Argentina torrent is situated at approximately 430 m and the real uphill climbs starts 2 km ahead, at around 450 m. For 8.5 km, the road climbs up to 1,080 m above

ABOVE, the Badalucco bridge.
PAGE OPPOSITE, towards Mount Ceppo.

POINTS OF INTEREST

For the more practiced cyclists, or even by car, we suggest a further stretch up to Triora to visit the **Ethnographical and Witchcraft Museum** *(corso Italia 1, t. 018494487). The two upper floors host traces of the mountain civilization of the valley, while the lower floor gathers documents that recount the punishments and the history of witch hunts. At Molini di Triora, connoisseurs can find their "small paradise" in the* **Bottega di Angelamaria** *(piazza Roma 26, t. 018494021): the Witch Liquor, the snail milk and other brews made with local herbs. You must try out the "bruzzo", ricotta cheese fermented in boxes made of larch wood.*

sea level, up to the crossroads on your left (before the Langan hill) to the sanctuary of San Giovanni dei Prati and the hill crossing of Mount Ceppo (1,505 m above sea level). At the topmost point of the route, take a short break: the right moment to recover salts, put on a wind repellent jacket and start the long and pleasant downhill stretch.

After riding for just over 7 km, you reach a crossroads where you turn left (if you turn right you reach Baiardo) and go straight towards the valley of the Oxentina torrent. Just after passing the hamlet of Vignai, continue riding up to the junction on the S.S. 548 main road, returning into the Argentina Valley. Now turn right on a downhill stretch, until you reach **Taggia** (6.2 km), then ride on the short stretch of road you already covered at the start.

Technical info

Route
67 Km: Taggia - Badalucco - Molini di Triora - Moneghetti - Mount Ceppo pass- Badalucco crossroads - Taggia. Entirely on asphalt road.
Difficulty
This itinerary requires good physical conditions and your being used to staying on a saddle also on uphill stretches. There are no too tough slopes, but the overall rise is approximately 1,400 m. Most of the uphill stretch is spread over the 15 km between the crossroads for Molini di

Triora and the pass of Mount Ceppo (1,075 m rise).
Cycling period
From late spring to fall.
Map
Atlante stradale d'Italia, Northern volume, 1:200,000, TCI.
Bicycle + Train
The Arma di Taggia railroad station (Genoa-Ventimiglia line) is situated at 3.5 km from Taggia, starting point of the itinerary.
Technical assistance
Grosso Sport, via Aurelia Ponente 145,

Arma di Taggia;
t. 0184448830.
www.grossosport.it
Tourist information
• APT Riviera Dei Fiori Villa Boselli, via Boselli, Arma di Taggia;
t. 018443733.
• Pro Loco Triora, corso Italia 1, Triora;
t. 018494487.
www.comune.triora.im.it
• APT Riviera dei Fiori, Palazzo Riviera, largo Nuvoloni 1, Sanremo;
t. 0184571571.

Finalese   23 Km
On the traces of the Romans

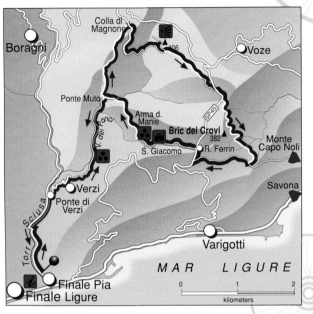

Colla di Magnone
Boragni
Voze
Ponte Muto
Arma d. Manie
Bric dei Crovi
S. Giacomo
R. Ferrin
Monte Capo Noli
Savona
Verzi
Ponte di Verzi
Varigotti

MAR   LIGURE

Finale Pia
Finale Ligure

0   1   2
kilometers

The itinerary runs in one of the wildest areas of the Finale hinterland, one of the most interesting areas from an environmental point of view, and one of the richest in historical traces throughout the Ligurian Riviera.

Technical info

Route
23 Km: Finale Pia - Ponci Valley - Ca' du Puncin (Acqua bridge) - Colla di Magnone - Bric dei Monti - Bric dei Crovi - San Giacomo Church - Arma delle Manie – crossroads of the Muto bridge - Finale Pia. Mixed route, mainly dirt roads, mule tracks and pathways, well beaten and marked. The starting point is a stone's throw away from the Aurelia main road at Finale Pia. From the Aurelia bridge over the Sciusa torrent, you'll spot at a close distance the more ancient parallel bridge, from where you take the road that climbs up the torrent.

Difficulty
The technical parts are situated only on the mule track in the Ponci Valley, with stretches of emerging rocks: some acquaintance is required when using a mountain bike. Some sudden spurts call for due attention. The overall rise is 501 m.

Cycling period
Winter, spring, fall.

Map
• *IGM* 92 - I - SO and 92 - I - SE.
• *Itinerari escursionistici collegati all'Alta Via dei Monti Liguri*, Pollupice Mountain Community.

• Arturo Borbonese, *I sentieri di Finale*, Bacchetta.

Technical assistance
• Sport e Natura, via Brunenghi 59, Finale Ligure; t. 019690007.
• Riviera Outdoor, via Nicotera 3/5, Finale Ligure; t. 0196898024.

Useful addresses
• IAT Finale Ligure, via S. Pietro 14, Finalmarina; t. 019692581.
• Associazione Alberghi e Turismo, via Saccone 1, Finalmarina; t. 019692615.

POINTS OF INTEREST

The **five Roman bridges** *on Via Iulia Augusta (I century B.C.) along the Ponci Valley. The Fairies' bridge (the first) is perfectly kept and is awe-inspiring for the impressiveness and the refinement used in its construction. At the top of the route, between the third and fourth bridge, you find the* **Roman caves** *where the Romans once used to extract stone for road paving.*

From the **Finale Pia** bridge, ride up the Sciusa torrent on the road to Vezzi Portio. After 2.1 km, turn right (bridge) to Verzi, on the small asphalt road that climbs up amid olive groves, up to the hairpin bend where you leave, to your left, the dirt road of the Ponci Valley (road sign "Via Iulia Augusta", 3 km). After passing the menhir of the Idolo di Pen, an ancient god of the Ligurians, enter the wild deep narrow valley of the Ponci, or "bridges". The first bridge you meet is the magnificent Fairies' bridge,

after which you enter the "rian" (bottom of the valley) of Punci, reaching marked crossroads (4.5 km), where you keep left, parallel to the streamlet, up to the Sordo bridge (collapsed), then followed by the well-kept Muto bridge. Soon after you reach a crossroads (5.1 km): now turn left on a rutted trail where, among the emerging rocks, traces of Roman carts are still visible, and climb up to the Roman caves. It's an easier ride to reach the Acqua bridge, near Ca' du Puncin. Now continue on a broad track that passes an uphill stretch in the wood to Colla di Magnone (318 m above sea level, 7 km). The meadow saddle is cut by a pathway that you take on your right. Once you arrive in front of a gate, turn left on the trail leading to the summit of the Bric dei Monti (406 m above sea level, 8.8 km).

Now go back for about 100 m and after a bend you'll notice a trail on your left amid the vegetation (a trail mark with crossed circle). This is where

an exciting long and winding downhill road starts; by constantly following the main trail, you reach an unsurfaced track that climbs up to the S.P. 45 provincial road (280 m above sea level, 12.2 km). Continue on asphalt road on your right, and after the first bend, turn left on a steep dirt road, then right, before the visible panoramic crossroads, on a broad trail that climbs up to Bric dei Crovi.

At the crossroads on the summit crest, keep right and climb up for a short stretch before starting a new descent along a track dug like a tunnel in the undergrowth. At the end, proceed on the dirt road to Mount Capo Noli, riding on your right to get back on the S.P. 45 provincial road, and then right again to the Ferrin restaurant. Opposite, a fast dirt path leads you to the San Giacomo Church (260 m above sea level, 16.2 km), from where you continue on asphalt road up to the near Arma delle Manie, a vast cavern once inhabited by Neanderthal man (16.5 km). From this spot, ride straight onto the dirt road, which then switches to mule track that leads you back on a downhill stretch to the crossroads of the Muto bridge (18.1 km). You then finally return to **Finale Pia** along the same route of the outward journey.

LEFT, riding amid olive groves.
PAGE OPPOSITE, under the gates of Finale.

Giovo
At the gates of the Beigua Nature Park

36 Km

In the mountains, just a stone's throw away from the sea. This is the leitmotif that accompanies the cycle tourist on the hillsides that form the territory of the Giovo Mountain Community, an area which, in its small way, holds the characteristics of the whole region of Liguria, locked between the sea and the mountains in a really tiny area.

The tour develops in the vicinity of the Mount Beigua Regional Park, winding in the woods of the former Selva dell'Orba, once inhabited in prehistoric times and the

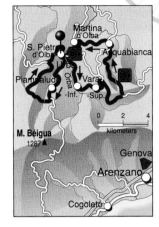

favorite hunting grounds of the Longobards. It's a very suggestive route, winding across virtually intact envi-

ronment with woods, glades and breathtaking views on the gorges of the River Orba. The traces of man are the old farm dwellings and the typical "alberghi", dry rooms made of stone for chestnuts. You start your ride from the square of the church of **San Pietro d'Olba**, an old village that still preserves traces of the distant past. In medieval times, the village was an agricultural and artisan center of the nearby Cistercian community of Tiglieto; between the XVII and XIX centuries, it became a thriving centre for iron working. Now con-

Technical info

Route
36 Km: San Pietro d'Olba - Vara Inferiore - Vara Superiore - Acquabianca - Piampaludo - Alberola - La Carta - San Pietro d'Olba.
You reach the starting point by taking the A 10 freeway, Albisola exit, and then the S.S. 334 Sassello main road. Or the A 26, Masone exit, then the road towards Tigleto-Urbe.

Difficulty
This route requires some training; the more challenging stretches are the uphill climbs between Vara Inferiore and Superiore (approximately 2 km) and between the crossroads of Alberola and Piampaludo (approximately 3 km).

Cycling period
From spring to late fall.

Road Map
Il Giovo in Bicicletta - sette percorsi oltre l'Aurelia with maps, altitude and description of the itineraries: distributed by the Giovo Mountain Community and the local tourist boards.

Technical assistance
• Zanini, via Pescetto 31, Albisola Superiore;
t. 019486932.
• Formula Uno Bici, corso Ferrari 65, Albisola Superiore;
t. 019489022.

Bicycle rental
• Rifugio Sciverna,

haml. of Maddalena, Sassello;
t. 019720081.
Open from March 15 to November 15.
• Guided tours with AMI leaders, Claudio Merlo, t. 3495782693.
Vanessa Curto, t. 3478434459.

Tourist information
• Comunità Montana Giovo, corso Italia 3, Savona;
t. 019841871.
www.comunitamontanagiovo.it
• Ente Parco del Beigua, corso Italia 3, Savona
t. 01984187300. www.parks.it.
• Centro Visite "Palazzo Gervino" - IAT Sassello via G.B. Badano 45, Sassello;
t. 019724020.

POINTS OF INTEREST

A visit to the **Mount Beigua Regional Park,** *18 thousand hectares of high-ground woods and prairies. Mount Beigua (1,287 m) is the peak of a plateau that stretches for 25 km from the Giovo to Turchino, a natural saddle lying between the Ligurian Sea and the Po Valley. The plateau is just over 5 km away from the sea, and this environmental feature allows plant species that usually belong to different ecosystems to live and grow in harmony. Further mention must be made of rare plants such as the bertoloni violet or the sweet-scented daphne, a strong perfumed flower, symbol of the Park.*

tinue riding on your right after the bridge towards Vara Inferiore, then after a tough uphill climb, to Vara Superiore. The route runs towards Acquabianca (skip the crossroads to Marasca), following a very suggestive panoramic stretch, then a steep descent on a narrow road, with no guard rail on the edge, overlooking the valley.

From Acquabianca, the inner part of the hamlets of the Municipality of Urbe, continue on your left heading towards Martina d'Olba. Now turn left again, and after a slope of 2.5 km, at the bridge, take the left turn leading you to the crossroads for Alberola. This very scenic road has a circular layout and is a highly

suggestive route as far as the landscape is concerned: the beech wood alternates with vast meadow plateaus characterized in some stretches by isolated groups of century-old majestic beech trees. Towards Piampaludo, the wood thins out and is replaced by shrubby vegetation typical of wet and swampy areas. From Alberola, ride down the Carta pass, where you find a small chapel dedicated to San Michele. Tradition has it that the chapel was built by Queen Teodolinda at the end of the VI century. Continue your ride down keeping right until you reach **San Pietro d'Olba**.

BELOW, riding towards San Pietro d'Olba.

Between the Magra and La Spezia   45 Km
Montemarcello and the Poets' Gulf

Highly suggestive itinerary between the Mediterranean light of the Poets' Gulf and the serenity of the River Magra, on roads made to measure for cycle touring.

Start from **Montemarcello** taking the via Nuova to Lerici. Run down along olive groves and Mediterranean scrubland, then climb up cutting through a holm-oak and cluster-pine wood. Now ride downwards through the cultivated terraces of the Figarole up to Zanego. From here, you climb up again for a short stretch and then descend with a wide view of the gulf and the coastline between Tellaro and Maralunga. The route continues amid olive groves, until you reach Serra, and after passing the stone arch that goes over the provincial road, take the S.S. 331 Lerici main road, which you cover for a short stretch, then turn left on via Militare. The road now climbs up towards Pugliola, then continues on a level section offering you a view of the Lerici Gulf and of the castle. After passing Solaro, you reach the Tre Strade crossroads, where you turn right to Pitelli. Pass the town on via Biancamano, then turn right in

POINTS OF INTEREST

The **Montemarcello-Magra Nature Park** *was founded in 1982 to safeguard the river areas of the Magra and the Vara. Since 1995, the protected area has also comprised the Caprione promontory, from Bocca di Magra up to Lerici. The route running from the Magra to the Cisa pass is a very busy migratory route covered by herons, dwarf herons, cormorants and* Anatidae *that usually winter or nest on the banks of the river and in several ponds.*

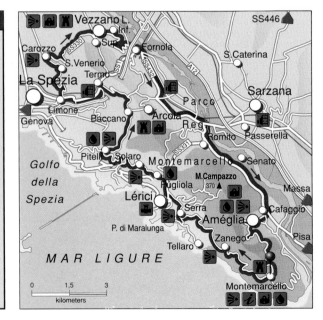

Technical info 🔄 ‖ 🚴

Route
45 Km: Montemarcello - Zanego - Serra - Pugliola - Pitelli - Bonamini - Baccano - Monti - Limone - San Venerio - Carozzo - Vezzano Ligure - Fornola - Senato - Ameglia - Montemarcello.
All on asphalt roads. You reach the starting point by exiting the freeway at Sarzana: continuation towards the south on the Aurelia alternative route, turning right on the S.P. 21 provincial road to Marinella up to Montemarcello.

Difficulty
There are no tough climbs, but it is a varied itinerary as far as altitude is concerned, with constant up and downhill stretches (except for the level section of 10 km from Fornola to Cafaggio). The most grueling climb runs from Limone to Vezzano Superiore (6.5 km, 230 m rise).

Cycling period
All year round.

Map
Atlante stradale d'Italia, Northern volume, 1:200,000, TCI.

Bicycle + Train
For train travelers, the itinerary can start from the Arcola station on the La Spezia-Pisa line.

Technical assistance
Eurobikes di Arpesella, via Provinciale 87, Romito (SP); t. 0187989477.

Tourist information
• APT Cinque Terre e Golfo dei poeti, viale Mazzini 47 C.P. 345, La Spezia; t. 0187770900.
www.aptcinqueterre.sp.it
• Information offices and tourist accommodation via Biaggini 6, Lerici; t. 0187967346; via Nuova 48, Montemarcello; t. 0187691071.
• Ente Parco di Montemarcello-Magra, via Paci 2, I Sarzana; t. 0187691071.
www.parks.it/parco.montemarcello.magra

the S.P. 16 provincial road. Now turn right until reaching Vezzano Superiore with its X century pentagonal tower and typical steeple. Continue along the S.P. 16 provincial road (stop at the Romanesque parish church of Santa Maria) until you reach Fornola, where you enter the S.P. 10 provincial road. Keep right and pass under the freeway loop. Turn immediately left on the S.S. 1 Aurelia main road that leads to Pisa. Turn

ABOVE, the Tellaro church.
PAGE OPPOSITE, view from the top of the Lerici port.

Piazza 4 Novembre and continue on an uphill stretch along via Canabrino. Now leave the coast side and ride towards the hinterland. Proceed on the ridge along via Fostella, crossing the villages of Pietralba and Bonamini. After reaching Baccano, turn left on the S.P. 19 provincial road that passes the town. Continue your ride approaching the 18th century Villa Picedi, the parish

church of Saints Stefano and Margherita and the houses of Monti di Arcola, then descend towards Termo.
Now turn left on the S.S. 1 Aurelia main road for 2 km. Pass the Termo, Melara and Limone, then turn right to San Venerio. Once in the village, turn left for via San Rocco, skirting the church. At Carozzo, enter the town and ride on the paved lane of via Vespucci until you take

right on the S.S. 331 main road and once you've reached Romito Magra, leave the road and make a left detour on the S.S. 432 main road, skirting the hamlet of Senato. At Cafaggio, leave the S.S. 432 main road and go right along via Camisano, until you reach Ameglia after a climb, then ride towards **Montemarcello**, passing through piazza della Libertà, via Cavour and via Colombo.

Lombardy

The Adda Nord Park
From Trezzo to Paderno
27 Km

The old power stations route is one of the most beautiful itineraries in the park, for both the presence of the river, bounded by wooded banks and alternating torrential and calm stretches across marshland, and for the numerous traces of industrial archaeology.

After leaving the XIX century Villa Gina, seat of the park at **Trezzo d'Adda**, turn immediately left along a pedestrian road that drops sharply down to the sanctuary. From this point, take the tow path that climbs up the course of the Adda and brushes the mouth of the Martesana Canal. Pass

the freeway bridge and reach the bridge at Trezzo, then continue your ride to via Alzaia. Should that not be possible, climb up on your left along a switchback towards the castle. Once out of the castle park, take on your right via Barnabò Visconti and return on the bank of the Adda near

Technical info

Route
27 Km: Trezzo d'Adda - Trezzo castle - Esterle power station - Bertini power station – Church of Santa Maria della Rocchetta - Paderno dam – Trezzo bridge. Except for the detour to Paderno on rugged country paths, the itinerary runs along the river on the "via Alzaia" for cyclists and pedestrians only. You can reach Trezzo sull'Adda by car from Milan by taking the A4 freeway to Venice, Trezzo exit. From the toll booth, turn left following the road signs pointing to the Concesa Sanctuary.

Difficulty
Except for the steep climb to Paderno, no other hardships await you on this itinerary. You could also try a gearless bicycle, although we suggest a good touring bike or a mountain bike.

Cycling period
All year round

Bicycle + Train
The Paderno railroad station is situated along the Bergamo-Milan line.

Map
IGM pages 89-91,1:25,000.

Technical assistance
Motta, via Dante 25, Trezzo; t. 029090443.

Bicycle rental
• Cooperativa Sociale Castello, piazzale Gorizia, Trezzo; t. 029090664, 3351210285, 029091543. web.tiscalinet.it/coopcastello Open every day.
• Bar Al Vecchio Lavatoio, via Alzaia 13, Trezzo (near the Taccani hydro-electric power station); t. 0290939892.

Tourist information
Parco dell'Adda Nord, Villa Gina, via Padre Calvi 3, haml. of Concesa, Trezzo; t. 029090766. www.parks.it/parco.adda.nord/

POINTS OF INTEREST

Built between 1887 and 1889, and designed by Swiss engineer Rothlisberger, the **iron bridge of Paderno** *is a refined construction modeled on similar contemporary works of the famed Eiffel. Rumor has it that the designer killed himself by jumping off the bridge, fearing it would not have stood the weight of trains. In actual fact, Rothlisberger's project, which cost 1,850,000 lire at the time, was never upset by any fatalities.*

the Taccani hydro-electric power station, built in 1906 (refreshment spot and bicycle rental). Continue riding up the course of the river on a smooth dirt path for bikes and pedestrians, and reach the Esterle power station (1914). Shortly after, the Paderno Canal flows into the Adda, which you follow on an asphalt road up to the Bertini power station (1898), built to produce energy for the tramway network of Milan. Pass the canal, continuing for a stretch between the canal

BELOW, along the Adda towards Paderno.

and the Adda, then go back to follow the right bank of the canal that moves away from the river and reaches the Sanctuary of Santa Maria della Rocchetta (XIV century). Just after the sanctuary, a path on your left allows you to walk to an interesting scenic spot on the Adda rapids. Now reach the old Paderno dam and the mouth of the homonymous canal, where you meet the small church of Santa Maria Addolorata, an information spot of the park's environmental guards (open on Sundays). Ride under the iron bridge of Paderno and near the mouth of the canal of the Esterle power station, then turn left, climbing up a steep uphill asphalt road that leads to Paderno. After reaching the church of the Alpines (XVIII century), in remembrance of the 1630 plague, enter via Airoldi on your right, then via Marconi, the first on your left passing over the railroad that ends at the traffic lights. Ride straight ahead on strada Fornace. Soon after, on your left, you'll see the Assunta farm, an extraordinary example of fin de siécle rural architec-

ture. Proceed along strada Fornace, then reach the intersection, where you turn left to reach Porto d'Adda. Now opposite the church, turn left entering via 25 Aprile and ride down towards Porto Inferiore. The road now switches to dirt path, and with a long rectilinear stretch, reaches the Esterle power station and the bank of the Adda. Ride back along the Adda to return to **Trezzo d'Adda**.

ALTERNATIVE

An extra stretch could be the wonderful ride from Paderno to Brivio d'Adda (about 5 km) with the ride back along the same road.

Montevecchia and the Curone Valley 14 Km
Mountain bike ride in the Park

The Montevecchia hill marks the border between the Po Valley and the Prealps, just north of Milan. It is an extensive relief, approximately 600 m high, bounded on the west by the Santa Croce Valley and on the north-east by the Curone Valley, where a nature park was created.

At the parking lot before the **Molinazzo**, on the S.P. 54 Cernusco-Montevecchia provincial road, starts via dei Carpini (n. 10), which runs high on the bank of the Curone torrent inside the Carpini wood. Ford the torrent four times, emerging from the wood under the Bagaggera farm. Soon after, you reach a cross-roads in the wood again, where you keep left, going back to the Curone, and then emerging on the broad dirt road that climbs up to the Valfredda farm. At the farm, turn right on the mule track that cuts the gentle slopes of Valfredda, with sweeping views on the upper Curone Valley and on Mount Brianza, and reaches, after going back into the wood, Ca' del Soldato, an old renovated farm that presently houses the Park Center. At this point, start following via dei Cipressi (n. 1), taking the broad level dirt road leading towards the aqueduct. Now

POINTS OF INTEREST

*On the terraces that cover most of the south-western slope of the Montevecchia hill, you can spot the typical **rosemary** cultivations, a particular crop (once made from a fine native species) passed down over the centuries. The **Curone Valley**, at the foot of the north-eastern slope of the hill, is one of the best preserved spots in Brianza.*

Technical info

Route
14 Km: Molinazzo (parking lot) via dei Carpini - Cascina Bagaggera - Cascina Valfredda - Ca' del Soldato - Ospedaletto – Cascina Busarengo - Cascina Rata - Pianello belvedere - Galbusera Bianca - Malnido - Guaidana - Cascina Belsedere - Molinazzo. You can reach the starting point by taking the eastern bypass of Milan towards the north; you then follow the S.S. 342 main road until you reach Cernusco Lombardone; just after the traffic lights, take on your left the S.P. 54 provincial road leading to Montevecchia, and after 1 km, you'll spot the Molinazzo parking lot.

Difficulty
This itinerary has many fords and must be covered by mountain bike. There are few rises (390 m), squeezed in just a few spurts. Most of the route stretches over rather narrow single-tracks.

Cycling period
From spring to fall.

Bicycle + Train
You can reach the starting point of the itinerary, near the Cascina Molizza, by train: Milan-Lecco line, Cernusco Lombardone station, situated at approximately 500 m from the Molinazzo.

Map
Parco Naturale di Montevecchia e della Valle del Curone - I sentieri, scale 1:40,000, published by the Park.

Technical assistance
Il Biciaio, via Statale 111, Merate (along the S.S. 342 main road, approximately 1 km after the traffic lights of Cernusco Lombardone); t. 0399901555.

Tourist information
• Centro Parco Ca' del Soldato, Valle del Curone; t. 0395311275.
• Parco di Montevecchia e Valle del Curone, via Donzelli 9, Montevecchia (near the town hall); t. 0399930384.

ride down a path to the right side of the Curone, skirting it until you reach Ospedaletto, concealed by the vegetation on the other bank. Ignore the bridge, keep left, and after the ford, continue your ride in the bottom of the valley, one of the most captivating areas in the park. Once you pass the glade, the route climbs up on the left side of the valley, and after a sharp hairpin bend towards the right, gets steeper, emerges from the wood and reaches the Busarengo farm. Continue on a dirt road that climbs up to the Rata farm, where you keep left until you reach the Pianello belvedere. Now take the level path on your right leading you to the ridge of the crag; you reach it keep-

Above, ridge road in the park. Page Opposite, Sanctuary of the Blessed Virgin of the Carmelo at Montevecchia.

ing left of the various crossroads. Go straight ahead on panoramic up and downhill stretches, until you reach a tip crowned by a circle of cypress trees, the ideal spot to enjoy a bird's eye view on Montevecchia.

Now ride down to the nearby Galbusera Bianca, keeping right under the hillock of the cypress trees. Before reaching the farm, turn left on a level dirt road that takes you to the asphalt path stretching down towards Malnido, and shortly ahead, to the Ca' del Soldato parking lot. Soon after, at the Fornace, get back on the dirt road that climbs up to the Valfredda farm; this time you ride past the farm, on the dirt road, and reach Guaidana, then just further up, the Butto crossroads (asphalt). Ignore the uphill climb on your right to Montevecchia Alta, take the left road to the Belsedere farm, opposite which you enter a path on your left that takes you back onto via dei Carpini and to the **Molinazzo** parking lot (14 km).

The Ticino Park Abbiatense

25 Km

This easy, enjoyable itinerary twists its way into the Abbiategrasso countryside, tween open expanses of land, rice fields, woods and old farms. There are two main destinations: the river, which you reach at the Capanna Vecchia, and the Morimondo Abbey, an outstanding example of history and art.

From the Visconti castle of **Abbiategrasso** (XIII century), just a stone's throw away from the railroad station, ride along via Matteotti up to the small roundabout opposite the Camillo Golgi Geriatric Institute. On the right side of the Institute, take via Annoni, then ride straight ahead, follow via Ticino and leave the town.

After riding for about 6 km, you'll spot on your right the road signs pointing to the Park Center for Environmental Education, housed in the former Enrichetta solarium, in the middle of the wood. At this point, follow the fitness path, reach the asphalt road, then the bank of the Ticino near the Capanna Vecchia refreshment spot, where you find a small harbor and a group of huts.

From the last huts towards the valley, get back on the fitness path and ride for a stretch along the bank of the river. Now return on the asphalt road and ride back to Abbiategrasso up to the small church of the Remondata farm, one of the oldest farms in the area. Turn right on the dirt road leading to the Bellotta farm. Continue your ride, brushing the Broggina farm, preceded by a wet taxodium wood, a swamp cypress that grows in flooded woods. Now proceed straight ahead along the dirt road, passing a level crossing, until you reach the S.S. 494 main road. Turn right and ride along the main road (watch out for traffic!) for 200 m, un-

Technical info

Route
25 Km: Abbiategrasso - Capanna Vecchia - Cascina Bellotta - Cascina Broggina - Cascina Santa Maria del Bosco - Cascina Casorasca - Morimondo - Abbiategrasso. On lightly-trafficked asphalt roads, with long dirt stretches. We suggest using a mountain bike or a robust touring bike. You can reach Abbiategrasso from Milan (23 km) by car, taking the S.S. 494 main road to Vigevano.

Difficulty
Ideal for everyone.

Cycling period
Spring and fall.

Bicycle + Train
The Abbiategrasso railroad station is situated along the Milan-Mortara-Alessandria line. Departures from the Porta Genova station.

Map
Parco del Ticino Lombardo, 1:17,000, Orizzonte, Milan.

Technical assistance
Cicli Battistella Euromoto, via Isonzo 2, Pontevecchio di Magenta; t. 029793776.

Bicycle rental
• Orizzonte,
c/o Cicli "Battistella",
Pontevecchio di Magenta;
t. 02/67391283.
• Camping Ticinia,
via Edison 1,
near the Vigevano bridge;
t. 0381347592.

Tourist information
• Parco Lombardo
Valle del Ticino, via Isonzo 1,
Pontevecchio di Magenta;
t. 0297210205.
www.parks.it/parco.ticino.
lombardo/
• Centro Visite
c/o Riserva La Fagiana,
Pontevecchio di Magenta,
open Saturdays and Sundays,
9.30-12,30 a.m. and 2.30-6.30
p.m.; t. 02972101.
• Centro Parco e Centro
di Educazione Ambientale
"Colonia Enrichetta",
Abbiategrasso;
t. 0294608518.
www.naturaaltrove.org

POINTS OF INTEREST

"Mori mundo" (to die in the world), this is the name the Cistercian monks gave to the abbey they founded in Borgogna, near Langres. In 1134, thirteen of them reached the Ticino, and after two years, founded this magnificent abbey we can still admire today, giving it the same name of their mother convent: **Morimondo**.

til you reach the first bend, where you take the farm road running straight to the Santa Maria del Bosco farm. Through the poplar trees, reach the Casorasca farm, then an intersection. On your right, you'll spot the Cascina Lasso farm holidays (meals to be reserved). Instead, the itinerary follows the left path that enters the wood and arrives straight at the gates of the mill of the Prato Ronco farm.

Don't cross the irrigation ditch, just skirt the farm fence and ride up on a short climb in the wood. After reaching the crossroads of the Cerina di Sopra farm, go straight ahead along a pleasant and shaded asphalt path, until you reach a former quarry that has been transformed into a lakelet. At this point, you reach a crossroads and take the road on your right leading to Morimondo, where you'll find good eating-houses and restaurants, and to the magnificent abbey. Once you leave the town, near the cemetery, cross the S.S. 526 main road and take the cycle-pedestrian track of the Naviglio Grande. After riding for 500 m, reach the bank of the Bereguardo Canal and turn left. Following the cycle lane for 5 km along the canal, get back to **Abbiategrasso**, cross the main road (watch out for traffic again!) and go straight ahead, until you reach viale Mazzini. Now turn left, and after passing the level crossing, return to the castle.

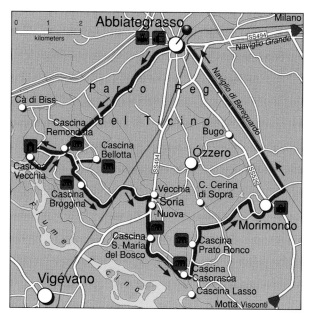

ABOVE, technical stop near a crook of the Ticino.

Lodigiano   33.5 Km
Between Lodi and Abbadia Cerreto

A land shaped by nature and man, the Lodigiano preserves a harmony and an aura to be experienced by slowly moving along small roads and great spaces.

You start off from **Lodi** passing porta Cremona and taking corso Mazzini. After about 600 m, turn left on the narrow and lightly-trafficked Vecchia Cremonese. Continue riding for 1.2 km, then, after crossing the last houses, turn left on a small road that cuts through the countryside towards the Maldotta and Coldana farms. Now ride along the dirt road and reach the edges of the terrace at the Costino farm.

Just a short stretch after, you can take a left detour to Ca' del Conte and continue your ride up to the Adda. At this point, you'll find the Mairana farm and, if you like, you can continue your tour on the dirt road that reaches Morta di Soltarico. Once back on the main road, continue riding on your left, entering the Nuova Cremonese leading to Caviaga. Ride along the irrigation ditch and reach the crossroads for Soltarico. A small road makes its way into the countryside towards the woods along the river, crosses the small built-up area and enters the lush river vegetation up to the dead arm of the river. Now ride back on the

Nuova Cremonese, until you reach the crossroads for Cavenago d'Adda. Once in the town, opposite Villa

POINTS OF INTEREST

Lodi's **Piazza della Vittoria,** *a typical example of "platea maior" dating back to the Dark Ages. Other interesting spots in Lodi are the* **Cathedral,** *the* **Church of the Incoronata** *and the* **Town Museum** *(Corso Umberto I, t. 0371420369), with its majolicas and ceramics (XV to XIX centuries). At Abbadia Cerreto you can stop and visit the* **Cistercian Abbey of Saints Pietro and Paolo.**

Technical info

Route
33.5 Km: Lodi - Caviaga - Cavenago d'Adda - Persia - Casaletto Ceredano - Abbadia Cerreto - Ronchi - Isella farm - Corte Palosio - Cadilana - Fontana - Revellino - Lodi. On mostly asphalt by-roads.

Difficulty
Easy itinerary, ideal for everybody.

Cycling period
All year round, preferably in spring and fall.

Bicycle + Train
The railroad station is situated along the Milan-Bologna line, 36 km away from Milan.

Map
IGM, 1:50,000, pages 140 Lodi and 141 Crema.

Bicycle rental
Cooperativa L'Ortica, Parco Isola Carolina, viale Dalmazia, Lodi; t. 0371410540, 3394341145.

Technical assistance
• Boccardo Giuseppe, via San Bassiano e Alberto 31, Lodi; t. 0371610230.
• Dilie Francesco, piazza Fiume 1, Lodi; t. 0371420619.

Tourist information
• APT Lodigiano, piazza Broletto 4, Lodi; t. 0371421391. www.apt.lodi.it
• Ciclodi - FIAB, c/o Spagnolello Pina, via Vecchio Bersaglio 12, Lodi; t. 0371411812.
• Turbolento Veloclub, via Cosimo del Fante, Milan; t. 0258309584. www.turbolento.net
• Parco Regionale Adda Sud, via A. Grandi 6, Lodi; t. 037135747. www.parks.it/parco.adda.sud

Greppi, turn right on the road that takes you to the Sanctuary of the Madonna della Costa.

After getting back to town, pass the town hall and reach the church. Ride down towards the bridge over the Adda, around the terrace that rises up like a natural fortification. After passing the river, turn left towards the Persia farm, then to Ca' de Vagni, where you turn left again, taking the road to Casaletto Ceredano (2.7 km from Persia). Ride for less than 2.5 km up to Abbadia Cerreto, where you stop and enjoy the beauty of the abbey. Once back on the main road, cross the bridge over the Tormo brook. After passing the bridge, go left reaching the embankment of the Adda. Now that you're back in the square, leave town until you reach two de-

tours. At the second detour on your right, ride across cultivated expanses of land, grazing San Cipriano, and then climb around a small prominence entering the large courtyard. Now proceed on a dirt road that passes near the Ronchi, Dosso and Molina farms, where you turn left on a secondary track

that leads you back on the provincial road, opposite the Isella farm.

At this stage of the ride, go straight ahead until you get to the Ancona farm. After crossing the farmyard, turn left, reaching the Casellario farm (eating-house on the banks of the lake). Once you return to the Ancona farm, continue the ride on your left towards Corte Palasio (about 1 km). Cross the town and turn left reaching Cadilana (3.5 km, passing by the San Marcellino farm) where your tour continues towards Fontana (1.5 km).

Now reach the main road, then turn left, then left again towards several sheds that you skirt, until you reach the Tre Cascine crossroads. Ride straight ahead to Revellino, the bridge over the Adda and **Lodi**.

LEFT, view of the characteristic Lodigiano countryside.

The Adda Sud Park   51 Km
Cycling up to the Po

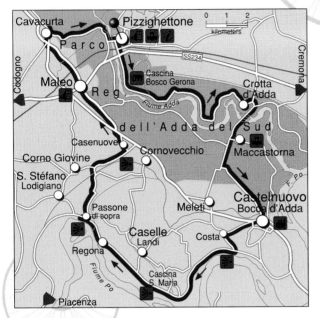

The Adda Sud Park, on its southern edge, spreads out close to the Po. Farming is the staple activity practiced between the two rivers, although plain woods can still be seen, while in many stretches, the banks of the river bear witness to the evolution of this "waterland".

You start your tour from **Pizzighettone**, *riding along the left bank of the Adda.*

After passing the city walls near porta Soccorso, continue riding near the river and up the embankment; now cross the S.S. 234 main road and proceed along the course of the Adda.

Pass near the Adda Morta Nature Reserve, a marshy basin born of a river flood. After approximately 10 km, leave the embankment and enter Crotta d'Adda, a town situated near a crook of the

BELOW, aerial view of a stretch of the Adda.

56

river. In via Acquanegra, after leaving the built-up area, stop and admire Villa Stanga, a wonderful example of Baroque architecture. After reaching the junction with the S.P. 47 provincial road, turn right following the road signs for Castelnuovo, then cross the bridge over the Adda. It would be worthwhile, shortly after, to take a left detour to the Maccastorna castle (XIII century), one of the most important small Visconti fortresses of the dukedom of Milan.

Now continue your ride along the S.P. 196 provincial road up to the crossroads on your left for Castelnuovo Bocca d'Adda, getting there by taking the S.P. 243 provincial road.

Cross the town, continuing your ride on via Umberto I. Towards the end of the built-up area, turn left for the Costa farm, riding towards the embankment of the Po, getting there after 3 km.

Now ride upstream along the course of this vast river for about 10 km, passing near the Palazzo farm (after 5 km), with its pigeon tower that rises in the central body of the rural building. Further ahead, you can distinguish, among the poplar groves, the "bodro delle Punte", a circular basin, the remains of a bed abandoned by the river. After leaving Regona, near a sand quarry, turn right on the S.P. 113 provincial road that passes between the houses

Technical info

Route
51 Km: Pizzighettone - Crotta d'Adda - Maccastorna - Castelnuovo Bocca d'Adda - Regona - Casenuove - Maleo - Cavacurta - Pizzighettone. On roads made for cycling. You can reach the starting point (60 km from Milan) by taking the A1 freeway: Casalpusterlengo exit, further stretch on the S.S. 234 main road leading to Cremona.

Difficulty
No problems on this itinerary, all the roads are virtually level. It's just a question of getting used to staying on a saddle for 3 hours.

Cycling period
All year round, preferably in the intermediate seasons, fall and spring.

Bicycle + Train
The Pizzighettone railroad station is situated along the Milan-Codogna-Cremona line.

Road map
G. Camuri, G. Musitelli, *Tra rosse presenze e verdi silenzi*, APT Lodigiano: 5 artistical-environmental itineraries in the Lodigiano.

Map
Atlante stradale d'Italia, Northern volume, 1: 200,000, TCI.

Technical assistance
Zignani Carlo, via V. Emanuele 33, Pizzighettone; t. 037274339.

Tourist information
• APT Lodigiano, piazza Broletto 4, Lodi; t. 0371421391; www.apt.lodi.it
• Ciclodi - FIAB, c/o Spagnolello Pina, via Vecchio Bersaglio 12, Lodi; t. 0371411812.
• Turbolento Veloclub, via Cosimo del Fante, Milan; t. 0258309584 www.turbolento.net
• Parco Regionale Adda Sud, via A. Grandi 6, Lodi; t. 037135747. www.parks.it/parco.adda.sud

of Passone di Sopra. After a short stretch, turn left for Corno Giovine, riding along the winding path that crosses extensive maize plantations. After the bridge over the Gandiolo Canal, you reach a crossroads. Keep right, riding towards Casenuove surrounded by tall poplars and alders. From Casenuove, continue riding on your left towards the S.P. 27 provincial road, then turn left, and immediately afterwards (100 m), turn right, follow the

road signs pointing to Chiesuolo and reach Maleo. Once you reach Cavacurta, take the cemetery road and follow the road signs indicating the Portina farm. At the first crossroads, carry on riding, ignoring the detour on your left leading to the Castellina farm. At the second crossroads, turn right, at the third, right again, and at the fourth, turn left towards the Adda.

Just less than 2 km and you reach **Pizzighettone**.

The Lariano Triangle   38 Km
The crossing from Brunate to Bellagio

The Lariano Triangle is a portion of mountains wedged between the two southern arms of Lake Como. It's a mystical world, made of valleys and hills, whose position, at the edge of the Lombard plain, offers breathtaking views.

From the forecourt of the **Brunate** cable railroad, take the road to San Maurizio (CAO Refuge road signs). After reaching the square, continue your ride on asphalt road up to the CAO Refuge, on the western slopes of Mount Uccellera. At this point, you ride on a tough dirt road that climbs up to the

Bondella chalet, then to the Boletto chalet, situated just before the homonymous peak (1,236 m above sea level). This stretch cuts the panoramic slope that bounds to the south the reliefs of the Lariano Triangle: you can enjoy the spectacular sights on the Lombard plain and on the Apennines. A grueling,

though short climb takes you to the crossroads under the peak of the Boletto, where you keep left on the mule track that takes you to the Molina pass and to the nearby San Pietro hut (8 km). At the pass, follow the left path that straddles the ridge descending from Mount Bolettone, running along its we-

Technical info

Route

38 Km: Brunate - Molina pass - Lemma pass - Palanzo pass - Faello hill - Mount Croce - Colma dei Cippei - Colma del Bosco - Alpe Spessola - Rovenza - Brogno - Bellagio: 965 m rise on dirt road. If you take the rack railroad, you gain a 513 m rise between Como and Brunate. From Bellagio, you return by boat, a service run by Navigazione del Lago di Como (from Easter through October, last ride at 4.30 p.m.).

Difficulty

Tough route, requiring

a leaning towards cycling on mountain paths and mule tracks, and good practice. Covered in 4.30-6.30 hours.

Cycling period

From late spring to fall.

Bicycle + Train

The Como Nord/Lago railroad station is really close to the Como-Brunate cableway, on the eastern lakefront.

Map

• *Lago di Como - Lago di Lugano*, page 91, 1:50,000.

• *IGM*, page 32, tables I - NO, I - SO and II - NO, 1:25,000.

Technical assistance

• Martinelli, viale Lecco 95,

Como; t. 031264417.

• Riccardi, via Diaz 90, Como; t. 031260105.

Tourist information

• Como, piazza Cavour 16; t. 031269712.

• Bellagio, Imbarcadero landing, piazza Mazzini; t. 031950204.

• Navigazione Lago di Como, piazza Cavour, landing n. 3, Como; t. 031304060.

• Lungo Lario Manzoni 1, Bellagio; t. 031951980.

stern flank. At this point of the ride, you reach another crossroads, where you keep left on the path again that crosses, on hard ground, a splendid beechwood with a series of ups and downs and twists and turns. From the Lemna pass (11.5 km), at the crossroads marked on the ridge between Mounts Bolettone and Palanzone, go straight ahead on the dirt road that abruptly climbs up to the Palanzo pass. After emerging from the wood, ride straight towards the summit of the Palanzone, then go west, cutting, on an uphill stretch, the grassy slope up to the Riella refuge (13.8 km). From the terrace, enjoy the sweeping view on the lake, the Lugano Prealps and the Rosa Group. The climb ends near a monument with tombstones, where you turn right across the Faello pass, at the foot of the Bûl summit. With a series of ups and downs, reach the Caglio pass, under Mount Croce, then get ready for the uphill climb directly on the ridge, reaching the peak (16.4 km). At the group of beeches, take

the steep descent on a mule track that takes you to the col between Mounts Croce and Pianchetta. Now turn left, dodging the summits of Mount Panchetta and of Mount Falo, and emerge at the Colma del Piano (19 km). Pass over the asphalt road, and aside the La Colma restaurant, take a cart road with a smooth and panoramic route. Now climb up to the Colma dei Cippei, the Colma del Bosco and the Alpe Spessola (22.9 km), then ride straight ahead and get ready for the tough climb to Mount Ponciv. At the crossroads, keep on the left path leading to the summit (1,453 m above sea level). At this point starts the long descent along the path that moves away from the pool, across the fir-wood of the San Primo Park, and enters the road, where you keep left towards Alpe delle Ville. Follow the road signs and climb back to the Martina Refuge, then take, on your right, a downhill path that joins up with the broad dirt road with a few asphalt stretches, and drops down towards Rovenza. At the fountain, keep left and ride down the cart road that crosses the built-up areas of Gravedona, Seller and Brogno. Follow the paved track up to Perlo, and then take the asphalt road that runs behind Villa Melzi and reaches the **Bellagio** pier.

LEFT, cycling at the Molina pass.
PAGE OPPOSITE, view of Bellagio.

POINTS OF INTEREST

During your crossing from Bellagio to Como, you'll have time to admire on the western side: Villa Carlotta di Tremezzo; Villa del Balbianello, on the promontory covered by the splendid garden; Comacina island; Villa d'Este and Villa Erba, at Cernobbio; Villa Gallia, La Rotonda and Villa Olmo, the apotheosis of Neoclassicism, overlooking the lake where the city of Como starts. On the eastern bank, just before Torno, Villa Pliniana, the most wonderful example of Mannerism on the Lario.

Monte Isola   9 Km
The mountain tour around Lake Iseo

A short ride in search of an oasis of serenity that seems to float in the blue waters of Lake Iseo. Monte Isola is the largest lake island in Europe and is a golden opportunity to take off with your bike and spend a peaceful day outdoors on a true island, a paradise for trekkers and cycle tourists in search of genuine places.

At the end of your short ferry-boat crossing, time-space dimensions seem to expand, so just relax and rediscover slowness.
To explore Monte Isola, you can plan an easy and extremely pleasant tour along the coast road, a classical itinerary well-known by cycle tourists who cycle near Lake Iseo. Every moment is a good moment, but bear in mind that boats carry bicycles only during weekdays.

Technical info

Route
9 Km: Sulzano - Peschiera Maraglio (ferry boat) - Sensole - Menzino - Sinchignano - Siviano - Carzano - Peschiera Maraglio - Sulzano (ferry boat).
On quiet roads.

Difficulty
Easy itinerary, ideal also for families with children along.

Cycling period
All year round, although during the holidays, the boats suspend the bicycle transport service.

Bicycle + Train
Basso Sebino railroad,
Info TrenoBlu;
t. 0354243937.
Group reservation;
t. 3388577210.
fti@ferrovieturistiche.it

Map
Comunità Montana del Sebino Bresciano,

Map of the paths,1:25,000, ed. Risorse e Ambiente.

Bicycle rental and transport
During holidays, the boats suspend the bicycle transport service. At Monte Isola, you'll find the following bicycle and scooter rental spots, open from April to September:
• Mazzucchelli, Carzano;
t. 0309825144.
• Guizzetti, Sensole and Peschiera Maraglio;
t. 0309825228.

Tourist Information
• Ufficio Informazioni e Accoglienza Turistica di Iseo; Lungolago Marconi 2, Iseo;
t. 030980209.
• Ufficio Turistico di Monte Isola, via Peschiera M. 150, Peschiera Maraglio;
t. 0309825088.
(open in summer).

You can reach Sulzano by train or by car. The ideal starting point is the free parking lot situated near the railroad station, which you reach by turning right on the uphill climb, at the traffic lights in the town center. Go down to the port and catch the boat to **Peschiera Maraglio**.
Once on the island, start your tour by taking the lakefront road southwards,

POINTS OF INTEREST

The walk to the **Sanctuary of the Madonna della Ceriola,** *whose festival is celebrated on the second Sunday of July. You get there after a 2 hours' walk from Peschiera Maraglio, crossing Cure.* **"Menzino in festa",** *the last weekend of July and the first in August: these are the only chances to visit the Old-ofredi-Martinengo fortress.*

cycling amid cultivated olive terraces up to the town of Sensole (approximately 1.5 km) overlooking the islet of San Paolo.

At this point, we suggest taking a detour towards the town, along a path leading to the boat wharf. A steep, though asphalt alleyway takes you back on the main road. Now ride up until reaching Menzino, then after crossing Sinchignano, continue on a level road for Siviano (roughly 2.5 km from Sensole), the island's municipal seat, with its typical Martinengo tower.

Cross the town up to the war memorial opposite a small church, where you turn left on a slight descent. Just after Siviano, leave, on your left, the detour towards the port and continue riding downhill to Carzano (1.5 km). It's an interesting thing to know that in this village, every five years, on the occasion of the

Festival of Santa Croce, its 240 inhabitants blanket the entire town with flowers: Carzano thus becomes a magnificent wood in full bloom.

This old tradition dates back to 1835, when the miraculous end of a cholera epidemic was celebrated with the procession of the Santa Croce. The next event is

scheduled for September 2005. Your nice trip proceeds following the lakefront road. Leave Carzano and return to **Peschiera Maraglio** with a delightful 3 km ride along the waters. One interesting feature, just before reaching the town, is the Archetti yards where wooden boats are, still today, built by hand.

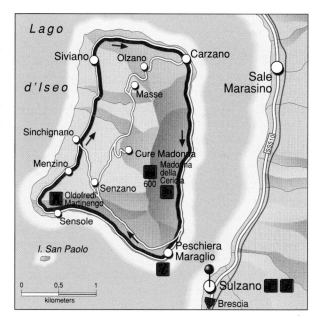

ABOVE, Peschiera Maraglio.
PAGE OPPOSITE, typical vessel at Carzano.

🚲 Franciacorta   17 Km
Amid the vineyards of Corte Franca

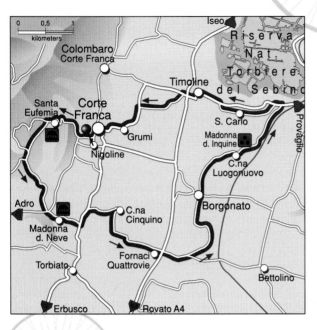

A land of gentle hills blanketed with vineyards, medieval towers and patrician villas, Franciacorta is a moraine amphitheatre south of Lake Iseo, where top quality wines are produced, wines such as the excellent sparkling DOCG Franciacorta, king of its category in Italy. The itinerary crosses a slightly wavy countryside embraced by reliefs covered with woods, which give these places an aura of peace and serenity.

You start your ride from **Nigoline**, seat of the Municipality of Corte Franca, following via Santa Eufemia, which reaches the mountain slopes. Now take a slight climb on a pebbly road leading to the Sanctuary of Sant'Eufemia (XII century).

After passing a crossroads, turn left on the dirt road that drops down to vineyards, keeping on the main track.

Following the trail mark (n° 7), turn left on a path that goes back up the prominence. At the end of the vineyards, the road, which runs perpendicular to the slope of the hill, reaches a nice scenic spot on the plain.

Ride down on your right, passing near the Saline farm and reaching the asphalt road of Nigoline - Adro. Continue by following the road signs pointing to the Sanctuary of the Madonna della Neve (XVII century). Now take a downhill stretch, leaving the church to your right, along via San Zeno, up to a crossroads, where you turn left, then right on the asphalt road towards the Cinquino farm.

Crossing the countryside, you intersect the Rovato-Iseo provincial road near Fornaci Quattrovie. After riding for 1 km towards Passirano, turn left on a cart road, which initially runs parallel to the road, then climbs up in a wonderful oak wood. The wood covers a hill surrounded by vineyards, forming an extremely

POINTS OF INTEREST

Tasting the **DOCG Franciacorta**, *a famed wine produced with Chardonnay, Pinot Bianco and Pinot Nero grapes. The slow bottled fermentation (18 months rest on yeasts and at least 25 months of process from vintage to marketing) is a refined art that requires perfect primary material. There are six versions of Franciacorta, each with its own typical peculiarity.*

Technical info

Route

17 Km: Nigoline - Sanctuary of Sant'Eufemia - Cascina Solive - Fornaci Quattrovie - Borgonato - Cascina di Luogonuovo - Timoline - Borgonuovo. You can reach the starting point by taking the A4 Milan–Venice freeway, exiting at Ospitaletto or Rovato.

Difficulty

No special effort is required on this itinerary, ideal also for people with no training at all.

Cycling period

All year round, preferably in fall (grape harvest) and spring.

Map

Franciacorta e Riserva Naturale delle Torbiere del Sebino, 1:16,000, Orizzonte; routes designed by Promozione Franciacorta: available at the Tourist Board offices at Rodego Saiano.

Technical assistance

Lissignoli Gino, viale Europa 110, Passirano; t. 0306850658.

Tourist information

• Promozione Franciacorta, Via Castello 8/a, Rodengo Saiano; t. 0306811005.

• IAT Office, Lungolago Marconi 2, Iseo; t. 030980209.
• APT Bresciano, corso Zanardelli 38, Brescia; t. 03045052. www.bresciaholiday.com
• Amici della Bici, via B. Maggi 9, Brescia; t. 03047191. www.youthpoint.it/amicidellabici
• Associazione Strada del Vino Franciacorta, via Verdi 53, Erbusco; t. 0307760870.

---

interesting natural environment. Continue your ride northwards, until you skirt a stone wall that seems to show the way to enter the town of Borgonato. Continue riding northwards across countryside; stop and admire the Madonna del Corno opposite, on the stratified rocks of Provaglio and, further above, the massif of Mount Guglielmo. The vicinal path forms a wide curve passing near the large quarries, then near the Luogonuovo farm and the small abandoned church known as Madonna delle Inquine. After about 1 km, you arrive, on your left, at the road for Timoline, which gives you

the chance to take a detour on the dirt road that stretches overhead near the road, and allows you to look onto the peat-bog environment. At Timoline, cross the provincial road again, and just after the crossroads, via Conicchio, reaching Grumi, then the built-up area of **Nigoline**, where your ride ends.

RIGHT, Provaglio, the monastery of San Pietro in Lamosa.

The Stelvio National Park: the lakes 30 Km of Cancano and San Giacomo di Fraele

The Stelvio National Park is the largest protected area in Europe: 134,620 hectares of mountain landscapes featuring wonderful woods, pastures, lakes, glaciers and snow-capped peaks. Established in 1935 as the fourth national Italian park, today it stretches from the provinces of Sondrio, Brescia, Trento and Bolzano.

From the **Mount Scale refuge** (1,938 m above sea level), ride down to the dam of Lake Cancano (1,900 m above sea level), dropping vertically on the deep ravine dug by the River Adda, crossing to the other bank, where you turn left on the dirt road that runs along the north-eastern side of the basin. After 4 km, you reach an L-shaped tunnel, 500 m long (torches ready), and after a second short tunnel, the Val Fraele refuge

(1,960 above sea level, 6 km), near the dam of Lake San Giacomo di Fraele. Continue your ride passing the refuge (road signs for the Fraele pass, Gallo Valley), on an easy level stretch along the bank, reaching the top of the lake, where the Chapel of San Giacomo stands, near the Fraele Pass (1,952 above sea level, 9.6 km), which connects the Fraele Valley to the Gallo Valley.

Now proceed along the lake, until reaching the bridge situ-

Technical info

Route:
30 Km: Rifugio Monte Scale - Lake Cancano dam - Rifugio Val Fraele – Fraele Pass – pass of the Alpisella Valley - Pettini Valley - Case Doscopa - Rifugio Monte Scale (385 m rise). You can reach the starting point from Bormio (17 km) by taking the S.S. 301 main road leading to Livigno up to Torripiano di Premadio, where you turn right, after the Church of the Madonna della Pietà, on a dirt road (road signs for the Lakes Cancano and Torri di Fraele) leading to the Mount Scale refuge.

Difficulty
None in particular, except for the climb at the pass of the Alpisella Valley (333 m rise), which is covered, as for all this itinerary, on excellent dirt road.

Cycling period
Summer and fall.

Map
• *Bormio - Livigno*, scale 1:50,000, Kompass n. 96.
• *Alta Valtellina*, scale 1:50,000, TCI.

Technical assistance
• Bobo Moto, via Milano 56, Bormio; t. 0342905064.
• Martin Bike and Sky, Pedenosso - Isolaccia, Valdidentro; t. 0342929629.
Tourist information
• Mountain Bike Alta Valtellina, via Monte Braulio 34, Bormio. In the summer season, near Lake Cancano, the seat of the MTB school opens (information spot, guided trips, bicycle rental, mechanical assistance, tips on how to plan itineraries, training and specialization courses for adults and children with SIMB instructors); t. 0342901336, 335710856 (Silvio Mevio). www.mtb.stelvio.net
• APT Valtellina, via Roma 131/B, Bormio; t. 0342903300. aptbormio@provincia.so.it.
• Pro Loco Valdidentro, via Nazionale 18, Isolaccia Valdidentro; t. 0342985331.

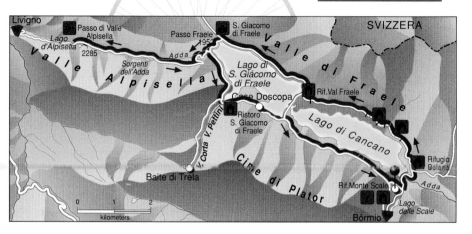

ated in the narrow Alpisella Valley, from where the waters of the Adda drop (merely a stream at this point). A marked mule track (10.2 km, road sign for the Alpisella Valley) moves away on the right and abruptly climbs up, firstly with hairpin bends in a wonderful larch wood, then straight along the right side of the valley, rising above the upper limits of the vegetation. The mule track cuts the slope up to a pool in the rocks, preceded by a detour on your right (13.2 km, writings on the rock) leading to the sources of the Adda. The climb ends at the pool: you

now continue your ride at the centre of the valley, in a wonderful environment under the immense scree on the left side, on a mule track that starts on level road, then gets

slightly steep, up to the pass of the Alpisella Valley (2,285 m, 15.2 km). Just after the pass, the basin that hosts Lake Alpisella opens up (2,267 m). The mule track continues downhill to Livigno, but the itinerary runs backwards on the road you have already covered. At the bottom of the descent, take, on your right, the road that follows the south-western bank of the lake. On level road, reach the deep cut of the Pettini Valley, crossed by an arm of the lake. At this stage, the dirt road moves away from Lake Fraele, climbing up in gentle wavy meadows and thickets of trees to the refreshment spot of San Giacomo. After passing the Doscopa houses, go back to the dam that separates the Fraele and Cancano basins (1,960 m, 24.8 km), and after another 4 km, back to the **Mount Scale refuge**.

LEFT, cycling along the banks of Lake Fraele.
ABOVE, view of the lake.

The Mincio Park: the cycle lane   39 Km
between Peschiera and Mantua

A uniquely fascinating itinerary, stretching between the provinces of Verona and Mantua, along the River Mincio.

The itinerary starts at **Peschiera del Garda**, seat of the ancient stronghold, from where the Mincio and Lake Garda separate. After crossing the town center and exiting from porta Brescia, the road rises for a short stretch on your left. A road sign at the entrance of a dirt path (on your left) indicates the start of the cycle lane. A short downhill stretch leads to an unsurfaced section along the town's defense systems. After a few hundred meters, go back on a lightly-trafficked road. Pass under the S.S. 11 main road and the Milan-Venice freeway, and pass the barrier that closes the road to traffic after about 3 km.

From this moment, continue your ride on the cycle lane. During this first stretch, the track curls along the towpaths of the river flowing on

Technical info

Route
39 Km: Peschiera del Garda - Monzambano - Borghetto - Valeggio sul Mincio - Pozzolo - Marengo - Soave - Mantua. This is an easy itinerary, winding almost entirely on level road, with a dirt stretch of about 7 km between Marengo and Soave. The itinerary runs constantly along the towing-paths of the waterways, while the various built-up areas can be visited by taking short detours.

Road signs
The round stickers with white arrow on green background are preferable, for itinerary purposes, to the yellow signs.

Cycling period
All year round, especially in spring and fall.

Map
Dal Garda al Po,
carta dei percorsi ciclabili,
1:25,000, Parco del Mincio.

Bicycle + Train
You can reach Peschiera by train and start your ride from Mantua to the main destinations (Milan - Verona - Venice - Modena - Bologna).

Technical assistance
World Bike,
via Bell'Italia 31,
Peschiera Del Garda;
t. 0456401837.

Tourist information
• Parco del Mincio,
via Marangoni 36, Mantua;
t. 037622831.
www.parks.it/parco.mincio/
• Amici della Bicicletta,
c/o Mattioli Daniele,
viale Pompilio 33, Mantua;
t. 0376263130.
• IAT, Piazzale Bettelloni 15,
Peschiera del Garda;
t. 0457551673.
• Pro Loco Valeggio
sul Mincio;
t. 0457951880.
• APT Mantua,
piazza Magenta 6,
Mantua;
t. 0376328253.

POINTS OF INTEREST

Excellent bicycle rental service, every weekend from April to October. You collect your bike at the Peschiera railroad station and leave it at the Mantua station; booking is recommended. Planned and run by Zeppellin, tour operator specialized in easy biking holidays. To receive a free copy of the cycle lane map: t. 0444526021, www.zeppellin.it.

your left. After passing the power station, cross the dam and continue your ride on the opposite bank.

You ride across moraine hills, and after about 4 km, the imposing Visconti bridge (XIV century) welcomes you to Borghetto. You can reach Borghetto along a short dirt stretch or along the asphalt track of the fitness route, by taking left, at the remains of an old farmhouse, the short uphill climb.

The cycle lane emerges on the municipal road: towards your right, you enter the town center of Borghetto, a real jewel of alleys and old mills. If you turn left and ride for 200 m uphill, you reach Valeggio sul Mincio (we suggest a visit to the Sigurtà Park). If you go straight ahead, crossing the former forecourt of the railroad station, and turn right along a

short downhill bend, you get back on the cycle lane.

At Pozzolo, after 8 km, the great river takes a detour, while the route continues along the waters of the Bianco Canal.

Near Marengo, cross the S.S. 236 Peschiera-Mantua main road and get back on the lane following the canal.

After reaching Soave, follow the opposite bank, crossing the bridge on your right, then riding back on asphalt road. A short stretch after, a road sign indicates a possible detour to your left towards the Fontana wood (rich in oaks, maples and undergrowth that can be visited on foot); if you go straight ahead, you reach the S.S. 236 main road. Pay due attention to the pathway, concealed by the trees, which drops on the right just a few meters before the main road.

At the bar, turn right again, riding on narrow paths along the irrigation canals of the Mantua countryside. At the

point where the cycle lane stops, to enter town, turn right on the S.S. 236 main road and then right again on the S.S. 62 main road. By entering via G. Bono and turning left, 200 m further ahead, you cross Lake Superiore along the railroad. From the underpass, you can continue riding along the lake up to the Sanctuary of Santa Maria delle Grazie, or you can pass under the railroad and enter the old town center of **Mantua**.

RIGHT, a "madonnaro" at Santa Maria delle Grazie.
PAGE OPPOSITE, stop near Goito.

Veneto

Lake Garda   25 Km
The Olive Riviera

This itinerary runs along the gentlest and most "Mediterranean" bank of Lake Garda. Covering the first half of the route by boat, you can admire the coast from the waters before exploring it by bike on the mainland, stopping every now and then in small harbors and at the heart of warm, welcoming medieval villages.

POINTS OF INTEREST

The Veronese Riviera of Lake Garda is famed for its wine production, in particular for the Bardolino DOC, a dry and palatable red. You can find it at the F.lli Zeni wine cellars of Bardolino (via Costabella 9, t. 0457210022), which also host an interesting **Wine Museum.** *Another typical native produce is olive oil that you can buy at the Cisano del Garda oil mill (S.S. 249, t. 0456229047). The oil mill also houses a very interesting* **Oil Museum.**

From **Peschiera**, bring your bike along with you and catch the boat for Torri del Benaco, arriving after a pleasureful 90 minute crossing.

A picturesque town pervaded by a medieval aura, Torri del Benaco still has a XIV century castle that houses the local museum. Following the lakefront southwards, leave the town and take the S.S. 249 main road, taking a short detour on your right and reaching Punta San Vigilio, one of the most suggestive spots of Lake Garda. Now continue your ride along the main road and reach Garda after approximately 3 km. When entering the town, on your left, you see Villa Albertini, which hosted King Carlo Alberto during the first war of independence. Spare a worthwhile effort to penetrate the small alleys of the old town center, then continue your tour reaching the panoramic spot of Rocca di Garda. From the Garda lakefront,

move on southwards along the cycle-pedestrian lane made out of the old railroad track; riding along the bank of the lake, you reach Bardolino, another characteristic medieval-type village.

At this point, continue riding along the bank of the lake towards a dirt track for cyclists and pedestrians, then reach the graceful town of Lazise, still today almost entirely surrounded by the Scaliger walls. If you start feeling whacked out or are merely bewitched by the romantic atmosphere of the town harbor, you can stop for a spell and wait for the boat to Peschiera (approximately 25 minutes' crossing). Otherwise, exit Lazise through the Lion gate (south) and turn left reaching the S.S. 249 main road, following it towards the right and climbing up for about 1 km until you reach the Casa Mia hotel. Now take a left detour, entering the asphalt road leading to Colà. After about 500

m, you reach a rise before riding down for a short stretch, then turn right and take the strada delle Greghe, a small asphalt road running along the ridge of a hill amid fields and vineyards.

Once you reach Pacengo,

pass two crossroads: at the first crossroads, enter via Mantovanella, at the second, take via Mantovana and leave the built-up area riding towards via Pigno, a dirt road that reaches a group of houses standing amid vineyards (Pigno hamlet). Now turn right and cycle across vineyards up to the parking lot of the Gardaland amusement park. Turn right, along the parking lot fence and get back on the 249 main road near the Gardaland entrance. Following the main road to your left, you reach **Peschiera** after approximately 2 km.

LEFT, the small Lazise harbor.

Technical info

Route
25 Km: Peschiera del Garda - Torri del Benaco (by boat) - Punta San Vigilio - Garda - Bardolino - Lazise - Pacengo - Peschiera del Garda (15 km on cycle lane or roads with no traffic, 10 km on main road). You can reach the starting point by taking the A4 Milan-Venice freeway, Peschiera exit.

Difficulty
Not a tough itinerary. Whoever wishes to knock 10 km off the route, can stop at Lazise and continue the tour by ferry boat up to Peschiera.

Cycling period
All year round. We suggest avoiding the peak seasons such as August and the late spring and

summer weekends, when the S.S. 249 main road (approximately 10 km) is really bustling with cars.

Bicycle + Train
The Peschiera railroad station is situated along the Milan-Venice line on the stretch between Brescia and Verona.

Map
• *Lago di Garda - Monte Baldo*, 1:50,000, page 102, Kompass.
• *Atlante stradale d'Italia*, Northern volume, 1:200,000, TCI.

Technical assistance
• Bauer Josef Michael, via Venezia 21, Peschiera del Garda; t. 0456401970.
• World Bike, via Bell'Italia 31, Peschiera del Garda; t. 0456401837.

• Tandem, piazzetta Beccherie 13, Lazise; t. 0456470173.

Bicycle rental
Piccoli Mauro, via Venezia 13, Peschiera del Garda; t. 0457551813. (only in summer)

Tourist information
• IAT Riviera degli Olivi, Lungolago Regina Adelaide 3, Garda; t. 0457255773, 0457256672. www.aptgardaveneto.com
• APT Lazise, via Fontana 14, Lazise; t. 0457580114.
• IAT, piazzale Bettelloni 15, Peschiera del Garda; t. 0457551673

The Po delta 50 Km
Between Loreo and Caleri

The Po delta is a dimension built on delicate balances, where earth, water and man shape a unique landscape, an ideal place to cover by bike.

You start your ride from the Botanical Garden of **Porto Caleri**, where you take the S.P. 65 provincial road, riding straight ahead and ignoring the detours to Rosolina Mare. The road winds its way between the pine forest (on your right) and the Boccavecchia and Passarella valleys (on your left). At the crossroads for Casoni, turn left, riding along the S.P. 65 provincial road, then turn right into via Ca' Diedo, which passes a canal, and after a pizza house, climbs up the embankment of the Adige. Now cross via Romea, taking due care of a dangerous crossroads, and continue cycling along the embankment of the river (via Adige).

Pass the lock with a drawbridge on the Po Brondolo Canal, and just further ahead on your left, you'll spot the houses of Corte di Cavanella, where precious Roman relics were unearthed.

After reaching the Loreo Canal, leave the embankment and turn left in via Tornova, which runs along the canal. Pass the hamlet of Tornova with its Villa Vianelli, then reach the crossroads and turn right, and continue following the canal, entering Loreo and riding on the Marconi riviera.

Loreo used to be an important river port of the Serenissima in the Polesine; its past

Technical info

Route

50 Km: Porto Caleri - Rosolina Mare - Portesine - Loreo - San Gaetano estate - via delle Valli - Portesine crossroads - Rosolina Mare - Porto Caleri. On asphalt roads, not always in good conditions. The starting point is 25 km from Chioggia and is reached by leaving the S.S. 309 Romea main road at the junction with the S.P. 65 provincial road leading to Porto Caleri.

Difficulty

No problems on this itinerary as far as heights are concerned. But no matter how easy, 50 km do require a minimum amount of training. Heat in the hot season and wind in general may cause you some problems.

Cycling period

A ride in summer is absolutely out of the question, since this is not a shady route.

Bicycle + Train

The Loreo railroad station is situated along the Chioggia-Rovigo line.

Map

Atlante stradale d'Italia, Northern volume, 1:200,000, TCI.

Technical assistance

• Crivellari Giuseppe, strada del Sud 218, Rosolina Mare; t. 042668462, 0426632216.

• Mancin, viale Marconi 2, Rosolina; t. 0426664004.

• Walter, via Riviera Nuova, Rosolina; t. 0426334237.

Tourist information

• APT Rovigo, via J.H. Dunant 10, Rovigo; t. 0425386290. www.apt.rovigo.it

• IAT Rosolina Mare, viale dei Pini 4, Rosolina Mare; t. 0426326020.

• Ente Parco Delta del Po, via Marconi 6, Ariano nel Polesine; t. 0426372202. www.parks.it/parco.delta.po.ve/ www.parcodeltapo.org

POINTS OF INTEREST

The Coastal Botanical Garden of Porto Caleri *lies between the mouth of the Adige and the Po di Levante, situated on a strip of beach looking onto the open sea. Three paths (A short, B average, C long) allow you to discover the typical habitats of the Po delta: from the pine forest to the sandy dune and the lagoon (info: t. 042668408). Open from April to September; visits: Tuesday, Thursday, Sunday, 10.00 a.m.-1.00 p.m. and 4.00-7.00 p.m.*

can be witnessed by the wonderful Venetian-style houses overlooking the canal. At the bridge over the navigable Loreo Canal (piazza Matteotti), turn left and ride along via Roma; after 250 m,

you reach a roundabout and turn left in via XXV Aprile which, after a bend, becomes via Arzeron. Now pass the level crossing, and just shortly ahead, turn left on the S.P. 45 provincial road (very risky crossroads and road). Turn right for Rosolina Mare and cross, over the bridge, strada Romea, continuing your ride towards Albarella.

ABOVE, canoeing in the river park.
PAGE OPPOSITE, weels at Porto Caleri.

Soon after, near the San Gaetano estate, leave via delle Valli (nice, although busy road) and take on your left the reclamation road, until you reach the abandoned Moceniga Church. Just before the church, pass near the Veniera "casone", a typical example of a Veneto rural building, once a very popular construction in the delta, where fish used to be picked, sorted and then sent to the markets. Continue your tour turning left and taking via delle Valli along the embankment and touching the Segà, Spolvetina and Cannelle valleys, where you'll easily spot animals in the reed-bed and the salt cedar hedges. Now reach the Portesine crossroads and turn right, following the busy S.P. 65 provincial road leading to the crossroads for Porto Caleri, then turn right and enter via Boccavecchia. At the detour on your left for Rosolina Mare, ride straight ahead, following the road signs for the Botanical Garden of **Porto Caleri**, and finally reach the parking lot.

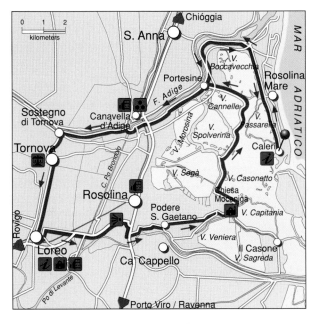

Between Mestre and Treviso   31 Km
The cycle lane of the villas

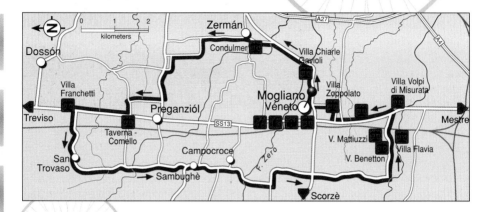

An aristocratic ride partly along the historical Terraglio artery. For over 2,000 years, a vital channel of communication between Venice and Treviso, it was named after "Terraleum" during the Roman age, Regia Strada Postale del Terraglio during the magnificence of the "Serenissima", and Strada Napoleonica during the French reign.

You start your tour from **Mogliano Veneto**. Ride

eastwards towards the A27 freeway, then follow via Zermanesa and skirt Villa Chiarle-Gavioli (on your left at the end of via Moranti). Ride along the provincial road for 3 km and take the detour to Zerman. On your left, you'll spot Villa Condulmer, currently a hotel with golf course. At Zerman, you can view two sacella painted by Paolo Veronese: one at the crossroads opposite the church, the other on

the road skirting it. Now take via Preganziol leading to Dosson, ride until you cross a small bridge, then turn left on via Pesare. The path emerges on via Schiavonia; at this point, turn left, reaching Preganziol. On your left-hand side starts a nice cycle lane that leads you to Preganziol passing by Villa Marcello Del Majno. After cycling for 100 m after the next traffic lights, get on the right-hand side to stop and admire Villa Tasso. Once you're back at the traffic lights, turn left, entering via Palladio, which crosses, after 1 km, via Collegio. Now turn left and reach the Terraglio, with the park and Villa Taverna-Comello on your right. Following the main road on your right towards Treviso, you reach Villa Franchetti, preceded by a small church. Ride up to the traffic lights and turn left un-

POINTS OF INTEREST

Villa Franchetti, *situated along the Terraglio, at the border between the municipalities of Preganziol and Treviso, with the park open to the public; the* **Vecchia Filanda** *center at Campocroce;* **Villa la Marignana**, *Mazzocco, housing the Wrought Iron Museum of Tohl Benetton (t. 0419 22111);* **Mogliano e le sue Ville in carrozza**, *a costume display with period carriages, held every second Sunday in September.*

til you get to San Trovaso. After the railroad underpass, follow the main road and cross Sambughè and Campocroce with the Vecchia Filanda, an artisan center. Continue cycling on your right in via Molino (for Scorzè). At the crossroads with via Tagliamento, turn left, and after a long straight stretch, follow the road signs for Scorzè. Turn right on the provincial road, and immediately after, turn left to ride along via Osoppo, which comes out on via Ghetto. After reaching via Marignana, go past Villa Benetton, which you recognize on your left by its iron sculptures in the garden. Further ahead, pass by the Flavia and Mattiuzzi villas.

After crossing the railroad underpass, go back on the

Terraglio by turning left towards Mogliano. With a quick ride, pass, in sequence, by the Gris (left), Marchesi, Milanese, Veronese and Zenoni-Politeo villas (all right). Once you're back at Mogliano, pass a petrol station and turn right in via Mameli going past Villa Zoppolato. Ride on your left along via Verdi and along the park, and after the traffic lights, go back to **Mogliano**. An interesting sight to see is Villa Stucky (hotel) and the adjacent Benedictine cloister, dating back to 997.

ABOVE, **Villa Franchetti** at Preganziol. PAGE OPPOSITE, the Terraglio parish church.

Technical info

Route

31 Km: Mogliano Veneto – Zerman – Preganziol – Campocroce – Marocco – Mogliano.
You can reach the starting point by taking the A27 freeway, Mogliano exit, then by turning left on the provincial road and riding for 3 km up to the cemetery parking lot.

Difficulty

The route is entirely on level road. Hectic traffic on workdays along the Terraglio.

Cycling period

All year round, preferably from spring to fall.

Bicycle + Train

The Mogliano and Preganziol railroad stations are situated along the Mestre-Treviso line.

Map

• *Treviso ed il Piave*, Series n° V222, 1:50,000, Belletti Editor
t. 0541615696

Technical assistance

Cicli Trabucco, via Zermanesa 72, Mogliano Veneto; t. 0415900150.

Tourist information

• Assessorato al Turismo di Mogliano Veneto, via Terraglio 3, Mogliano Veneto; t. 0415930802.
• Consorzio Provinciale di Promozione Turistica "Treviso una Provincia Intorno"; t. 0422541052.

Along the Sile   28 Km
From Treviso to Albaredo

Peaceful ride along the course of the Sile, one of the rare resurgence rivers (the biggest in Italy) originating in lowlands.

To exit the center of **Treviso**, ride along via Calmaggiore, via XX Settembre and corso del Popolo, then, after crossing the scenic bridge over the River Sile, the Lungosile Mattei closed to motorized traffic. Now turn left in via dei Cacciatori, and after passing a level crossing, take via Sant'Angelo that passes under the ring-road and continues on a tree-lined stretch, up to the junction, and the traffic lights, with the S.S. 515 main road, at Quinto di Treviso. Cross the main road following the road signs pointing to Ongarie and Badoere (via Cornarotta). Now that you're out of the town area, ride across the countryside and catch a glimpse of the numerous farms and the ponds formed by the Sile (on your right). Soon afterwards, you reach the gates of the Cervara Nature Oasis, on an equipped rest area. Continue your ride, following via Cornarotta, and after passing by the houses of Ongarie, turn right and reach piazza Indipendenza, at the heart of the small village of Badoere. The village preserves a pe-

Technical info

Route
28 Km: Treviso - Quinto di Treviso - Cornarotta - Ongarie - Badoere - Spada - Torreselle - Lorenzoni – sources of the Sile - Casacorba - Albaredo. Return trip to Treviso by train. For those who prefer cycling it back: at the Casacorba chapel, turn right in via Sile and on the cycle lane through Viciliegie and Corriva, where you turn right heading towards Cavasagra, then straight ahead to Quinto and Madonna dell'Albera: 300 m after the chapel, turn right in via Munara towards the Sile. Again on via Bassa, then turn right in via Barbasso and left in via Pescatori. At the bridge (between the Sile and Settimo), ride straight ahead passing Palazzi, Santa Cristina and Quinto di Treviso, then take via Noalese until you reach Treviso.

Difficulty
Easy itinerary, ideal for everyone, with no significant rise.

Cycling period
All year round, preferably in spring and fall.

Bicycle + Train
You return by train from Albaredo to Treviso on the Vicenza-Treviso line.

Map
Atlante stradale d'Italia, Northern volume, 1:200,000, TCI.

Technical assistance
• Pinarello, borgo Mazzini 9, Treviso; t. 0422543821.
• Motorbike, via Riccati 38, Treviso; t. 0422540330.
• Conte, via XI Febbraio 28, Quinto di Treviso; t. 0422379227.
• Pozzo, via V. Emanuele 72, Quinto di Treviso; t. 0422379033.

Tourist information
• IAT Treviso, piazzetta Monte di Pietà 8, Treviso; t. 0422547632. www.sevenonline.it/tvapt
• APT Treviso, Palazzo Scotti - via Toniolo 41, Treviso; t. 0422540600. www.sevenonline.it/tvapt
• Parco del Sile, via Tandura 40, Treviso; t. 0422321994. www.parks.it/parco.fiume.sile/

POINTS OF INTEREST

*The **Cervara Oasis**, on the Santa Cristina island. In the willow tree, poplar and alder wood, there is a birdwatching path. The Oasis is populated by herons and by grey, dwarf and black-crowned night herons, and also by purple herons, great white herons and cattle egrets. Open Saturday (2.30–6.30 p.m.) and Sunday (8.30–12.00 a.m. and 2.30–6.30 p.m.). Info: Gruppo Ecologico Tiveron, t. 0422477001.*

culiar urban layout due to its being a market area since 1689. Other notable features are the "barchesse", farm buildings used as warehouse, shop and dwellings, built in 1756 by the Badoer family. You exit Badoere, turning right in via Palazzo, then left in via Marcello and left again in via Rialto, which passes the River Zero and crosses a cultivated area of asparagus, meadows and poplar groves.

Emerge in via Levada and turn right. After approximately 200 m, turn right (unmarked crossroads) in via Menaredo, and near a small chapel, right again in via Foscolo, which emerges in via Munaron, where you continue left. The road ends in via Piave, at Spada. Now continue right, skirting the houses of Torreselle and Lorenzoni where, at a flashing traffic light, you turn right in via Montegrappa, which winds across the countryside with numerous bends. After riding for 2.2 km in via Montegrappa, turn towards the sources of the Sile (about 700 m). Turn on the dirt road on your right and at the next crossroads on your left. Now that you're back in via Montegrappa, which then becomes via Santa Brigida, ride up to the small chapel of Case Seccafien. Turn right heading for another chapel at Casacorba, where you turn left for **Albaredo** and the railroad station to get back by train to Treviso.

ABOVE, the Sile at Quinto di Treviso. PAGE OPPOSITE, Palazzo del Podestà at Treviso.

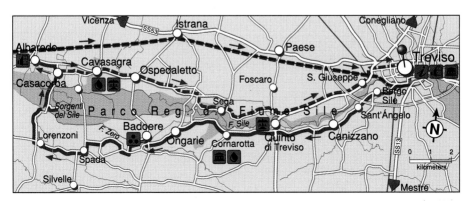

Plateau of the 7 Towns-Asiago 1   158 Km
Stage trip by mountain bike

The shape of the plateau helps you organize a genuine traveling trip by mountain bike across the most stunning spots in the area. The stage points are the "malghe" (small mountain dairy farms) or refuges: you can ride for days immersed in nature, far from motorized roads.

When one imagines a park for bikers, the mind's eye conjures up the remote Californian single-tracks or the pathways that cut through the Colorado forests. If you load your mountain bike into your car and drive towards the imposing spurs of the Veneto Prealps, you soon reach a place that can really stand up to any "American biker's dream". The karstic shelf rising up from the Veneto plain is such a tempting island of rock for cart road and pathway adventurers. Pastures and forests cover

the light-colored rock of the Asiago Plateau, an enormous basin that seems to embrace the sky: over 600 kilometers of dirt forest and military roads; the ideal environmental conditions to ride and practice sport at an altitude ranging from 1,000 to the over 2,000 m of the highest peaks.

The itinerary has a large circular layout stretching on the plateau and requires at least 4 days' riding; no matter how tough, the trip can be easily arranged, with the precious logistical help from the Asiago 7 Towns Tourist Consortium, which provides luggage transport and, if necessary, an expert guide.

Your trip starts at the forecourt of the **Asiago** railroad station. You immediately ride on the dirt road once crossed by the railroad

POINTS OF INTEREST

The **Astrophysical Observatory of Pennar**, built in 1942 on the plateau, is the major observatory in Italy and one of the leading optical astronomy centers in Europe (t. 042446221, www. pd.astro. it/visitasiago). The altitude, the clear skies, the absence of polluting agents and the small presence of city lights are the ideal conditions to watch the stars. The dome houses the great Galileo telescope, visited during the day and used at night by the astronomers. You can also visit the nearby Multimedia Hall, used for teaching and popularization aims; it has two telescopes through which you can watch the sun during the day, and the planets, nebulas and galaxies during the evening visits.

tracks. Just before reaching Cesuna, turn towards the Boscon refuge. The road penetrates a thick wood and runs along the English military cemetery, immersed in a dreamlike peace. Various paths wind from the refuge: the second on the right climbs on a not too backbreaking slope and skirts behind Mount Lemerle before dropping down to the Magnaboschi Valley and climbing up again in the stunning panorama of the malga Zovetto following the military path of Esele.

The enjoyable dirt road continues to gently climb towards the Paù area, to the rocky limits of the plateau. At the Paù pass, space rises up vertically and the view drops down 1,000 m to the plain crossed by the waters of the Astico. A spectacular ride on the road that brushes the edge of the karstic wall up to the malga Fondi, before turning again towards the heart of the plateau. If the weather's nice, it would be worthwhile to climb up to Mount Corno, otherwise you can continue your ride up to the Pozza di Favero refuge, an ideal spot to snack. After closing a circle at the Boscon refuge, advance in the Barenthal Valley up to the golf course, a short distance from the Astrophysical Observatory of Pennar, before reaching the hamlet of **Bertigo**.

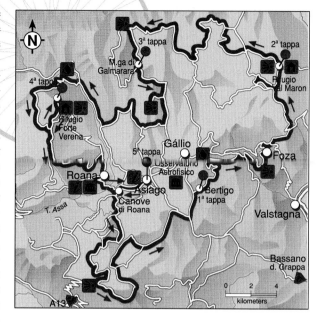

The itinerary continues on hard ground across the Frenzella Valley up to the hamlet of Giannesini, then in the intimate and secluded atmosphere of the Piana Valley, an area of small villages and huge pastures. From the bottom of the valley, follow the irregular pattern of short hairpin bends that go high up the road to Foza. Just a few more smooth kilometers on the 1,000 m contour line, crossing the built-up area of Foza and the Lazzaretti area, then you start your climb up to the Marcesina plain. After a very scenic initial stretch over the roofs and the steeple of the hamlet of Gavelle, the road penetrates

the thick wood and climbs up to the Maron Valley.

From the **Maron Valley refuge**, you start immediately on an uphill climb towards the Forcellona, and after the hill crossing, descend towards a rough cattle track until you reach the Marcesina plain. From the Campo Grande tableland, ride on the malga Buson, where you start the climb up to the highest point of the tour. A military path ascends to Roccolo Cattagno and, shortly after, you reach the asphalt link road leading to the malga Fiara. From this point, climb up to the crossroads for Ortigara (we suggest a detour if the weather's nice) and then take the downhill stretch to the **malga Galmarara**, an ideal stage point.

LEFT, from the peak of Mount Verena. PAGE OPPOSITE, Paù pass.

You now leave the peace and quiet of Galmarara to make the crossing towards Mount Zebio, another dramatic chapter in the war history of this plateau. Gently descend, skirting round the wooded slopes of Mount Mosciagh, to return into the Galmarara Valley.

The ride downhill continues in the cool shade of larches, silver and red firs, up to the Assa Valley where, on a slight asphalt slope, you get to the malga Pusterle, an ideal spot to freshen up before tackling the last challenge: the tough climb to Mount Verena. The first stretch is rather smooth, the second gets tougher, on stony rough ground. Once you get to the top, near the last hairpin

Technical info

Route

158 Km: Asiago - Rifugio Boscon - Magnaboschi Valley - malga Zovetto - Paù pass - malga Fondi - Rifugio Pozza di Favero - Rifugio Boscon - Barenthal Valley - Bertigo - Frenzella Valley - Giannesini - Piana Valley - Foza - Lazzaretti - Maron Valley - Forcellona - Marcesina plain - Campo Grande - malga Buson - Roccolo Cattagno - malga Fiara - malga Galmarara - Mount Zebio - Galmarara Valley - Assa Valley - malga Pusterle - Forte Verena - Croce del Civello - Mount Erio - Roana lakelet - Assa Valley - Roana - Asiago.

Difficulty

You should have at least some practice in you before challenging the routes along the plateau; the stages are never too lengthy, the climbs never so rough, but some physical effort is required, as 90% of the route winds along dirt roads (we suggest using a mountain bike with shock-absorbing forks).

Cycling period

From end of May to October.

Cycling time

From 2 to 5 days.

Map

• *Altopiano dei Sette Comuni*, map n. 78, scale 1:50,000, Kompass, for trekkers, cyclists, skiers.

• *Altopiano dei Sette Comuni*, map n. 623, scale 1:25,000, Kompass.
Ideal for trekkers and cycle tourists.

Logistics

The Plateau Tourist Consortium provides cyclists, who request it, with well-organized logistical support; maps, information material, reservation of hotels and refuges, baggage transport service, and if necessary, assistance from a biker-guide along the itinerary. On demand, you can also book personalized tours according to your time requirements. The Tourist Consortium's offer includes 3 "Caroselli Free Ride" varying from 2 to 4 or 5 days. Moreover, the more trained cyclists can have a stab at a longer and more challenging tour of approximately 250 km. Service is first-class: half-board, special breakfast for bikers, workshop assistance and bike cleaning, luggage transfer; guide service not included but available on demand, MTB rental and packed lunch provided by the hotel. Since you can count on luggage transport, you would only need to carry a light rucksack with a change of clothes, a cycling rain and wind jacket. Don't forget your ordinary maintenance kit: pump, spare inner tubes, patches for flats, lubricant for chain and gear. Along the route, you'll usually find "malghe" equipped to offer you a snack or even a hot meal you need for a midday refreshment. A good map is required.

Technical assistance

• Stella Carlo,
via dei Patrioti 31, Asiago;
t. 0424462812.

Bicycle rental

• Hotel da Barba,
Poeslen-Kaberlaba, Asiago;
t. 0424462888.

Tourist information

• Consorzio Turistico
Asiago 7 Comuni,
via Trento e Trieste 19, Asiago;
t. 0424464137.
www.asiago7comuni@keycom m.it

• IAT Altopiano di Asiago,
via Stazione 5, Asiago;
t. 0424462221, 0424462661.
www.ascom.vi.it/asiago

STAGE POINTS RECOMMENDED

• **From Asiago to Bertigo**
38 Km, 560 m rise
Cycling time: *3-4 hours*
Notes: *average difficulty; variable altitude with constant climbs, exciting descents and perfectly cycling road surface.*

• **From Bertigo to the Maron Valley refuge**
30 Km, 640 m rise
Cycling time: *3-4 hours*
Notes: *average difficulty, with some uphill stretches, not long, but quite challenging.*

• **From the Maron Valley refuge to the malga Galmarara**
30 Km, 870 m rise
Cycling time: *4-5 hours*

Notes: *tough stretch, owing to the rise and unpredictable weather conditions at around 2,000 m.*

• **From the malga Galmarara to the Forte Verena refuge**
40 Km, 1,250 m rise
Cycling time: *5 hours*
Notes: *challenging final stretch with the climb up to Mount Verena, owing to the rise and the rough, stony track.*

• **From the Forte Verena refuge to Asiago**
20 Km, 150 m rise
Cycling time: *2-3 hours*
Notes: *a stage with no altitude difficulties, except for the last stretch to Canove.*

bend, you can finally stop to admire a really spectacular sight from up above, on the deep green colors of the Assa Valley and the Lavarone and Luserna plateaus. The climb ends near the **Forte Verena refuge**.
The final stretch of the journey is a magnificent ride downhill. You start at 2,000 m from the Verena refuge.

This section requires great caution on the stony ground and puts quite a lot of pressure on the mountain bike's shock-absorber forks. After reaching Croce del Civello, continue your ride on the downhill stretch of Mount Erio to the Roana lakelet. Proceed downhill to the bottom of the Assa Valley, where you travel back in time to thousands of years ago, gazing in wonder at the ancient graffiti carved into the rock of Tunkelbad.
At this stage of the trip, you challenge the last fairly short, but quite steep wall, before closing the circle and ending this great adventure at the heart of **Asiago**.

BELOW, the Marcesina plain.

Plateau of the 7 Towns-Asiago 2   18 Km
The former railroad track

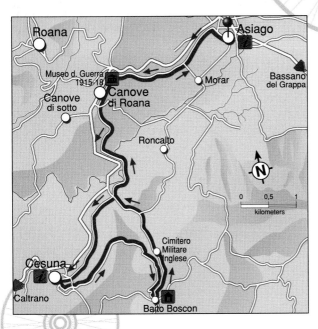

Easy ride at the heart of the plateau, immersed in the muffled atmosphere of the wood, not far from the built-up areas, mostly on roads closed to traffic.

You start your ride from the forecourt of the **Asiago** railroad station, where, until July 31, 1958, a rack railroad used to arrive from Piovene Rocchette. At the back of the APT offices starts the former railroad track, transformed into dirt road with gradients that never exceed 3%. Metal road signs with green background and the symbol of a mountain bike over a railroad engine indicate the "train road".

Take the railroad track, crossing the new parking lot and passing in front of the Asiago Dairy Consortium. After a very short stretch,

the road levels out towards Canove, amid pastures and meadows. Just less than 2 km and you reach the swimming pools of Canove di Roana. Now continue, keeping left and following the road signs (watch the crossroads with asphalt roads).

On a gentle descent, you reach Pian dei Costa (about 3 km from the starting point). After approximately 500 m, cross a small wooden bridge that marks the start of the gentle ride up to the heart of the wood.

Another 800 m and you cross a cement and stone bridge. Now ride for about 1 km and pass near a former gateman's box, then cross the "pine forest" of Cesuna di Roana, with its silver firs, recognizable by the two white stripes on the lower part of the leaf.

Continue your tour on the cycle lane, until reaching on your left a small amusement park. From this point, start riding on a stretch of asphalt road. Pass under a small cement bridge and keep right as you enter a section open to traffic.

At the Cesuna square, take the first bend on your left on a slight uphill stretch, and after about 80 m, turn left again for via Larici. After 500 m, the asphalt road ends and closes again to motor-

POINTS OF INTEREST

The **Great War Museum,** *via Roma, Canove di Roana (t. 0424692405).* **Museum of the Cimbra Traditions,** *piazza Santa Giustina, Roana (t. 042466106).* **Cuchi Museum,** *popular wind instruments from all over the world, via XXVII Aprile 16, Canove (t. 0424694283, www.museodeicuchi.it).*

ized traffic. Follow the main road, ignoring the steep pathway on your right.

Just after 3 km and along gentle slopes, you reach the Boscon-Bivio 5 strade refuge.

Take the first bend on your left towards *Boscon British Cemetery,* and you soon reach the Boscon British Cemetery, in remembrance of the allied victims of World War One.

After approximately 1 km, ignore another dirt road on your right leading to Kaberlaba di Asiago, and stay on the main path (avoid any possible detour). After roughly 250 m (1.5 km from the Boscon cemetery), enter a path on your left, leaving the main road. After approximately 100 m, you meet the former railroad track and turn right to **Asiago** (5 km, wooden signs with a red MTB and the word "return").

ABOVE, view of the plateau from Kaberlaba. PAGE OPPOSITE, towards the Boscon refuge.

Technical info

Route
18 Km: Asiago (piazzale della Stazione) - Consorzio Caseifici Asiago - Canove swimming pools - Pian dei Costa - Cesuna pine forest – Cesuna - Rifugio Boscon - Bivio 5 strade - Boscon British Cemetery - Asiago. The road bed is 80% unsurfaced, with cyclable gradients. You can easily reach the starting point by car: from the A4 Serenissima freeway, at Vicenza Est, take the A31 Valdastico freeway up to the last toll booth of Piovene Rocchette; drive along the S.S. del Costo n° 249 main road until you reach the Asiago Plateau at Treschè Conca di Roana.

Difficulty
Ideal itinerary for families also with children along; a mountain bike would be the best two-wheeler due to the many dirt stretches.

Cycling period
From May to October. Healthy air and cool temperatures, since you ride mainly in woods.

Map
• *Altopiano dei Sette Comuni,* sheet 78, scale 1:50,000, Kompass.
• *Altopiano dei Sette Comuni,* sheet 623, scale 1:25,000, Kompass.

Technical assistance
Stella Carlo, via dei Patrioti 31, Asiago; t. 0424462812.

Bicycle rental
Hotel da Barba, Poeslen-Kaberlaba, Asiago; t. 0424462888.

Tourist information
IAT, Asiago Plateau, via Stazione 5, Asiago; t. 0424462221, 0424462661. www.ascom.vi.it/asiago

The Belluno Dolomites Park
The Mis Valley

52 Km

A journey across the intimate and wild nature of the Belluno Dolomites, following the magic of the waters that cross the Mis Valley with its crystal clear waterfalls.

You start your ride from **Agordo**, the main center of the Cordevole Valley. From piazza della Libertà, take via Battisti (after a short stretch, it becomes the S.S. 203 main road), which is usually a busy road. After covering a downhill stretch of 3.3 km from Agordo, pass near Valle Imperina, an old mining village, once a thriving extractive center (cupriferous ore and silver lead ore, then, until 1962, sulphuric acid). The downhill stretch continues along the Agordo Canal up to the Castei tunnel, where we suggest taking the disused

road that passes on the other side of the Cordevole torrent, with a panoramic bridge over the gorges. Get back on the main road and, shortly after, go past La Stanga, with a view on the wild Piero Valley. At Candaten, skirt the equipped area of the park and continue your ride towards Ponte Mas, where you turn right, following the road signs pointing to Sospirolo, then immediately right, passing the bridge over the Cordevole, towards Lake Vedana. After reaching the Carthusian monastery, turn left, riding along the outside walls. A short detour on your left leads you to the placid waters of Lake Vedana. The

road continues with a series of up and downhill stretches to Mis, following on the right the road signs indicating the Mis Valley; take another turn on the right to Volpez and enter the S.P. 2 provincial road running along Lake Mis with

ABOVE, the Mis canal.
PAGE OPPOSITE, Agordo, Mount Moiazza.

short tunnels. Just shortly after the bridge over the Falcina Valley, on your right, you encounter an equipped rest area. The artificial reservoir ends at Gena Bassa. Continue your ride along the S.P. 2 provincial road that climbs up the Mis Valley. On your right, you can admire the small abandoned village of Stua, and on your left, waterfalls dropping down to the Mis watercourse.

The route faithfully follows the valley that becomes increasingly narrow, while the road cuts through the rock through tunnels. Shortly after exiting the Mis Canal, the roads climbs up with a series of ups and downs, crossing a few hamlets, while the view opens out towards the mountain ranges of Piz de Mez and Sas de Mura. At Tiser, take

the S.P. 3 provincial road that reaches the Franche col, the highest spot of the itinerary (990 m). The descent gets steeper at Rivamonte Agordino, where a series of hairpin bends curl towards the bottom of the valley, offering a splendid view (to your right) on the deep ravine of the Agordo Canal. At the bottom of the valley, cross the bridge over the Cordevole, then turn left on the S.S. 3 main road leading to **Agordo**, closing the circle and your trip.

Technical info

Route
52 Km: Agordo - Muda bridge - La Stanga - Candaten - Peron - Mas - Lake Vedana - Pascoli - Lake Mis - Gena Bassa - Franche col - Rivamonte Agordino.
On asphalt road (360 to 990 m altitude).
Difficulty
The itinerary has just one long uphill stretch towards Titele, getting tougher towards the Franche pass. The most challenging part is the 11 km section between Gena Bassa and the pass of the Franche col. The final stretch is entirely downhill. You ride through tunnels, so equip yourself with front and tail lights.
Cycling period
Spring and fall.
Map
Atlante stradale d'Italia, Northern volume, scale 1:200,000, TCI.
Technical assistance
• Tekno Sport, via IV Novembre 6, Agordo. t. 043763465
• Free Time, piazza IV Novembre 10,

Cencenighe Agordino t. 0437580118
Tourist information
• Tourist Information Office, via XXVII Aprile 5/a, Agordo; t. 043762105.
• Parco Nazionale delle Dolmiti Bellunesi, piazzale Zancanaro 1, Feltre; t. 04393328.
• Centro Visitatori, piazza 1° Novembre, Pedavena; t. 0437304400.
www.parks.it/parco.nazionale. dol.bellunesi/

The Euganei Hills   63 Km
From Este to Valsanzibio and Arquà Petrarca

Nature, history and culture are the dominant themes of this cycling tour in the Regional Park of the Euganei Hills, between Este and Padua.

Leave the center of **Este,** riding along via Guido Negri and skirting the castle walls. Turn left in via Vigo di Torre, then immediately right in via Ca' Mori and via Rana Ca' Mori. Now turn left at two farms in via Rana, leading to Preare and to Baone. At this stage, follow the S.P. 21 provincial road towards the San Giorgio Valley up to Ponticello, where you turn right for Arquà Petrarca. The provincial road, after an uphill stretch, descends amid vineyards facing Arquà. At Aganoor, just after a restaurant, turn left along the uphill road leading to the village of Arquà. Go straight ahead on a steep downhill stretch, then turn right towards the Duomo. From the Duomo square, turn left and, soon after, at an unmarked crossroads, turn left again following the road signs indicating the "I Ronchi" farm holidays. Firstly on an uphill stretch, then downhill, you reach the S.P. 25 provincial road at Monte Baraldo, where you follow the signs pointing to Valsanzibio. After reaching Villa Barbarigo, continue your ride along the S.P. 25 provincial road towards Galzignano. At the next junction with the pro-

Technical info

Route
63 Km: Este - Preare - Baone - Arquà Petrarca - Valsanzibio - Galzignano Terme - Roccolo pass - Torreglia - Praglia abbey - Teolo - Vò Vecchio - Lozzo Atestino - Rivadolmo - Este (730 m rise). On asphalt roads (except for the link road between Lozzo Atestino and Rivadolmo, avoidable by choosing the alternative)
Difficulty
A rather challenging itinerary. A few series of up and downhill stretches alternate with enjoyable level surfaces, but brace yourself for the tough gradients of the Roccolo pass.
Cycling period
The intermediate seasons, spring and fall, are ideal.
Bicycle + Train
The Este railroad station is situated along the Mantua-Padua line.
Map
• *Colli Euganei,* 1:30,000, Kompass.
• *Atlante stradale d'Italia,* Northern volume, 1:200,000, TCI.
Technical assistance
• Ciclo Shop, via Zuccherificio 2, Este; t. 04292937.
• Aerelli Bike, via Mirabello 67, Torreglia; t. 0495212154.
Tourist information
• Parco dei Colli Euganei, via Fontana 2, Arquà Petrarca; t. 0429777144.
www.parks.it/parco.colli.euganei/
www.parcocollieuganei.com
• Pro Loco
piazza Maggiore 9/a, Este; t. 04293635.
• Tourist Office,
c/o Palazzetto dei Vicari, Teolo; t. 0499925680.
• Tourist Office
via Guido Negri, Este; t. 0429600462.

vincial road, turn left towards Fontanafredda, riding along the S.P. 99 "Cingolina" provincial road, on a slightly uphill stretch.

The gradient increases, and once you get up the hill, turn right in via Roccolo, firstly on a series of up and down-hill stretches, then on a steep ascent to the Roccolo pass (393 m above sea level).

Now ride down to the provincial road, where you turn right until reaching Torreglia. After crossing the

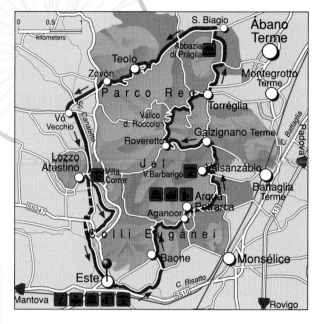

POINTS OF INTEREST

Villa Barbarigo *(t. 0499 130042) at Valsanzibio, surrounded by a magnificent XVII century Italian-style garden.* **Arquà** *with the house of Francesco Petrarca (t. 0499718294), where the poet spent the last four years of his life until 1374. The guided visit to the* **Praglia Abbey** *(t. 0499900010), now a laboratory for the restoration of old books.*

town, turn left (S.P. 43 provincial road) until you reach the crossroads for Praglia, where you turn left (S.P. 25 provincial road). After crossing the hamlet of Tramonte, turn left towards the Praglia Abbey, which is worth a visit. After turning back, move on towards the S.P. 89 provincial road (watch out for traffic!), turning left up to Treponti. After Villa, the road climbs up, with a view on the old caves and woods, to Teolo, the ancient Roman *Titolum* on the "via Montanara" for Este. From Teolo, continue your ride downhill until you reach Zovon, where you can visit caves of Euganean trachyte. Now proceed straight

Left, Villa Barbarigo at Valsanzibio. PAGE OPPOSITE, Este, the castle walls.

ahead up to Vò Vecchio, riding along the final stretch of the itinerary with no other difficulties in store.

From this point, stick to the road signs for Lozzo Atestino, following the Cataletto drain. After approaching Villa Lando-Correr, cross the bridge and take via Botte, turning left on the via Argine Bisatto dirt road, which follows the homonymous canal and leads to **Este**, closing the circle and your ride.

ALTERNATIVE

Instead of taking via Botte, turn right in via Val Calaona along the Lozzo drain and the S.S. 247 Riviera main road. At Rivadolmo, after crossing the main road, ride along the cycle lane, closed to traffic, which follows the Bisatto Canal up to the center of Este.

The Pusteria Valley   45 Km
The San Candido-Lienz cycle lane

A classical cycle touring route, straddling Italy and Austria. Ideal for everyone, it's a small, yet grand journey that offers the thrill of crossing the border in the presence of proud mountain peaks, and rouses the fantasy of leaving on a traveling ride to the heart of Europe.

The route stretches along the cycle lane that starts from **San Candido**, at the heart of the Pusteria Valley, along the course of the River Drava. Cross the border between Italy and Austria, and reach Lienz, a small town located in eastern Tirolo, across the enchanting scenario of the Dolomites.

The route is 44 km long, but not challenging (in fact it is known as "the family road"): the starting point is situated 500 m higher than the destination point. At Lienz, or even in the towns you meet along the route,

you can catch a train with your bike along and get easily back to the starting point. You start your ride from the main square of San Candido (Innichen for

Technical info

Route
Approximately 45 Km:
San Candido - Versciaco - Sillian - Abfaltersbach – Mittelwald - Aue - Gallizenklamm - Lienz.
You can start the itinerary from the Dobbiaco railroad station, and after 2.5 km of cycle lane, you can get to San Candido.

Difficulty
The itinerary is ideal for everyone: 500 m of rise spread over 44 km of track with a pretty good surface.

Cycling period
From May to October.

Bicycle + Train
Train timetables and fares from Lienz and to San Candido:
www.dolomiti.it/ita/zone/pusteria/it6.htm

Map
• *Brunico-Dobbiaco*, 1:50,000, sheet 57, Kompass.
• *Dolomiti di Sesto*, 1:25,000, sheet 010, Tabacco.

Technical assistance
• Papin Sport, M.H. Hueber 1, San Candido;
t. 0474913450.
Also offers assistance along the route.
• Trojer Martin,
via Duca Tassilo
(near the church),
San Candido; t. 0474913216.

Tourist information
• Associazione Turistica,
Piazza Magistrato 1,
San Candido;
t. 0474913149.
www.dolomiti.it
• APT Trentino,
via Romagnoli 11, Trento;
t. 800845034 (freephone number),
t. 0461497353.
www.trentino.to/

PAGE OPPOSITE, **stop near Sillian.**

POINTS OF INTEREST

San Candido is situated near the **Dolomiti di Sesto Nature Park,** *where it would be worthwhile to take a trip or two. San Candido also has other sights to see: the* **Duomo,** *Romanesque architecture, and the conventual complex of the Franciscans, dating back to the end of the XVII century. We suggest a trip to the* **Bagni di San Candido** *with its five mineral water springs. At Lienz, don't miss a visit to the XII century castle (Schloss Bruck).*

the Tyrolers), and following the road signs pointing to the state border, ride for 4 km up to Versciaco. Pass under the main road and the railroad, and then continue your ride along the left side of the Drava and on the track that offers you a few easily rideable dirt stretches, until you reach the border.

You are now riding in Austrian territory. Soon after the border, turn left and cross the Drava, then ride towards Sillian, the first town in the Tyrol region,

with the typical local architecture.

After covering 13 km from the starting point, you reach Sillian. You then ride for another 4 km, until you cross the main road at the Forellenhof hotel and continue following the course of the Drava.

Once you get to Abfaltersbach, near the sawmill, you find a cycle assistance spot. The road surface is good and the landscape suggestive: incredibly green meadows framed by impressive mountains. Now continue

your ride on a gentle descent down to Thal, where you find another assistance spot, this time near the Gasthof Aue.

Your destination is approximately 14 km away, and the road offers pleasant downhill stretches to reach Gallizenklamm and then continue for the last 4 km up to the **Lienz** railroad station. From here, you can get back to the starting point, loading your bike on a train and stopping to have a glimpse of the center of this enchanting Tyrolean town.

The Aurina Valley 25 Km
The Gais-San Giacomo cycle lane

The route develops on the cycle lane running along the northernmost valley in Italy, in the province of Bolzano. The destination of the itinerary is San Giacomo, a town immersed in the green expanse of the Aurina Valley, an ideal place to be discovered at a walking pace.

The cycle tour starts from **Gais**, situated at the center of an enormous plain a few kilometers from Brunico. This is where the cycle lane starts, marked by special signs, which leads to the Aurina Valley crossing the Tures Valley. A few hundred meters' ride and you approach an artificial lake, a favorite destination of kayak enthusiasts. Continue your ride towards Villa Ottone, and after getting near the town, you'll be able to spot the Canova castle concealed

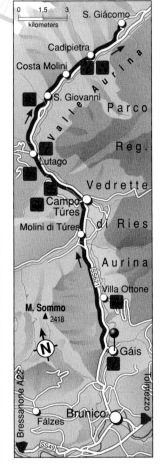

Technical info

Route
25 Km (50 Km return trip):
Gais - Villa Ottone –Molini di Tures – Campo Tures – Lutago – San Giovanni – Cadipietra – San Giacomo. On cycle lane. You can get back to Gais by bus (departures every 30 minutes) or you can cover the same road backwards.
Difficulty
The environment and the serenity of the places make this itinerary an ideal route for families with children along.
Cycling period
From May to October.
Map
Valle Aurina, 1:25,000 sheet 36, Tabacco.
Technical assistance
• Rainer Bike, via Talfrieden 12, Gais; t. 0474504526.
• Hofer Hubert,

via Aurina 106, Cadipietra; t. 0474652126.
Useful addresses
• Consorzio Promozione Turistica Cadipietra, via Aurina 95, Cadipietra; t. 0474652081. www.tures-aurina.com
• Associazione Turistica Valle Aurina, via Aurina 22, Lutago; t. 0474671257. www.ahruntal-info.com
• Associazione Turistica, via Josef Jungmann 8, Campo Tures; t. 0474678076.
• Associazione Turistica Valli di Tures e Aurina, via Aurina 95, Cadipietra; t. 0474652081.

by the luxuriant trees. Another 10 km on a gentle uphill stretch leads you to Campo Tures, main city of the homonymous valley, with its imposing castle. A crown of mountains forms a scenario to the ride, while you start looking forward to the Southern Tyrolean landscape. At this stage, after crossing the built-up area of

Campo Tures, the panorama changes dramatically. The valley narrows and the lane starts following the route of the Aurino torrent, amid mixed woods of fir trees, pines and larches that alternate with vast meadows. For a short stretch, your view is covered by the lush and imposing vegetation, but all of a sudden, appearing on the upper left-hand corner, the splendor of the Sasso Nero glacier.

The course of the track, which runs parallel to the main road, now turns slightly westwards, following the base of the Palù massif, up to Lutago, in a green basin. After a necessary ride across the center of Lutago, the road continues northeastwards. At this stage, you have to challenge the only uphill stretch, which is, however, only a few hundred meters long.

Before the ski-lift facilities of Speikboden, the track drops down again and changes side of the torrent. After crossing the main road to penetrate in another wood along the river, move on without any particular variations in gradient and on a fairly good road surface. Now cross again, in rapid sequence, San Martino, and after just more than 1 km, San Giovanni, followed by the hamlet of Cadipietra, once famous for its copper mines (now closed) and, after the last 3 km, the small, enchanting town of **San Gia-**

ABOVE, San Giacomo Church.
BELOW, artificial lake near Gais.

como. You can get back to the starting point covering the same route, on a mainly downhill stretch.

POINTS OF INTEREST

The **Campo Tures castle** *(XIII-XV century) was built in two different periods: the defense tower and the Romanesque residential section under the lords of Tures, the four-sided tower and the two Gothic turrets under the Counts Fieger and the bishops of Bressanone. Inside the castle, which is open to the public, there are 64 rooms, of which 24 completely covered with wood.*

Also make the interesting visit to the remains of the copper mines of Cadipietra, mainly exploited during the medieval ages, which still preserve a few constructions dating back to the XVI and XVII centuries.

The Adige Valley 1   38 Km
From Merano to Bolzano

The journey along the second largest river in Italy (410 km) runs from Alto Adige to Veneto, crossing Trentino. The river is faithfully followed by a cycle route that runs from Lake Resia down along the Venosta Valley and penetrates the vaster Adige Valley. This is a classical cycle touring route in Italy, combined with train transport, therefore simple and practical, just like the most famous cycle routes in Europe.

From the center of **Merano**, follow the left side of the Passirio, turning left to cross the overpass of the freeway, then continue your ride towards Marlengo and Lana. From Lana, take the Strada del Vino that leads to Nalles and Andriano, and after 2 km, to Lana di Sotto/Niederlana, where you meet the parish church dedicated to Maria Assunta, with its great wooden altar of Schnatterpeck.

Continuing your ride along via Brandis/Waalweg, which flanks the church, you arrive near the Fruit-Growing Museum of Alto Adige, built inside a medieval construction.

After the stop, continue your ride on an easy stretch along expanses of apple trees. At the junction with the road that leads to Gargazzone, ride straight ahead towards Nalles, without crossing the town center. After riding for a few

POINTS OF INTEREST

The Castel Trauttmansdorff Gardens *(via S. Valentino 51a, Merano, t. 0473235730, www.trauttmansdorff. it), a vast botanical garden, east of Merano. Visitors may be assisted by an audio-guide to best follow the two equipped routes.*

Centro Recupero Avifauna Castel Tirolo *(Schlossweg 25, Dorf Tirol, Merano, t. 0473 21500), the only centre in the Alpine arc specialized in the recovery of birds. Flight demonstrations of birds of prey at 11.15 a.m. and 3.15 p.m.*

Technical info

Route
38 Km: Merano – Lana – Nalles – Andriano – Frangarto – Bolzano. On asphalt track with dirt stretches. You can easily reach the starting point by taking the trains coming from Bolzano every hour, or you can take the A22 Brennero freeway, Bolzano Sud exit, continuing on the freeway up to Merano.
Difficulty
Apart from some short gentle uphill stretches, the route doesn't require particular effort, and is ideal also for "family" or group outings.
Cycling period
Starting from April with the splendid views of the

blossoming apple orchards, until fall.
Map
Ciclopista del Sole – sheet 1, 1:100,000, Ciclomappe Ediciclo Editore (t. 042174475).
Bicycle + Train
You go back to the starting point on the Bolzano-Merano line.
Technical assistance
• Merano: Bike Point Meran, via Portici 337, Merano; t. 0473237733.
• Josef Staffler, piazza Tribus 2a, Lana; t. 0473562592.
• Velo Sportler, via dei Grappoli 56, Bolzano; t. 0471977719.
Useful addresses
• Consorzio Turistico

Merano e Dintorni, via Palade 101, Merano; t. 0473200443. www.meranerland.com
• Consorzio Turistico il Giardino del Sudtirolo, via Pillhof 1, Frangarto; t. 0471633488.
• Azienda di Soggiorno e Turismo di Bolzano, piazza Walther 8, Bolzano; t. 0471307000.
• Alp Bike - Ciclotrekking, via Flavon 101, Bolzano; t. 0471952266, 0471272024. www.alpbike.it
Sports association engaged in MTB cycle touring, with the assistance of national experts. Also orienteering courses for children, young people and grown-ups.

kilometers and reaching Andriano, at the crossroads leading to Terlano, a famous centre for the production of asparagus and excellent wines, turn right, then immediately left. Follow the gentle uphill climb leading to a path that curls along the edge of the mountain.
After the ride down, and after crossing the hamlet of Unterrain, you reach the S.S. 42 main road that leads, on an uphill stretch, to Caldaro/Kaltern. Cross the main road and enter a path that links the cycle lanes of Bolzano to the route along the Strada del Vino coming from Caldaro. Now take the

ABOVE, Lana, path between orchards. PAGE OPPOSITE, the Adige Valley near Bolzano.

right turn and climb up towards Appiano and then Caldaro, to finally reach Termeno (after Bolzano).
If, instead, you continue your ride on a straight downhill stretch, after crossing the Adige and the railroad, where you turn right, you shortly reach the intersection with the track that descends from **Bolzano** along the Isarco: by continuing on your left, you reach the town center in 20 minutes. The way back can be covered by train, or you can extend the itinerary, as you wish, along the cycle lane (see Bolzano-Trento itinerary on the following page).

The Adige Valley 2   63 Km
From Bolzano to Trento

The ride down to Trento along the Adige Valley is a stretch fraught with meaning. It's a stage of the very long "Ciclopista del Sole" path (work in progress), which entails the link from the Brennero to Sicily. The path is part of the more complex and extensive Euro Velo project, the great European cycle route network. In particular, Trento is a historical stage of the north-south route of passage, and has always acted as a link between the Mediterranean and Mitteleuropean cultures. A ride along this stretch of the Adige cycle lane has, therefore, a strong symbolic meaning.

The cycle lane coming out of **Bolzano** follows an embankment halfway between the Isarco and Adige rivers,

which later meet a few kilometers downstream. After crossing the bridge that takes you on the right side of the Adige, continue your

ride up to Laives. Here, a new bridge takes the route on the other bank, where it continues along a nice stretch of apple and pear orchards. As you approach Ora, cross a railroad underpass and, keeping right, reach Termeno/Tramin.

From Termeno, ride along the road that takes you to the Egna-Termeno railroad station, where you turn left to cross the freeway and the Adige.

After crossing the bridge, you reach Egna/Neumarkt, not such a popular place as far as tourism is concerned, but highly interesting for its suggestive porticoes in the pedestrian center.

Now that you're back on the cycle route along the river, with the lush woods of the Monte Corno Nature

POINTS OF INTEREST

The **Museum of Traditions of the People of Trentino** at S. Michele all'Adige, a former convent of the Augustine friars (via Edmondo Mach 1, t. 0461650314, www.museo sanmich ele.it), is worth a stop after a few hours' ride: open from 9 to 12.30 a.m. and from 2.30 to 6 p.m. (closed on Monday). It is one of the most important ethnographical museums in Europe, which bears witness to the life, the traditions, the work in bucolic-rural world of an Alpine people.

PAGE OPPOSITE, cycle lane near Salorno.

Park dominating on the left, you can spot in the distance the steeple of Salorno. Just a few more kilometers and you leave Alto Adige and enter Trentino.

Continue your ride along the cycle lane with many lay-bys, and after a large crook of the river towards the left, you reach the area of Mez-zocorona, an important wine-producing center (entirely cultivated with Teroldego vine) situated at the mouth of the Non Valley. After 1.5 km, the cycle lane crosses the built-up area of Grumo, where you turn towards San Michele all'Adi-ge, which is worth a stop to visit the Museum of Traditions of the People of Trentino (see box). At Nave San Rocco, cross the Adige again and stay on the left side until you reach Trento. Within sight of Lavis, due to the great bed of the Avisio that flows into the Adige, you have to climb up the course of the torrent and cross it at the first footbridge.

Now that you're back on the right direction, after passing under the railroad and the freeway, ride for a few kilometers with the great artery nearby before reaching **Trento**.

Technical info

Route
63 Km: Bolzano - Termeno - San Michele all'Adige - Nave San Rocco - Lavis - Trento. On asphalt cycle track (except for short stretches during the crossings). Once you leave Bolzano, the track skirts the towns, except for the above mentioned localities. You can easily reach the starting point by car, taking the A22 Brennero freeway, or by train on the Verona-Brennero line. After leaving the railroad station, turn left until you reach the track that descends from the Talvera torrent, at the intersection with the Isarco cycle lane, and continue on your right up to the junction with the Adige.

Difficulty
Easy route, mostly along the embankments of the river. The relative distance requires at least your being used to staying on a saddle.

Cycling period
From April, with the splendid views of the blossoming apple orchards, through October.

Map
Ciclopista del Sole – sheet 1, 1:100,000, Ediciclo Editore (t. 042174475).

Bicycle + Train
To get back to the starting point, take the train on the Trento-Bolzano stretch.

Technical assistance
• Velo Sportler, via dei Grappoli 56, Bolzano; t. 0471977719.
• Theresia Vescoli,

piazza Principale 18, Ora; t. 0471811233.
• Tuttobici, via Rosmini 103, Lavis; t. 0461241999.
• Cicli Giovanni Baldo, c.so 3 Novembre 70, Trento; t. 0461915406.

Useful addresses
• Azienda di Soggiorno e Turismo di Bolzano, piazza Walther 8, Bolzano; t. 0471307000.
• Consorzio Turistico il Giardino del Sudtirolo, via Pillhof 1, Frangarto; t. 0471633488
• APT Trentino, via Romagnoli 11, Trento; t. 800845034 (freephone number), t. 0461497353. www.trentino.to/

The Upper Venosta Valley   30 Km
From Burgusio to Lake Resia

This route plunges into the serenity of the Upper Venosta Valley and, in particular, "circumnavigates" Lake Resia, whose most famous symbol is the characteristic semi-submerged church steeple that emerges from the waters.

lake, you reach San Valentino alla Muta/St. Valentin a. d. Haide, situated between the small lake expanse of Muta and the larger Lake Resia/Reschensee. Now ride along the cycle lane, and after just less than 5 km, you reach

the village of Curon/Graun, the locality famous for the steeple that emerges from the lake. Continue your ride along the lake, and after approximately 4 smooth kilometers, you reach the built-up area of Resia/Reschen,

You start your ride from **Burgusio**, and immediately after, you have to take on the most challenging part of the itinerary: a 265 m rise from the starting point to the lake (approximately 5 km), with some steep hairpin bends. In any case, the not too trained cyclists can use the very comfortable bicycle cab service (see box). Riding along the

Technical info

Route
30 Km: Burgusio – Dörfl – S. Valentino alla Muta - Curon - Resia - S. Valentino alla Muta - Burgusio. On asphalt surface. You reach the starting point by taking the S.S. 38 and 40 main roads which, from Merano, climb up to the Resia pass. After leaving Malles, turn left and shortly after reach Burgusio. You can park before the climb up to Slingia.

Difficulty
Average difficulty, recommended for cyclists with the basic training required to manage the rise between

the starting point and the lake, and the steep hairpin bends along the right side. The fast and long downhill stretches require a two-wheeler equipped with excellent brake systems.

Cycling period
From mid-April through October.

Bicycle + Cab
• Taxi Armin, via Stazione 63/A, Malles; t. 0473.831106
• Taxi Flora, via Pardelles 5, Malles; t. 0473.831171

Map
No maps are needed, thanks to the scores of road signs

found along the Adige cycle lane. However, a sheet map in German is available, the *"Etsch-Radweg Von Landeck (A) nach Verona"*, 1:75,000, Verlag Esterbsuer GmbH, at the Athesia di Bolzano bookshop; t. 0471927286.

Technical assistance
Sport Tenne, via Generale Verdross 1, Malles; t. 0473830560.

Useful addresses
Consorzio Turistico Val Venosta, via dei Cappuccini 10, Silandro; t. 0473633101.

POINTS OF INTEREST

The Monte Maria/Marien-berg Benedictine Abbey, *1.5 km from Burgusio towards Slingia; don't miss the visit to the crypt with its precious Romanesque frescoes (guided visits, lasting about 30 minutes, t. 0473831306). Founded in 1149/50 by Ulrich von Tarasp, the abbey welcomed the first monks coming from the Suevian convent of Ottobeuren. The portal and the frescoes in the crypt still bear witness to the Romanesque period.*

where you ride along the lakefront, with broad views on the snow-capped, majestic peaks of the Ortles-Cevedale mountain range. Following a lightly-trafficked road, after passing a ski-lift facility, the road climbs for approximately 1 km, up to a clear hairpin bend on your right at a cross-

BELOW, the semi-submerged steeple of Lake Resia. PAGE OPPOSITE, cycling along Lake Resia.

roads. The itinerary advances on your left towards San Valentino alla Muta. The road now drops along a steep downhill stretch crossing a coniferous wood, until you get back near the lake.

At this point, faithfully follow the general direction of the coast, until you reach the end of the lake. Turn left, crossing the dam and taking the S.S. 40 main road again to go back to San Valentino. Now continue on a downhill stretch past Lake Muta on the road you have already covered. A few hundred meters after the lake, turn right along a dirt road that follows the course of the Adige.

The final part of the itinerary continues along the wood on asphalt road. It would be wise to pay due attention to the passage of tractors, especially during the hay harvest. Take the downhill road and return to **Burgusio**.

ALTERNATIVE

The itinerary is easier if

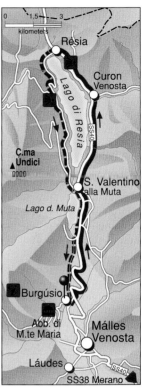

you restrict your tour to Lake Resia, with starting point and destination at San Valentino alla Muta (18 km).

Valsugana 29 Km
The loop of the Sella Valley

This corner of Trentino holds all the ingredients to live an experience in close contact with nature. Pathways and dirt roads run from the placid waters of the Levico and Caldonazzo lakes to the woods and the malghe of the great plateaus. The Valsugana is a real natural gymnasium.

The tour of the Sella Valley develops from the bottom of the valley, stretching between Borgo Valsugana and Novaledo, to the mountainous crest that extends from

Pizzo di Levico (1,908 m) to Cima Dodici (2,336 m), curling along woods and malghe. You start your ride from **Barco**, near the church. Now continue straight ahead until you meet a crossroads, then turn left and ride towards Lago Morto. After crossing the bridge over the River Brenta, go straight and before the level crossing, take the first path on your right that flanks the embankment of the river. Continue your ride towards the Novaledo railroad station on bad asphalt surface. At the level

crossing, turn right, and after reaching a crossroads, turn left and enter the built-up area of Oltrebrenta. After 100 m, start riding on dirt road. After getting to the

Technical info

Route
29 Km: Barco - Oltrebrenta - Roncegno railroad station - Borgo Valsugana - San Giorgio - Malga Costa - Barco. On asphalt and dirt roads.
Difficulty
Average difficulty, requiring about 3 cycling hours. The itinerary curls along middle mountain settings, with a total rise of approximately 650 m.
Cycling period
From late spring to the beginning of fall.
Roadmap
Valsugana Mountain Bike, 15 routes for MTB, with detailed description and altitude profiles, APT Trentino.

Bicycle + Train
The route runs mainly along the Trento-Bassano del Grappa railroad station, touching the stations of Levico Terme, Novaledo, Roncegno and Borgo Valsugana.
Technical assistance
• Pepe Cicli e Motocicli, viale Città di Prato 29, Borgo Valsugana; t. 0461754268.
• Debortoli Cicli e Articoli sportivi; corso Ausugum 20, Borgo Valsugana; t. 0461752275.
• Cetto Cicli, corso Centrale, Levico Terme; t. 0461701314.

Useful addresses
• APT Terme di Levico, Vetriolo e Roncegno, Panarotta 2002, Lago di Caldonazzo; t. 800018925 (freephone number). www.valsugana.nu
• APT Lagorai Valsugana Orientale e Tesino, via Dante 10, Castello Tesino; t. 0461593322. www.lagorai.tn.it/
• IAT Borgo Valsugana, piazza Degasperi, Borgo Valsugana; t. 0461752393.
• Associazione Arte Sella; t. 3392099226; www.get.to/artesella.

Roncegno-Marter railroad station, proceed until reaching a level crossing, then take the road to Borgo Valsugana up to the crossroads on your right for Fontana di Sotto. At the traffic lights, at the center of Borgo Valsugana, turn right for the Sella Valley and ride on asphalt road until you reach San Giorgio. Now continue up to the Legno hotel, the Val Paradiso hotel and then to Malga Costa (on dirt road).

From this point, ride on a rough asphalt road, until you reach a crossroads where you keep left. Pass near a malga, jump over a fence and follow the SAT signs "Barco di Levico - 203", then ride along a mule track which, after a stretch in the wood, ar-

ABOVE, the Arte Natura Route in the Sella Valley.

rives at a panoramic hill (996 m). Continue riding on a downhill stretch, along pathways in the grass, passing near a few scattered cottages, up to a dirt road, where you ride on your left for 350 m until reaching a crossroads on a stream (950 m).

This is the start of the real downhill part to Barco di Levico (on your right the falling rocks sign), on a bumpy stretch that brushes a meadow with cottages (Bellis houses). After passing a crag (steep descent on rugged road), ride down into a solitary valley. Now ride along a service road towards gravel quarries. After crossing the gully, emerge close to the built-up area of **Barco**, near an isolated farmstead, then return to the starting point.

POINTS OF INTEREST

Arte Sella is an international biennial of contemporary art, held in the meadows and woods of the Sella Valley, along the valley crossed by the **Arte Natura Route.** *The works, usually made with leaves, stones, branches and trunks, suffer the decomposition associated with the cycle of the seasons, until they are transformed by the surrounding environment, which decrees their final departure. Guided visits (prior to booking) every weekend in the months of May and October and every day in the months of June and August (Municipal Public Library of Borgo Valsugana, t. 0461754052; borgo. valsugana@biblio.infotn.it).*

The great Trentino plateaus   20 Km
Mountain biking in the Lavarone loop

A great enchantment along the route of the first permanent mountain cycle lane designed and built in Italy. Former military roads, forest pathways and tracks, cross the plateaus of Folgaria, Lavarone and Luserna on the Austro-Hungarian borderline. They form the route of the "100 km dei Forti". This is the place where, every year, expert bikers meet and challenge themselves for one day (100 km!). During the rest of the year, in spring and summer, it is a splendid cycle lane for mountain bikes. The entire route requires excellent training, but it can be split

up into three different circles that curl along the three plateaus of Folgaria (44 km, 1,055 m rise), Lavarone (20 km, 360 m rise) and Luserna (27 km, 575 m rise).

The Lavarone loop (less challenging compared to

Folgaria and Luserna) starts from **Bertoldi**. After leaving your car in the parking lot of Slaghenaufi, near the military cemetery, start climbing along the forest road. After approximately 400 m, you reach a crossroads: keep right on the Lavarone circle (on your left, near a bar, the "100 km dei Forti" route continues towards Sommo Alto). Now continue your ride on the main routes, ignoring the detours on your right.

After approximately 1.5 km, enter the "100 km" route, then cross the road of the Cost pass (asphalt), taking the dirt road that drops down to Camini, recognizable by a vast glade in the wood. After a scenic passage on the Astico Valley, you reach the asphalt road, where you turn left towards the forte Belvedere. Following the "100 km" route, pass by Masi di Sotto, riding amid the typical "laste", slabs of stone that mark off property. Now pass by Lake Lavarone and the crossroads of Mount Rust, where you start riding on an uphill stretch of 500 m with a 9% average gradient.
After taking the downhill stretch, near a ski-lift facility (at a bend on your right),

LEFT, passage at Masi di Sotto.
PAGE OPPOSITE, Lake Lavarone.

POINTS OF INTEREST

A visit to the interesting **Forte Gschwent-Belvedere Museum** *of Lavarone. This is the only border fortress out of the seven that was saved from partial demolition, owing to the stripping of "iron for the Fatherland" carried out by the Fascist regime during the Thirties. The museum is open from Easter through September from 9 a.m. to 6 p.m.; closed on Monday except for the months of July and August.*

leave the main road and take the route that passes under the facility.

This stretch requires great attention in order not to lose your bearings (watch out for the ski-lift facility!). The last stretch of the itinerary is highly suggestive and runs in the shade of a magnificent wood. You reach Carbonare (asphalt), where you continue your ride on your right, ignoring the "100 km" sign that points to the left. After reaching the crossroads, cross the main road and reach the first crossroads, where you find the "100 km" sign that points to the right.

At this stage, follow the "100 km" signs, then ride back to **Bertoldi** and to the parking lot of Slaghenaufi where you close the circle and your trip.

Technical info

Route
20 Km: Bertoldi - Cost pass - Camini - Forte Belvedere - Masi di Sotto - Lake Lavarone - Mount Rust crossroads - Carbonare - Bertoldi.
18.8 km on dirt road and 1.2 on asphalt. You can easily reach the starting point from Folgaria (10.5 km) to Carbonare, where you continue towards Virti and the Slaghenaufi Cemetery.
Difficulty
This is a short route, although running almost entirely on dirt roads and paths. The uphill stretches are altogether 4.5 km, but the itinerary is, all in all, quite rough, with frequent changes in gradients and short, though tough spurts.
Cycling period
From May to October.
Map
• *"100 km dei Forti"*, cycle lane for MTB, 1:33,000, APT Folgaria, Lavarone and Luserna. With altitude layout and description of routes, distributed by the Local Tourist Board.
• *Altopiani di Folgaria, Lavarone e Luserna,*
tourist and path map, 1:25,000, sheet 631, Kompass.
Technical assistance
• Taccone Sport, via Trento 51, Folgaria; t. 0464720551.
• Moda Sport, via Maffei, Costa di Folgaria; t. 0464721321.
Useful addresses
• Azienda di Promozione Turistica degli Altopiani, via Roma 67, Folgaria; t. 0464721133.
Gionghi 73, Lavarone; t. 0464783226.
www.altipianitrentini.tn/it

Friuli-Venezia Giulia

The Livenza
From Sacile to the sources of the river

This ride brushes the up-lands of the Cansiglio wood and follows the clear waters of the River Livenza, a historical watercourse across which most of the wooden trunks that support Venice were carried.

The itinerary starts from **Sacile**, once the "Giardino

della Serenissima", a typical Venetian town, with its characteristic streets with porticoes and noble palaces facing the Livenza. An extraordinary example is the XIV century Municipal Loggia in piazza del Popolo. Spare some time to also visit the Gothic Duomo frescoed by Casarini, the Baptistery and the Church of the Madonna della Pietà.

Start riding from the town centre towards Nave, then continue cycling until you reach Polcenigo, after about a smooth 10 km trip. Set in a magnificent scenery and lapped by the waters of the Livenza, Polcenigo offers some quite interesting spots, such as the San Floriano Park (which you reach by turning left before entering the town).

Now move on towards Gorgazzo, an ideal spot to observe one of the most fascinating sources of the Liven-

ABOVE, the bridge over
the Livenza at Polcenigo.

100

Technical info ⟳ ‖ 🚲

Route		
34 Km: Sacile - Polcenigo - Gorgazzo - Sarone - Caneva - Fiaschetti - Nave - Sacile. You can easily reach the starting point from Pordenone (12 km), Conegliano Veneto (17 km) and Vittorio Veneto (17 km).	is located along the Treviso-Pordenone railroad line. **Map** *Veneto e Friuli-Venezia Giulia*, 1:200,000, TCI Regional maps **Roadmaps**	Livenza, piazza Plebiscito 2, Polcenigo; t. 0434748788. • APT Piancavalle Cellina Livenza, piazza Duomo, Aviano; t. 0434651888. www.piancavallo.com
Difficulty Not too challenging, just one tough, short uphill stretch between Sarone and Caneva.	C. Favot, *Itinerari cicloturistici dalle Alpi all'Adriatico, Livenza in Bicicletta*, ed. Arti Grafiche Risma - Roveredo in Piano. **Technical assistance**	• Associazione Aruotalibera, C.P. 161 Posta Centrale, Pordenone; t. 0434540483. www.aruotaliberapn.it
Cycling period All year round.	Bravin Mauro, via Gorgazzo 30, Polcenigo; t. 0434748751.	• Museo del ciclismo "Toni Pessot", c/o Auditorium comunale,
Bicycle + Train The Sacile railroad station	**Tourist information** • Comunità Pedemontana	Caneva; t. 043479002.

za, an underwater pool with crystal-clear emerald green reflections.

Your trip continues along the "Pedemontana" (piedmont road) riding towards Sarone and Caneva. After a few kilometers, you meet the detour that leads to the XVI century Church of the Santissima (we suggest visiting the wooden altar inside dating back to the XVII century) and the sources of the Livenza. A path that starts with a small bridge opposite the church allows you to "circumnavigate" the sources in just a few minutes' time.

Once you're back on the "Pedemontana", ride up a short ascent, followed by a crossroads where you keep right to reach Sarone.

After crossing the town, follow the road to the Cansiglio, then get ready to challenge a tough uphill ride that takes you to another crossroads. Now continue on your left on a downhill stretch towards Caneva (on your right the road stretches towards the Cansiglio),

POINTS OF INTEREST

*The most traditional festival that takes place at Polcenigo is the **Sagra dei Sèst**, which has been held for over 300 years during the first week end of September. It was once a fair where farmers used to buy the "thestons", containers for the grape harvest. Thousands of people gather in the square to admire and buy the typical local handicraft, from wickers to rush, from wood to ceramics and leather.*

where you can stop and freshen up. A sight to see here in the 19th century church is the "Caduta degli angeli ribelli" (1840) by the Belluno painter Giovanni De' Min and two Renaissance works by Francesco da Milano, as well as the "Toni Pessot" Cycling Museum, displaying jerseys and items once owned by famous cyclists (open from Monday to Friday, 2–6 p.m.). From the church, ride on your left towards Fiaschetti, a small hamlet that heralds the last part of the tour: at the junction with the traffic lights, turn right following the road signs for Fontanafredda. Shortly afterwards, take via Deciani (on your right) and continue riding up to Nave where you turn right for the final part up to **Sacile**, end of circle.

Aquileia 23 Km
The pine forest of San Marco and Belvedere

A fascinating ride towards the Grado lagoon, formed by the mouth of the Isonzo, across paths made for bicycles, through the pine forest of San Marco and Belvedere.

You start from **Monastero** (piazza Pirano), riding along via Salvemini and via Sacra that flanks the river port reaching the town center of Aquileia, with its urban layout typical of great Roman cities, inscribed in the World Heritage List of UNESCO. From via Roma, reach piazza Garibaldi, and after crossing the bridge over the River Natissa, enter corso Gramsci, until you reach an intersection opposite the vine-

yards of the Ca' Tullio wine producing firm: now turn right, riding for 200 m until you enter a gravel road. Continue your ride amid fields for 1.5 km, passing a

water pumping station near a small bridge on a canal: at this point, the road turns right, then shortly after, left, until reaching, after 2 km, the embankment of the reclaimed land facing the Grado lagoon. Ride along the embankment on your right for 800 m and reach the mouth of the Natissa. If you turn left, ride for a further 300 m, and after passing the last slip road, you reach the small Church of San Marco, surrounded by the homonymous pine forest. From this point, you can enjoy a magnificent view on the lagoon; the meadow is blanketed with spider orchids in full bloom, and you can easily spot hares and pheasants. Now take the gravel road behind the church, which runs straight across the fields for 1.5 km, until reaching the main road. Before the crossroads, on your left, you'll find the so-called "house with 100 windows", a rural building that dates back to the reclamation period. By turning left, you get back to Aquileia after approximately 2 km. The itinerary continues by turning right on the main road heading to Grado. After 600 meters, turn left

Technical info

Route
23 Km: Monastero - Aquileia – mouth of the Natissa – small Church of San Marco - Tiel Belvedere bridge - Boscat - Fiumicello - Monastero.
On by-roads, both dirt and asphalt.
Difficulty
Ideal itinerary for everyone.
Cycling period
Spring is the best period to admire nature in full bloom, while winter is indicated for birdwatching enthusiasts.

Map
Atlante stradale d'Italia, Northern volume, 1:200,000, TCI.
Technical assistance
Canesin, via Garibaldi 1, Cervignano del Friuli; t. 043132572.
Tourist information
• Tourist Information Office, piazza Capitolo, Aquileia; t. 0431919491.
www.aquileiaturismo.info
• APT Grado, viale Dante 72, Grado; t. 04318991.
www.aptgrado.com

ABOVE, Roman river port at Aquileia. PAGE OPPOSITE, stop near the embankment of the reclamation land.

POINTS OF INTEREST

A trip across the waters of the mouth of the Isonzo, an interesting nature area. This is the northernmost wet area of the Mediterranean basin. At Grado, contact the Motoscafisti Gradesi (local motorboat pilots, t. 0431 00115) for a trip to the island of Barbana, which has different natural habitats: freshwater marshland and marine environment.

and take the S.P. 22 provincial road, following the road signs pointing to Belvedere and arriving in front of Villa Savorgnon Fior Pasi. Half hidden in the cluster pine forest on your right, you can spot the liberty station of the Austrian railroads. Now take the provincial road, riding along the quaint tree-lined avenue, passing by a wash-house and reaching, after just less than 1 km, the Belvedere camping site. From here, the road continues facing the lagoon.

Once you cross the Tiel

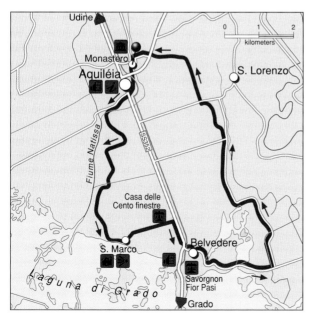

Belvedere bridge, after riding for 3 km across fields and vineyards, get to a left turn to Fiumicello, reaching Boscat (200 m): now leave the province of Gorizia to enter the province of Udine (the provincial road is now the 119). Turn left, passing aside a water pumping station, and riding between the canal on your right and the vineyards on your left, with the steeple of Aquileia coming into view. Ride for 9 km up to Fiumicello. At the stop, turn left to Aquileia (S.P. 91); at the next stop, go straight along the canal and after 1 km, at the crossroads, take on your left the gravel road (not the road to Fiumicello) which, in less than 2 km, along vineyards and peach orchards, crosses the S.P. 8 provincial road. End your tour in the **Monastero** square riding along via Sacco e Vanzetti and skirting the park of villa Hofer Valvassina.

ITINERARIES
Friuli-Venezia Giulia

Collio   37 Km
Between Gorizia and Cormons

On the border with Slovenia, the hilly area of the Collio offers cycle tourists a very relaxing panorama, where noble vineyards stretch across majestic beech and oak woods. Many people believe that the quality of the fine Collio wines is deeply rooted in the "ponca" (the Eocene malmstone and sandstone in Friuli dialect), a soil rich in precious salts. This perfect environment also hosts stone villages and medieval castles that dot a rolling territory.

You start your ride by exiting **Gorizia** towards the north and following the road signs pointing to San Floriano. After a few kilometers, pass the Isonzo, reaching the Piuma Park, with its pleasant paths that skirt the Isonzo. Now proceed on a cyclable uphill stretch towards Oslavia (2 km), with the imposing memorial gathering the rests of 60,000 victims of World War I. Continue on an uphill stretch reaching San Floriano del Collio, which faces expanses of vineyards on the Gorizia and Slovene sides.

Technical info

Route
37 Km: Gorizia - Oslavia - San Floriano del Collio - Uclanzi - Valerisce - Giasbana - Zegla - Cormons - Capriva del Friuli - Mossa - Pubrida - Gorizia.
On asphalt roads.
You can reach Gorizia by taking the A4 Turin-Trieste freeway, Villese exit, and expressway (20 km).

Difficulty
Average difficulty, with no particularly challenging stretches, altogether the itinerary has a quite varied altitude profile on the first stretch (up to Cormons), with various changes in gradients. This itinerary particularly suits people with no real training, but used to physical exercise.

Cycling period
All year round, preferably in fall and spring. The ride can be pleasant also in the sunny winter days with no wind.

Bicycle + Train
The Gorizia railroad station is well linked, with frequent trains from Udine and Monfalcone.

Map
• *Friuli Venezia Giulia*, 1:150,000, Tabacco.
• *Carta topografica e miniguida*

In viaggio nei Vini del Collio, Sviluppo 2000.

Technical assistance
• Cadajaco Ruote, piazza San Rocco, Gorizia; t. 0481536651.
• Cicli Cuk Elia, piazza Cavour 9, Gorizia; t. 0481535019.
• Cicli Novelli, via F. di Manzano 14, Cormons; t. 048161647.

Tourist information
• Azienda Regionale per la Promozione Turistica, via Roma 5, Gorizia; t. 0481386225, 0481386224. www.regione.fvg.it
• Cormons Tourist Office, piazza 24 Maggio 21, Cormons; t. 0481630371.

104

POINTS OF INTEREST

Tasting the fine Collio wine. *The place we recommend most is the public wine house of Cormons, piazza 24 Maggio 21, t. 0481630371: wine tasting and sale, but especially promotion of the culture of wine. At Cormons, you can also pay homage to Bacchus at the Wine Producers' Cooperative, via Vino della Pace 31, t. 048160579, the Paolo Caccese farming concern, at Paradis 6, t. 0481 61062, and the Castello di Spessa farming concern, via Spessa 1, t. 0481639914.*

After leaving the provincial road and the complex of the Formentini castle (hotel and golf club), ride (the first 2 km downhill) along the varied and scenic route that follows the Collio from east to west.

At this stage of the itinerary, you can stop at interesting wine producers' cooperatives and buy wine if you want. Now move on, passing by the towns of Uclanzi, Valerisce, Giasbana and Zegla. Just before Plessiva, with its wonderful nature park and false acacia and chestnut woods, turn left to Cormons on the S.S. 409 main road that crosses the Preval, a valley shaped by reclamation interventions which, in the past decades, have

ABOVE, the Wine Museum at San Floriano del Collio.
PAGE OPPOSITE, the Trussio castle.

strongly modified the territory through deforestation and the introduction of roads and canals.

At Cormons, near the army barracks, ride on your left towards the hamlets of Capriva del Friuli, Mossa and Pubrida, along a route with no altitude variations. At this stage, continue your ride towards **Gorizia**, entering the town center.

ALTERNATIVE

By train: the bicycle itinerary can be shortened by stopping at Cormons, without covering the last 13 km and catching the train to Gorizia.

A visit to the town that offered Giacomo Casanova "all the fun he could desire" is a must.

Also stop and take a relaxing seat in a downtown café and catch the sounds of people chatting in the Gorizia, Slovene and Friuli lingoes.

Emilia-Romagna

The Romagna hinterland   70 Km
From Riccione to the Marecchia Valley

This itinerary starts from the coast and stretches over the hills wedged between the sea and Mount Titano.

You start from **Riccione**, reaching the main road at San Lorenzo (a built-up area near the local sports center situated aside the old via Emilia main road). Ride along via San Lorenzo up to the crossroads with via Piemonte, 50 m after a small bridge over the Marano torrent. Now turn left in via Piemonte, which brushes the Rimini airport, flanking part of the disused military munitions depot. Turn right, then left to follow via Pontano. After crossing the overbridge on the A14 freeway, pass the crossroads with the S.P. 31 provincial road (Rimini-Coriano), then continue towards San Salvatore.

At the crossroads with the S.P. 41 provincial road (Rimini-Montescudo), turn right up to Gaiofana. Shortly after, turn left in via Santa Maria in Cerreto and pass the small cemetery. Keep right, riding for 1.5 km, and at the next crossroads, turn left and im-

---

Technical info

Route

70 Km: Riccione - San Salvatore - Gaiofana - San Martino in Venti - Sant'Ermete - San Martino dei Mulini - Santarcangelo di Romagna - Verucchio bridge - Verucchio - San Patrignano - Ospedaletto - San Salvatore - Riccione.

Difficulty

Rolling terrain, easy for trained legs, rather tough for cyclists with bad staying power.

Cycling period

All year round.

Bicycle + Train

Riccione, Rimini and Santarcangelo are situated along the Ancona-Bologna railroad line. The less trained cyclists can catch the train and reach Santarcangelo (from Riccione), then continue along the aforementioned itinerary towards Verucchio, Ospedaletto and Riccione.

Map

Atlante stradale d'Italia, Central volume, 1:200,000, TCI.

Technical assistance

• Cicli Migani, via Adriatica 145, Riccione; t. 0541602305.
• Mattoni M., via Marecchiese 359, Sant'Ermete; t. 0541750293.

Tourist information

• Riccione Bike Hotels (special service for cycle tourists), via Dante 128, Riccione; t. 0541642004. www.riccionebikehotels.it
• APT Riccione, piazzale Ceccarini 11, Riccione; t. 0541693302.
• IAT Rimini, piazzale Fellini 3, Rimini; t. 054156902. www.riminiturismo.it

POINTS OF INTEREST

An alternate plan for the less trained cyclists could be to tackle the easy route of the Marecchia Valley linking Rimini to the Verucchio bridge, riding along the banks (the left bank, then the right) of the river on a 35 km route for MTB.

mediately after right, passing the crossroads with the Rimini-San Marino expressway towards Santarcangelo di Romagna. After 1 km, you ride an uphill stretch up to the crossroads with the S.P. 49 provincial road. The road now crosses countryside, passing near an ENEL power station. After a right turn, the road takes a steep climb for 800 m up to the crossroads with the S.P. 69 provincial road near the popular Squadrani restaurant. After the crossroads, the road starts descending towards Sant'Ermete. Cross the S.S. 258 Rimini-Arezzo main road and

continue your ride towards Santarcangelo (S.P. 49) crossing the bridge over the river Marecchia.

Now proceed up to the Verucchio bridge over the S.P. 40 provincial road. Exiting the town, you can ride along a cycle lane on your right for a few kilometers. After crossing the River Parecchia, keep right and continue crossing the S.S. 258 (Rimini-Arezzo) main road and riding along the S.P. 15 bis provincial road up to Verucchio (2.5 km). Cross the square and continue cycling towards San Marino on the S.P. 32 provincial road. After covering 2 km, keep left heading towards Rimini via Santa Cristina, on the S.P. 69 provincial road. Now get ready for the descent and the rugged ascents known as Coste di Sgregna, up to the Squadrani restaurant, where you go back on the S.P. 49 provincial road to Ospedaletto. After a 1 km steep descent, 1 km of appar-

ently flat ground and 1 km uphill, turn left, and after 200 m, right towards Dogana. Cross the Ausa torrent, then the S.S. 72 main road to get back to Cerasolo (1 km). At the crossroads, turn left on the S.P. 49 provincial road. The road now descends, skirting the seat of the San Patrignano Community until you reach Ospedaletto, where you take the S.P. 41 provincial road to Rimini up to the San Salvatore crossroads. To return to **Riccione**, follow the same road backwards.

ABOVE, Verucchio.
In the background, San Marino.

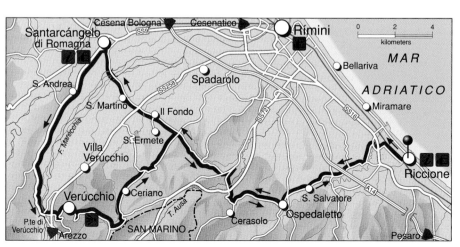

Ferrara 12 Km
The city of bicycles

POINTS OF INTEREST

Itinerando, via Voltapaletto 33, t. 0532202003, offers bicycle rental service, baby seats, trailers for children and guided theme visits. This is an ideal reference point for all cycle tourists in search of information and guides.

Urban trip at the heart of Ferrara, city of arts and history, just a stone's throw away from the Po, indissolubly tied to the culture of wheels and pedals, where cyclists are the masters of the roads.

From the **Centro Storico parking lot**, exit the town from porta Paola (forthcoming seat of the Bicycle Museum). Take on your left via Baluardi for 1.4 km, up to a widening, then turn right towards the bridge over the Po di Volano leading to the church and the cloister of San Giorgio, Ferrara's place of origin. Now turn back, crossing the bridge again and continuing for 350 m on viale Alfonso d'Este, up to the crossroads with via XX Settembre that you take on your left. In rapid sequence on your left, admire the

house of Biagio Rossetti (100 m), which hosts the Museum of Architecture, and Palazzo Costabili, seat of the National Museum of Archaeology (300 m). After covering via XX Settembre for 700 m, turn right in via Porta San Pietro, which enters via Carlo Mayr, then continue riding on your left. After reaching piazza Verdi (parking lot), turn right, then immediately left, passing near Palazzo Paradiso (Ariosto Municipal Library) and entering the characteristic via Volte, up to the crossroads in via San Romano,

the commercial hub of the old town.

At this point, turn right towards piazza Trento e Trieste and stop in the presence of the Cathedral. Keep left, reaching the town council and the square right in front of the Duomo façade. After going back towards the

Technical info

Route
12 Km: the itinerary firstly crosses the medieval side, then the Renaissance section of the city, following the walls for a good stretch.

Difficulty
None. Check the course on the map first, in order to orient yourself easily in the city environment.

Cycling period
All year round.

Bicycle + Train
Various interregional trains link Ferrara to Bologna, Venice, Florence, Rome and Trieste.

Roadmap
Luca Scardino, *Guida Turistica per Ferrara* - 8 itineraries to

discover the city; Liberty House; t. 0532764226.

Bicycle rental
At the Centro Storico parking lot, t. 0532765123, where you can purchase the Bicicard, which entitles you to bicycle rental, free entrance to town museums and 15% discount in many hotels and restaurants. Bicycle rental also at the railroad station.

Tourist information
• IAT, Castello Estense, Ferrara;
t. 0532209370.
www.comune.fe.it
• Amici della Bicicletta, via Muzzina 11, Ferrara;
t. 0532765770.

Cathedral, turn left, skirting the Este castle and emerging in corso Giovecca-viale Cavour, the axis that divides the two medieval and Renaissance sides of the town. After leaving the castle behind, ride along corso Ercole I d'Este (former Strada degli Angeli), the monumental axis of the "addizione erculea" (Duke Ercole's city extension) designed at the end of the XV century by Biagio Rossetti. Ride up to the unmistakable façade of the Palazzo dei Diamanti (National Picture Gallery, Municipal Gallery of Modern Art), next to the Risorgimento and the Resistance Museum. Opposite the ashlarwork of the Diamanti, you find Palazzo Turchi di Bagno (Geopalaeontological Museum and Arboretum), while past the Corso Rossetti-Corso Porta Mare axis, you see Palazzo Prosperi Sacrati with its beautiful portal. At the traffic lights, turn right, fol-

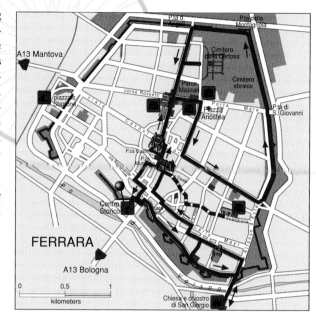

lowing corso Porta Mare and skirting on your right the Arboretum fence. Continue your trip until you reach piazza Ariostea, riding along it (via Palestro) up to the junction in corso della Giovecca, which you follow right to the end (1.1 km), up to the XVIII century arch known as

"Prospettiva". At this point, get off your bike and climb the flight of steps that leads (on your left) to the embankment of the walls, the green belt of the city. Follow the walls for approximately 3 km up to porta degli Angeli, then turn left in corso Ercole I d'Este, passing near the Carthusian monastery with the Church of San Cristoforo. Continue cycling on the main axis up to the castle, at the Cathedral square, then turn right towards via Cortevecchia, then left towards via del Turco, crossing via Volte and the axis of via Ripagrande.

Now turn left and return near Porta Paola and the **Centro Storico parking lot**.

LEFT, the Este castle.
PAGE OPPOSITE, stop near the walls towards porta degli Angeli.

The Po delta 1   8 Km
The Ostellato Valleys

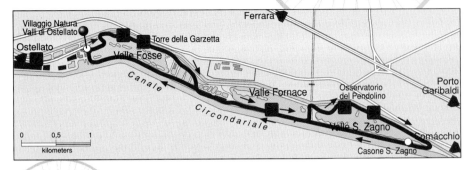

In the province of Ferrara, the "anse vallive" of Ostellato, the Mezzano and the Comacchio Valleys represent, in a different and suggestive way, the fascinating heritage of the historical Po delta: freshwater marshland, flat reclaimed expanses, swamps and saline valleys, landscapes bordering water and land.
A remarkable itinerary that develops inside this water world, precisely in the Ostellato Valleys, offering the opportunity to live an extraordinary environmental experience, especially as far as birdwatching is concerned, with many species populating the areas in different seasons.

You start your trip from inside the **Ostellato Valleys Villaggio Natura**, from the board with the map of the valleys, past the bicycle depot. The path on your left winds across hummocks and cane fields, with stretches on wooden footpaths, up to the first observation hut, built

on an islet facing the Fosse Valley. Continue your ride on a bridge on your left, reaching the northern side of the valley, just under the embankment of the navigable canal. Now turn right, riding along the wide ridge between the canal and the

POINTS OF INTEREST

Near Comacchio, the sta-zione Foce, a former surveillance house, hosts a Documentation Centre on the Comacchio Valleys. This is the starting point of your boat trip to the Museum of the Comacchio Valleys, an open-air museum route, whose stages are the valley country houses, original buildings once inhabited by the valley people during the eel fishing seasons. The visit gives you an exact idea of how the "lavorieri" (barrages) work, and of the life and hard work of the valley people in the fishing valleys.

valleys and reaching the other observations huts, such as the Garzetta tower, still facing the Fosse Valley. Where this ends, the cattle track turns right, cutting at the back of the heronry (observation posts) and emerging on the embankment of the district canal, which bounds the Ostellato Valleys on the south. After taking the dirt road towards your left, pass the fallow deer fence, reaching the southern side of the Fornace Valley, which you must completely cover, up to the strip of land cut by a canal separating it from the San Zagno Valley. On your left, after reaching again the embankment of the navigable canal that straddles this secondary canal (the waters flow at different heights), you can spot the brick building of the San Zagno draining pump (1925). Now ride down onto the opposite embankment

PAGE OPPOSITE, small wooden bridge along the nature route.

of the secondary canal and take, on your left, the Pendolino route, a tree-lined ridge that separates the San Zagno Valley from a smaller pond. In just a few minutes' time, you reach the Pendolino Observatory, the best observation spot in the valleys, from where you can watch the herons and cormorants standing on hummocks, while in fall and spring, mallards come to gather in great flocks. Following the path that runs again between the embankment of the navigable canal and the valleys, circumnavigate the San Zagno Valley, brushing the Cormorant Observatory and the San Zagno country house (former surveillance station), at the point where you return on the embankment of the district canal, following the whole stretch and getting back to the **Villaggio Natura**.

Technical info

Route

8 Km: Ostellato Valleys Villaggio Natura - Fosse Valley - Garzetta tower - Fornace Valley - San Zagno draining pump - Casone San Zagno. You can reach the starting point by taking the Ferrara-Porto Garibaldi expressway, Ostellato exit, which joins up with the A13 Bologna-Padua freeway at Ferrara Sud.

Difficulty

None, the route is entirely flat and runs along excellent dirt roads, cart roads and short stretches of beaten track, for a total of roughly 8 km. Any bike will do.

Cycling period

All year round, preferably in spring and fall, for both the climate and the observation of migratory birds.

Map

Lidi e Valli di Comacchio, scale 1:50,000, Belletti Editore.

Technical assistance

• Nordi Giuseppe, via Muratori 2, Comacchio; t. 0533311529.
• Ravasini Marino, via XX Settembre 59, Ostellato; t. 0533680127.

Bicycle rental

Villaggio Natura Valli di Ostellato, via Argine Mezzano 1, Ostellato; t. 0533680376, 0533680757.

Tourist information

• Tourist Information Office, piazzetta Folegatti 28, Comacchio; t. 0533310161.
• Assessorato al Turismo - Comune di Comacchio; freephone number 80015698.
• Consorzio del Parco Regionale del Delta del Po, via Cavour 11, Comacchio; t. 0533314003. www.parks.it/parco.delta.po.er

The Po delta 2   31 Km
Bosco Mesola and Po di Goro

Ride in the water labyrinths of the delta, in the area stretching between the Po di Volano and the Po di Goro. Your tour starts near the splendid hunting residence built in 1580 by Alfonso II d'Este. You then cross the Giardino del delta, an arboretum where the delta flora grows, the Boscone della Mesola, the last original plain wood.

You start from the **Mesola** castle, heading towards the embankment. Take the road on your left, riding towards the Carabinieri station, along a straight path that passes by the Canal Bianco. After crossing the bridge, turn right

Technical info

Route

31 Km: Mesola - Bosco Mesola - Gigliola – Boscone della Mesola - Po di Goro - Abate tower - Santa Giustina - Mesola (of which 4 km on dirt track). You can reach the starting point either from the south or from the north, by taking the S.S. 309 Romea main road. From Milan, take the A4 freeway up to Padua and then at Chioggia on the S.S. 516 main road. From Bologna, take the A13 freeway up to Ferrara Sud and then the expressway to Comacchio.

Difficulty

An ideal itinerary for everyone, completely flat.

Cycling period

Spring and fall ideal, also in winter too, when sunshine alternates with fog

Map

• *Il Delta del Po*, 1:50,000,

Belletti Gualtiero Editore (C.P. 46, Misano Adriatico).
• *Delta del Po*, 1:65,000, Litografia Artistica Cartografica di Firenze.

Technical assistance

• Granini, Mesola; t. 0533794719.
• Barboni Nello, via Nuova Corriera 15, Bosco Mesola; t. 0533794196.

Bicycle rental

Fattorie del Delta, piazza Santo Spirito 3, Mesola; t. 0533993176, 3394380724.

Tourist information

• Consorzio del Parco Regionale del delta del Po, via Cavour 11, Comacchio; t. 0533314003.
www.parks.it/parco.delta.po.er
• IAT, Castello Estense, piazza Umberto I, Mesola; seasonal, t. 0533993483.

in via Canal Bianco, a cycle lane that flanks the canal up to the next bridge where you turn left.

Now go straight ahead across the built-up area, following the road signs pointing to the Romea main road, which you reach after just over 1 km, and ride towards Ravenna. After approximately 1 km, turn left, leaving the S.S. 309 main road and taking the road that leads to the town of Bosco Mesola, after which you reach, at Gigliola, the crossroads for Volano. Turn left for the Boscone della Mesola. Just before entering the Boscone (wood), you meet the "Il Giardino del delta" arboretum. After a visit to the Boscone, ride northwards until you cross the road to Goro that reaches the embankment of the Po di Goro opposite the Rossi island. After approximately 2 km, as the road narrows, get on the embankment towards your left and take via Pescarina, which flanks the Canal Bianco and leads to the sewer of the Abate tower. From this point, after crossing the Canal Bianco again, you reach Santa Giustina and turn right, and after 200 m, left in via Gelosia, which takes you back on the embankment of the Po di Goro passing a bar. Ride along the embankment up the river until you reach **Mesola** along the unleveled cycle lane.

The stretch that follows the embankment is the final part of the cycle lane that winds along the right side of the Po, crossing for 125 km the whole province of Ferrara, from Rocchetta della Stellata to the mouth of the Po di Goro. This long cycle lane is part of the Eurovelo 8 route that crosses Europe from Cadiz to Athens (www.eurovelo.org).

POINTS OF INTEREST

The Center for Environmental Education *of Mesola, Este castle, t. 0533993644. The* Giardino del delta, *an arboretum on via Gigliola near the Boscone della Mesola t. 0533794918, 0533 996940. The* Boscone della Mesola, *via Gigliola, Bosco della Mesola, t. 0533794285.*

BELOW, Abate tower.
PAGE OPPOSITE, fishermen's boats in the Po di Goro.

From Forlì to Cesena   49 Km
Rolling Romagna

A pleasant itinerary on by-roads that gently follow the rolling profiles of the Romagna countryside, on a day to be slowly lived, exercising your body and freeing your mind.

You start the trip on the cycle lane that follows viale della Libertà near the **Forlì** railroad station; after getting to piazza della Vittoria, follow the road signs pointing to Predappio. Once you reach the Rivaldino fortress, take the cycle lane on viale dell'Appennino exiting Forlì. Your ride continues on the S.S. 9 ter del Rabbi main road up to Grisignano, where you turn left on the S.P. 125 provincial road, following the road signs indicating the Caminate fortress. The road now starts to climb and reaches the ridge between the Rabbi and Para rivers and continues in fits and starts, switching from tough spurts to long stretches on apparently flat ground.

Technical info

Route
49 Km: Forlì - Grisignano – Caminate fortress - Santa Maria di Fiordinano - San Domenico - Fratta Terme - Polenta – Mount Feriti - San Vittore - San Carlo - Cesena. On quiet by-roads. You can easily reach Forlì by taking the A14 freeway or by train: the railroad station is situated along the Bologna-Ancona line.

Difficulty
This is a choppy route, although with no big difficulty. There are two tough climbs: the first located at km 6 (Grisignano) with about 7% gradients, peaking at 10%; the second at km 24 (Fratta) with about 7% gradients, peaking in the

first stretch at 14%, certainly the most challenging part of the itinerary. The overall rise is approximately 700 m. You must have a bicycle equipped with uphill gears, and if you're not trained enough, tons of serenity when facing the toughest sections, which are providentially short and isolated.

Cycling period
All year round. During the winter period or after showers, you should ride with great care on the downhill stretches.

Bicycle + Train
You return to the starting point by train. The Cesena-Forlì line is short (10-15 minutes), direct and served by various regional and interregional trains, used also for transport bicycles.

Map
Atlante stradale d'Italia, Northern volume, 1:200,000, TCI.

Technical assistance
• Veloshop,
viale dell'Appennino 13, Forlì;
t. 054331495.
• Ciclomania,
via Roma 91, Meldola;
t. 0543490441.
• L'albero delle ruote,
via Pitagora 15, Cesena.

Tourist information
• Informazioni e Accoglienza Turistica,
corso della Repubblica 23, Forlì t. 0543712435.
www.delfo.forli-cesena.it/prov/
• Tourist Office,
c/o Town Council,
piazza del Popolo 1, Cesena;
t. 0547356327.

After passing by the Osteria delle Martinelle, you'll spot the Caminate fortress, but before reaching it, you have to ride on a short uphill stretch. Once you skirt the fortress park, go left towards Meldola on the S.P. 126 provincial road. After quickly getting to the Caminate inn, leave the main road and take the Sentiero degli Alpini by-road towards the Poggio firm (Church of Santa Maria di Fiordinano). Stop here and cross the hill, turning left towards Monteguzzo and reaching Meldola after a downhill stretch.

From Meldola, follow the S.P. 99 provincial road up to Fratta Terme, and continue following the road signs to Polenta, on the S.P. 83 provincial road and the second uphill stretch of the day. The first section is quite tough, while the second gets easier, offering a magnificent view on Bertinoro; the last part has still a challenging stretch in store near the Church of Polenta (fountain); after riding along a cypress-lined avenue, get ready for the nice downhill stretch. 800 m after Polenta, turn right on the S.P. 116 provincial road towards San Mamante. After a few up and downs comes the real downhill part, going down into the Savio Valley and losing altitude until you reach San Vittore.

At the roundabout sign, don't follow the road signs for Cesena, but turn right towards Rome (!), riding up to the town of San Carlo. At this stage, opposite the church, turn right and enter via Castiglione, passing under the expressway and the River Savio, then following the right side along via Roversano. You can easily reach the town center of **Cesena** passing near the Savio Nature Park.

ABOVE, the Malatesta fortress of Cesena. PAGE OPPOSITE, the XVI century fountain of Cesena.

POINTS OF INTEREST

The Romanesque Church of **San Donato** *at* **Polenta** *is a poetic corner of Romagna which gave the inspiration to Giosuè Carducci to compose his ode. Tradition has it that Dante, on his way back from Ravenna, was offered hospitality here by the Da Polenta family. Visit the church, with its majestic columns, all built with different plinths, supporting the refined capitals, the crypt and the vague, dim light penetrating through the narrow windows.*

[map showing: Bologna, A14, Forlì, Forlimpópoli, SS71, Grisignano, SS9, Ris. Nat. Bosco di Scardavilla, Fratta Terme, Bertinoro, Cesena, Rimini, Méldola, Rocca d. Caminate, Polenta, S. Vittore, S. Maria di Fiordinano, Chiesa d. Angeli Custodi, M. Granello ▲ 227, S. Carlo, Perugia, kilometers 0 2,5 5]

The Punte Alberete Oasis   11 Km
Immersed in nature near Ravenna

Here's a great chance for all those peace-loving cyclists to ride, surrounded in the most peaceful of peaces, across a flat and tempting part of Romagna, just 10 km away from the Byzantine Capital of Mosaic overlooking the Adriatic.

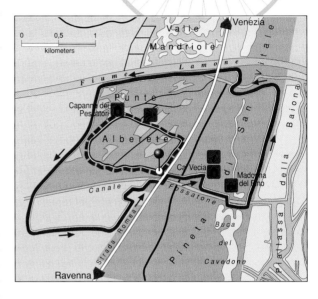

From the opposite side of the Fossatone di **Punte Alberete** parking lot, starts the northern part of the San Vitale pinewood. Cross strada Romea and enter the pinewood on a wide and beaten forest track. You reach Ca' Vecia, one of the period's oldest "case delle aie" where the pinewood was once used for the production of pine nuts (today it's an information center and the pinewood rangers' quarters). Now take

the track on your right leading southwards until you reach the Fossatone Canal. Ride along the left side of the canal up to the Madonna del

Pino, a small and suggestive chapel where some couples from Ravenna still wed.

Shortly after, pass the Fossatone on a small narrow wooden bridge and approach the Buca del Cavedone, a marshy area at the heart of the pinewood, where you can stop and watch lots of dwarf herons perched on the pine trees that flank the eastern side. Continue your ride eastwards until you reach a vast and flat valley, the Piallassa Baiona. Rising from the valley, like a stalk of a poisonous mushroom, looking southeastwards, the chimney of the Ravenna chemistry complex, built after the war where a wonderful pinewood once used to stand.

Technical info

Route

11 Km: Punte Alberete, Fossatone parking lot - Ca' Vecia - Madonna del Pino – bridge over the Fossatone – River Lamone - Punte Alberete pinewood - Punte del Fossatone - Serraglio dei Cavalli – Fossatone parking lot. Mixed route and quiet roads.

Difficulty

Very easy and safe itinerary. Ideal for families with children along.

Cycling period

All year round. Spring is a beautiful period

with nature in full bloom.

Map

Punte Alberete e Pineta di San Vitale, tourist map: available at tourist offices and at the Park's Information Center.

Technical assistance

• Galassi, via Pallavicini 20, Ravenna; t. 054432415.

• L'Albero delle Ruote, via Achille Grandi 88, Ravenna; t. 0544451588.

Bicycle rental

• San Vitale Cooperative, piazza Farini (at the railroad station),

Ravenna; t. 054437031.

• Bicycle rental, viale Italia 118, Marina Romea; t. 0544446562.

Tourist information

• IAT Ravenna, via Salara 8/12, Ravenna; t. 054435404.

• Centro Informazioni e Visita Ca' Vecchia, S.S. 309 Romea - via del Fossatone, Pineta San Vitale; t. 0544446866. www.parks.it/parco.delta.po.er/

• Amici della Bici, c/o Navacchia, via Sacile 3, Ravenna; t. 0544270260.

POINTS OF INTEREST

Birdwatching and walks in the Punte Alberete pinewood. Along the track that flanks the right side of the Fossatone Canal, you reach the wonderful "foresta allagata" with its elms and poplars and numerous lakelets populated by various species of animals.

Head towards the fishermen's hut, a place with delicate spring flowerings, to reach the observation hut near Chiari Sciafela, where you can admire white, purple and grey herons, dwarf herons, black-crowned night herons, crested herons and kingfishers.

PAGE OPPOSITE, birdwatching in the Punte Alberete Oasis.

After reaching Baiona, turn left and cross the Fossatone again. Now ride along the whole stretch of the Baiona embankment, along the so-called "Chiaro del Comune", where you can easily spot avocets, stilt-birds and spoonbills. At the end of the Chiaro, the path turns towards the heartland and takes you back to strada Romea near the bridge over the River Lamone (after which you can reach the observation tower on the Canna Valley). After crossing the Romea, enter the area of Punte Alberete, taking the gravel road that runs along the embankment of the River Lamone, the northern border of the Oasis. After about 1 km, you'll be able to spot, on your right, the dance of dwarf herons, black-

crowned night herons and cormorants: this is the place of the famous "garzaia delle Punte", which you can easily observe through binoculars from the embankment of the river. Now move on, up to the "partitore" (north-western border of the Oasis), where you turn southwards riding along the eastern border of the Punte up to Fossatone.

At this stage, leave the "foresta allagata" behind and enter an area that is currently undergoing renaturalization, along a country path up to the carriageable road called "Serraglio dei Cavalli" that emerges on the Romea. Continue along a stretch of main road northwards, then get back to the Fossatone di **Punte Alberete** parking lot, closing the circle and your tour.

Bologna and the Reno   35 Km
Riding along the Ciclovia della Seta

Nice ride at the gates of the city on roads and tracks following the Reno Canal.

From the Bologna town center (**piazza Maggiore**), ride along via Ugo Bassi (the entire route, up to and past the Palazzo de' Rossi, is marked by road signs indicating the Ciclovia della Seta).

By taking the cycle lane of via del Pratello, you reach viale Vicini, where, crossing via Sabotino, the cycle lane n.1 of Bologna to Casalecchio starts. Follow the signs and move along the Reno Canal. After reaching via della Barca, cross it and pass under an overbridge getting to via Canonica, situated in the territory of Casalecchio di Reno. Turn left, following the road signs pointing to via Corsica, then after about 100 m, to vialetto Baldo Sauro, and finally to vialetto Martinez Collado. On your right, you'll clearly see the canal bounded by the wall of Casa del Ghiaccio.

At the end of the Vialetto (6 km from the starting point), cross via Porrettana. Ride up via Panoramica and enter the Chiusa park, cycling down on the dirt road and approaching the monumental construction from where the Reno Canal starts.

Now skirt a meadow, and after 400 m, pass near a small fenced chapel. Follow the road signs on the fitness route, and after passing a house (number 32, with the

POINTS OF INTEREST

The famous **Casa del Ghiaccio,** *which has controlled the course of the waters flowing towards Bologna for over seven centuries, to prevent damage to the mills that draw their main energy from the canal.*

The medieval **Casalecchio lock,** *inside the homonymous park.*

Technical info

Route

35 Km: Bologna - Casalecchio di Reno - Chiusa park - Palazzo de' Rossi - Vizzano bridge - Vizzano park (fountain) - Rio Conco park – Roman aqueduct - Chiusa park - Bologna. 17 km asphalt, 18 km dirt road, the stretch from Bologna to Palazzo de' Rossi is part of the Ciclovia della Seta (from Venice to Leghorn by bike along paths and by-roads), a route full of road signs.

Difficulty

Easy route, with no particular difficulties in store.

Cycling period

All year round, except after heavy showers.

Map

Casalecchio di Reno, IGM 1:50,000.

Road map

• *Bologna visitata in bicicletta*, edited by Monte Sole Bike Group - 1999
• *La CicloVia della Seta*, Pendragon Editore - 2002.

Technical assistance

Due Ruote, via S. Stefano, 14/D Bologna; t. 051233337. www.dueruotebologna.it

Tourist information

• Ufficio Informazioni e Accoglienza Turistica, piazza Maggiore 6, Bologna, t. 051246541. www.comune.bologna.it
• Province of Bologna Tourism Department; t. 051218751. www.provincia.bologna.it
• Monte Sole Bike Group, piazza Allende 8, Ozzano Emilia; t. 051797103. www.montesolebikegroup.it

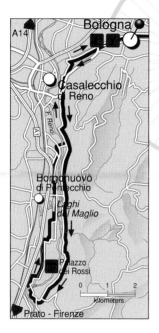

word "Cantelli" carved on a post), turn right again. The track now drops, heading straight to the blue cycle path on your right towards the south. Cross the river (8.1 km from the starting point), getting back on the very wide asphalt road (private) for a few kilometers. After 10.2 km, you reach the Maglio lakelets and continue on the cycle lane that runs parallel to the asphalt road. At 11.8 km, the track makes a wide right turn, then left, passing next to the entrance of the Sapaba and the Ciba (km 12.3). At the end of the cycle lane, follow on your right an asphalt road, and immediately after the parking lot of the chemical complex, turn left before the overbridge on the A1, reaching the complex of the Palazzo de' Rossi. Leave the village through the southern gates, climbing up between the castle and the church, then riding on your left for via Vizzano. Just a short stretch ahead, cross the River Reno on the suspended bridge, then continue towards via Vizzano up to the crossroads with via Ancognano. Now turn and head for via Ancognano towards the hill, then turn left northwards. Shortly after, the asphalt stretch ends, and the trip continues on a gravel path for via Rio Conco (leaving via Ancognano that climbs to your right). The road, initially flat, drops suddenly on cobbles and stones until reaching the level of the Reno. Continue your ride northwards on a gravel path, and after a left turn, you reach a glade. Go straight ahead on a road that gets increasingly narrow, until you reach the CAI path n° 112, where you start (21.4 km) slaloming (over 4 km) in the wood and, for some stretches, on the right side of the Reno. Ignore the paths starting on your right and reach (25.4 km) the blue cycle path you have already crossed. Enter the fitness route again and reach the Casalecchio lock and the way out of the park. Riding along via Panoramica, cross the Porrettana entering the cycle lane n°1 for Bologna, up to the boulevards of the Ring Road, then **piazza Maggiore**.

RIGHT, Bologna, piazza Maggiore, Nettuno fountain.

The seven hills of Bologna 52 Km
Amid ravines, vineyards and castles

This itinerary develops along the curves of a harmonic and highly interesting landscape: history, nature and local production enthrall cycle tourists, for a weekend of cycling and hearty eating.

You start your tour from **Monteveglio**, exactly from the San Teodoro Park Center. Ride down towards the town following via Abbazia, at the end of which you turn right in piazza della Libertà.

At the traffic lights, turn left, taking via Ponti, and after crossing the bridge over the River Samoggia, go right on the S.P. 76 provincial road following the torrent up to Stiore. At the end of the town, at the crossroads, go right and continue on the S.P. 76 provincial road along orchards and vineyards.

At the next crossroads between the 75 and 76 provincial roads, go left towards Montemaggiore, following

the S.P. 75 provincial road and then continuing the ride uphill, until you reach the town (to avoid the uphill stretch, you can go straight ahead towards Fagnano), and then ride down to Loghetto, where you turn right following the Landa brook. The road now starts again on an uphill stretch towards Monte San Pietro, reaching the summit side of the ridge following via Castello. Ride down among poplars, oak trees and majestic elms. After a short ascent, the road drops towards Ca' Silvestri and the bottom of the valley, where you continue on your left on via Sant'Andrea, passing near the Samoggia at the Jacone mill, and the hamlet of Stella. Now ride along the Samoggia, and shortly after Isola,

Technical info

Route

52 Km: Monteveglio - Montemaggiore - Monte San Pietro - Isola - Mongiorgio - Badia - Gavignano - Savigno - Tiola - Serravalle Castle - Monteveglio. On asphalt roads.

Difficulty

The route has a series of up and downhill stretches. There are seven climbs, never very long, but some are challenging. Two (Montemaggiore and Monte San Pietro) can be avoided by taking the Fagnano alternative. The outing is very pleasant if you are in good physical shape.

Cycling period

All year round; in the winter period, preferably on sunny days.

Map

Atlante stradale d'Italia, Northern volume, 1:200,000, TCI.

Technical assistance

Casarini, viale Costituzione 4, Monteveglio;
t. 0516707987.

Tourist information

• Parco Regionale dell'Abbazia di Monteveglio,
via Abbazia 28, Monteveglio;
t. 0516701044.
www.regione.emilia-romagna.it/parchi/abbazia/www.parks.it/parco.abbazia.monteveglio/

• Comunità Montana Valle del Samoggia,
Tourist Information Office
Information only by mail and phone;
t. 0516710411.
zona9@iperbole.bo.it

• Monte Sole Bike Group,
piazza Allende 8,
Ozzano Emilia;
t. 051797103.
www.montesolebikegroup.it

POINTS OF INTEREST

A trip on the **Strada dei Vini e dei Sapori, Città, Castelli e Ciliegi,** *an itinerary promoted by the Emilia-Romagna Region, which allows you to reach the local wine production areas. The TCI members have a 10% discount for guided visits. The Bologna hills produce three red DOC and thirteen white wines, including the fine Pignoletto.*

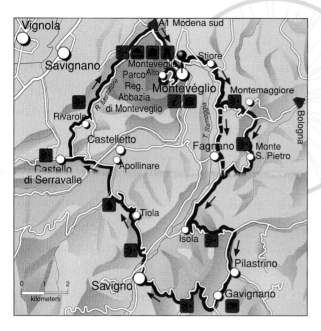

where you take, on your left, via Castello. At the crossroads, stop and admire the Church of Sant'Apollinare. Once you're back on the provincial road, go straight to Mercatello, where you start the ascent with hairpin bends that leads to the Serravalle castle. Now go back on the provincial road for approximately 500 m, then turn left (pay due attention to the dangerous bend) on via San Michele.

Following the ridge, you reach the Rivarolo Vecchio farms and then ride down to the bottom of the valley of the Marzatore, following the homonymous street, then turning left. Now ride on a gentle downhill stretch, skirting the Regional Park of the Monteveglio Abbey, reaching the S.P. 28 provincial road, where you turn right to **Monteveglio**. At the traffic lights, turn right and enter via Abbazia, riding up to the village.

continue on an uphill stretch to Mongiorgio, riding down towards the Badia, where you take, on your right, the S.P. 26 provincial road (via Lavino). The provincial road runs at the bottom of the valley up to the bridge over the Lavino at Pilastrino, where you turn right for Gavignano. The road follows the uphill climb immersed in chestnut trees, up to the ridge that heralds Merlano. At the end of the road, ride down along via Merlano (passage for Casa Maselli) to Savigno, where you reach the old town center.

Continue your ride taking, on your right, the S.P. 27 provincial road (via della Libertà) that passes the Samoggia and flanks it. Shortly after, turn left and enter via Tiola, taking the steep uphill stretch, then riding on rolling terrain up to Tiola. At the crossroads, go straight ahead on a downhill stretch, until you turn right on the S.P. 70 provincial road of Serravalle, continuing up to Castelletto di Serravalle,

RIGHT, Monteveglio, the abbey.

Bassa Reggiana
From Reggio Emilia to Brescello

74 Km

A fascinating ride across the linear landscape of the Bassa Reggiana, amid poplar woods, fortresses and palaces, where the history of the Gonzaga entwines with the stories of Peppone and Don Camillo and the life of the painter Ligabue.

You start from **Reggio Emilia**, riding through the unavoidable traffic of the internal ring road, before taking via Fogliani on your right. The road now enters via Cisalpina on your left and continues for about 2.5 km up to a crossroads with traffic lights, where you turn right heading towards the built-up area of Sesso. An underpass with cycle lane heralds a crossroads (4 km), where you continue on your left towards Cavazzoli and Roncocesi. After reaching Cadelbosco di Sopra (12 km), to avoid the busy S.S. 63 main road, take via Prampolini up to the crossroads with the main road at Zurco. Now turn left and ride for a short stretch (watch out for traffic) up to the detour on the right to Bagnolo. At the next crossroads, turn left again and go straight ahead through the countryside dotted by small hamlets such as Villa Seta. After passing a wide irrigation canal, cycle up to the small station of San Bernardino (avoid taking via Levata), then take a short dirt road of 1.3 km. After crossing the main road axis, enter the Agricola Riviera farm holidays, a typical example of the great landed estates of the past.

The reclamation of wet areas and lakes for fishing attracts a rich migratory birdlife coming from the nearby Novellara Valleys. These areas can be easily reached by taking

Technical info

Route
74 Km: Reggio Emilia - Cadelbosco di Sopra - Villa Seta - Novellara Valleys - Guastalla - Lido Po - Gualtieri - Brescello (including the detour to Novellara). On asphalt roads, except for a short stretch of 1.3 km.

Difficulty
None in particular, given the really smooth altitude. However, 74 km are not an easy job, so you should approach this itinerary with at least some training in your legs.

Cycling period
All year round, preferably in spring and the final part of summer.

Bicycle + Train
Reggio Emilia is situated on the Parma-Bologna railroad line. From Brescello, you get back by taking the train to Parma (just less than half an hour), where you change train and travel to Reggio Emilia (approximately 40 minutes).

Map
Reggio nell'Emilia Provincia, 1:100,000, Studio FMB Bologna.

Technical assistance
• New Cobianchi,
via Agnoletti 21, Reggio Emilia; t. 0522305671.
• GA-MA di Bonacini,
via Louis Pasteur 13/1, Reggio Emilia; t. 0522552105.
• Cicli Corradini,

via Emilia all'Angelo 33/a, Reggio Emilia; t. 0522382392.
• Manghi Claudio,
via Gramsci 25-27, Castelnovo di Sotto; t. 0522688593.

Tourist information
• Ufficio Informazioni e Accoglienza Turistica, piazza Prampolini 5/C, Reggio Emilia; t. 0522451152. www.municipio.re.it/turismo
• Pro Loco Brescello,
viale Soliani 2; t. 0522962158.
• Pro Loco Gualtieri,
piazza Bentivoglio; t. 0522828696.
• Tuttinbici, Casella Postale 1132, Reggio Emilia; t. 0522303247. www.tuttinbici.org

POINTS OF INTEREST

The museum, dedicated to the Naïf painter Antonio Ligabue *at Gualtieri, t. 0522 828696 and, next door, the Donazione Umberto Tirelli, boasting a good 50 works by artists such as de Chirico, Guttuso, Manzù and Mazzacurati.*
The Don Camillo and Peppone Museum *at Brescello, viale Soliani 2, t. 0522 962158 and 0522687526.*

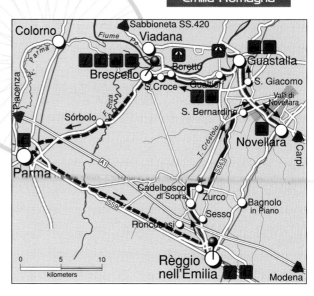

the provincial road and then the dirt road that enters the protected area and continues towards Novellara. Once you're back on the road, continue the ride up to the dusty via Spino Viazza until you reach Guastalla, crossing the hamlets of San Giacomo and Pieve. The lido Po, concealed by orderly rows of slim poplars, is the favorite spot for fishermen and people seeking peace and quiet.
After covering 3 km from the town center of Guastalla, you reach Gualtieri with its spectacular square that invites you to a stop. Now that you've freshened up, we suggest leaving the road of the embankment, choosing the lower route, which crosses Boretto and Santa Croce and reaches **Brescello** (12 km from Guastalla), where it would be worthwhile to stop and admire pi-azza Matteotti, the Church of Santa Maria and the interesting museum dedicated to Giovanni Guareschi, recognizable by the tank situated at its entrance. Now continue by train to Parma, then change train and get back to Reggio Emilia.

BELOW, view of the Novellara Valleys.

The Modena Apennine 27 Km
From Pievepelago to the Fiancata

Mountain atmosphere along this Apennine itinerary that winds across a highly suggestive environment, with extensive scenic views, unspoilt woods and mountain villages.

From the town center of **Pievepelago**, exit the town following via Roma, which then becomes the S.S. 12 Abetone main road. At the start of the ride, it would be wise for you to cycle at an agile pace, in order to get ready and set for the first sharp changes in gradient. After passing the watercourses of the Perticara brook and the Tagliole torrent, past the built-up area of Ponte Modino, the road climbs up towards Fiumalbo overlooking the Scoltenna Valley and Mount Cimone (2,165 m), the highest peak in the Northern Apennine.

POINTS OF INTEREST

*The village of **Fiumalbo**, which preserves the unscathed charm of a small mountain village, with its narrow, paved streets. A sight worth seeing in particular is the small XV century Chapel of San Rocco, decorated with a cycle of frescoes in 1535 by Saccaccino Saccacini da Carpi, an artist known for this single work.*

From Fiumalbo, with its typical sandstone roofs, continue your ride on the gentler uphill stretch, reaching the first houses of Dogana Nuova, founded as a mail and customs station of the Duchy of Modena. From this point, the more trained cyclists can have a stab at the climb up to

the Abetone (3 km and 340 m rise), while the itinerary proceeds towards the Fiancata, with a climb that requires tough muscles (3.2 km and 300 m rise).

From Dogana, follow the road signs pointing to Rotari. The road climbs up among houses and thick fir-woods and vast meadows. Ride straight ahead ignoring the detour on your left after approximately 1 km. The road now switchbacks up to the Fiancata of Mount Modino, offering a stunning view on the valley and on Mount Cimone. From the pass (1,362 m above sea level), ride down into the Tagliole Valley, where you enter the territory of the Frignano Park.

You quickly reach the ham-

BELOW, the Modena Apennine near Pievepelago.

Technical info

Route

27 Km: Pievepelago - Fiumalbo - Dogana Nuova - La Fiancata - Pian dei Remi - Le Tagliole - Pievepelago. On asphalt roads. You can reach Pievepelago by taking the S.S. 12 main road from Modena (80 km) and from the Tuscan side of the provinces of Florence and Pistoia. From the Upper Garfagnana, by taking the S.S. 324 "delle Radici" main road.

Difficulty

The itinerary is relatively short, with just a few uphill stretches that require muscles on your behalf. In any case, the altimetry includes only ascents and descents, so get ready to challenge them with at least a touch of practice.

Cycling period

From late spring to the beginning of fall.

Map

Alto Appennino Modenese, Map of the paths, 1:25,000, CAI Modena section.

Bicycle rental

Hotel Galassini, via Roma 95, Pievepelago; t. 053672354.

Tourist information

• Parco del Frignano, via Roma 84, Pievepelago; t. 053672134. www.parks.it/parco.frignano www.regione.emiliaromagna.it/ parchi/modenese/

• IAT Pro Loco, via Costa 25, Pievepelago; t. 053671304.

• Pro Loco, piazza Umberto I, Fiumalbo; t. 053673909 and 053673074.

---

lets of Rotari, Ronchi and Ca' di Gallo, where you can stop and admire a few interesting examples of rural buildings, and then continue downhill towards the bottom of the valley crossed by the Tagliole torrent. At this stage, the road climbs up again into the thick wood of Pian dei Remi (just over 1 km). After reaching the hamlet of La Fatalcina, keep left and ride towards Ca' Mordini. After about 700 m, turn left again and reach shortly after the oldest witch elm (*Ulmus glabra*) in Italy: about 450 years old, it is 30 meters tall and its majestic trunk seems to embrace the chapel standing right near it. Now go quickly back to La Fatalcina on the same route, riding on your left towards Le Tagliole and crossing a truly fascinating natural environment.

The view now broadens onto the valley dotted with hamlets and dominated by Mount Cimone. The downhill stretch comes to an end as the road enters the S.S. 324 Radici main road, which

you take turning right. After a short stretch, get back on the S.S. 12 main road riding on your left, crossing the bridge over the Perticara brook to easily reach the town center of **Pievepelago**.

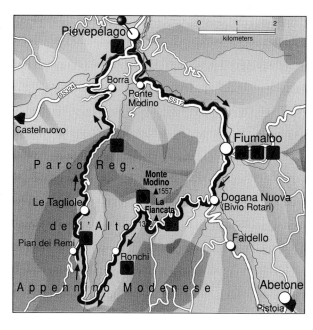

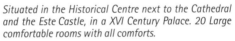

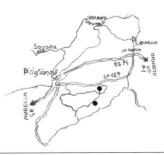

Tuscany

 ## The Etruscan Coast   37 Km
Wine and cypress trees

The Etruscan coast is an ideal destination for cycle enthusiasts: from families with kids along to the expert cyclists.

You start from San Giusto right at the foot of the hill where **Castagneto Carducci** is situated, near the Zi Martino restaurant-hotel. Take via Bolgherese, riding towards Bolgheri. After approximately 1 km, turn right, following the road signs pointing to the Le Pianacce camping site. You quickly approach a crucifix, where you turn left. At this point, start riding on a short uphill stretch along the Lamentano track amid old farms and olive groves. Ride for 2 km passing three crossroads, then turn left on a steep descent towards via Bolgherese, where you turn right. After crossing the Bolgheri Canal (a small watercourse), the road proceeds with steady up and downhill stretches between monumental oaks forming a true green tunnel, and amid fine

Technical info

Route
37 Km: Castagneto Carducci - San Guido - Bibbona - Bolgheri - Castagneto Carducci. Entirely on lightly-trafficked asphalt roads, except for the short stretch on the old via Aurelia.

Difficulty
Easy, with no particular uphill parts; along the Bibbona-Bolgheri (6 km) stretch, the altitude profile is marked by five short, but awkward up and downhill stretches.

Bicycle + Train
The Castagneto Carducci - Donoratico and Bolgheri railroad stations are situated along the Rome-Genoa line.

Cycling period
All year round

Map
• *Atlante stradale d'Italia*, Central volume, scale 1:200,000, TCI.
• *Pisa-Livorno* (Etruscan Riviera), 1:100,000, Multigraphic - Florence.

Technical assistance and cycling information
Ciclosport, via Aurelia 25, Donoratico (LI); t. 0565777149;
www.ciclosport.it
Specialized sale and rental center, cycle guides and technical information.

Tourist information
• Tourist Information Office, via della Marina 8, Castagneto Carducci; t. 0565744276 and 0565778218; castagneto.turismo@infol.it
• APT, piazza Cavour 6, 57125 Livorno; t. 0586204611.
• Consorzio Strada del Vino Costa degli Etruschi, San Guido 45; t. 0565749705.

POINTS OF INTEREST

Castagneto Carducci is the starting point of a road that has become a "must" for cycling enthusiasts: ride up to Sassetta, then venture along hundreds of curves and hairpin bends up to Suvereto on a superb technical route with an enchanting landscape. Together with via Bolgherese, it forms a stretch of the Ciclopista del Sole, the cycle road that connects the Brennero to Naples, in the larger frame of roads forming the Eurovelo cycle network.

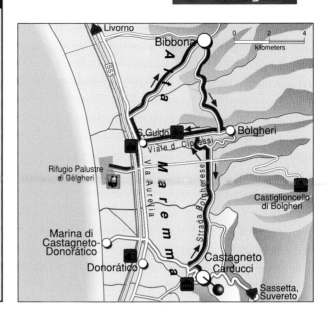

vineyards. After a double curve downhill, you can spot the famous Sassicaia vineyards. After the "passaggio Sassicaia", via Bolgherese enters with an intersection into the famous cypress avenue celebrated by Giosuè Carducci. Once you reach the cypress avenue that "stretches from San Guido to Bolgheri in a double row", turn left and downhill stretch to San Guido and the old Aurelia. From this point, you can easily reach the Marshland Refuge of Bolgheri, a natural oasis protected by the WWF, which can be visited from November to April. This is a stage point for many migratory birds and a nesting spot for the purple heron, the little grebe, the stilt-bird, the mallard and the bald coot. Now continue your ride on the old Aurelia on your right (northwards) for approximately 2 km, up to the crossroads (on your right again) to Bibbona. Ride along via Campigliese that climbs steadily up among cultivated fields, up to the next crossroads for Bibbona, where you ride straight ahead along a ravine road. After crossing the famous vineyards of the Ornellaia estate, go back on the cypress avenue and turn left until reaching Bolgheri. After visiting the village, ride downhill on the boulevard up to the detour on your left for **Castagneto Carducci**. Now take via Bolgherese again and continue along gentle up and downhill stretches, then on a light slope, until you reach the starting point.

LEFT, San Guido, at the start of the cypress avenue.

The Maremma atmosphere   41.5 Km
Touring around Massa Marittima

This magnificent ride starts from one of the most beautiful squares in Tuscany and unfolds a corner of Maremma which is truly appreciated by cyclists for the quiet roads that gently caress hills blanketed with olive groves.

You start your ride from the town center of **Massa Marittima**, moving towards Siena-Larderello. Shortly before entering the S.P. 439 provincial road that leads to Larderello, turn right towards Ghirlanda and Ribolla; for approximately 6.5 km, the road stays high and then drops (3 km) towards the old village-factory of Perolla appearing on your left. A short dirt path leads to the village situated in a scenic spot on the Grosseto Maremma. The road continues on a steep downhill stretch to an inter-

Technical info

Route
41.5 Km: Massa Marittima - Perolla – Lake Accesa - Massa Marittima.
Excluding the Castel di Pietra detour, the itinerary is 35.5 km long.

Difficulty
The route winds on asphalt roads (except for the Castel di Pietra detour). From an altitude point of view, this itinerary has a rolling profile and the only true challenge to face is the ravine stretch near Lake Accesa, plus the final uphill part at the town center of Massa Marittima (2.5 km).

Cycling period
All year round.

Map
• *Atlante stradale d'Italia*, Central volume, scale 1:200,000, ed. TCI.

• *Carta stradale provinciale*, scale 1:100,000, Multigraphic - Florence.

Technical assistance
Sumin Biciclette,
via Ferrinanti 31, Valpiana,
Massa Marittima;
t. 0566919111.

Organized cycle touring
Massa Vecchia,
S.S. 439, Massa Marittima;
t. 0566903385,
fax 0565901838.
A real "clinic center" for bicycles, with the possibility of accommodation, bicycle rental, outings with guides on MTB and/or road bicycles along the roads of Maremma.

Tourist information
Ufficio Turistico Comunale e Musei Civici, piazza Garibaldi, Massa Marittima;
t. 0566902289.

section. Now proceed on your right, following the road signs to Gavorrano. After exactly 1.1 km, you meet a track on your left, marked by a yellow road sign that indicates Castel di Pietra.
We suggest a short detour (3 + 3 km) to the castle. Ride for 2.3 km on a smooth dirt road flanked by cypress trees, then on your right

LEFT, the roofs and the Cathedral of Massa Marittima. PAGE OPPOSITE, towards Lake Accesa.

POINTS OF INTEREST

At Massa Marittima, the extraordinary Garibaldi square with the San Cerbone Cathedral (XII century), initially built in Romanesque style, then (1287) extended and enriched with Gothic elements by Giovanni Pisano; Palazzo dei Priori (XIII century), today an Archaeological Museum.
At the foot of the town, the Carapax Oasis, a center for the protection of tortoises. Info: t. 0566940083 and fax 0566902387.

starts the 0.7 km uphill stretch towards the medieval fortress. Leave your bicycle at the start of the track and continue on foot until you reach the remains of the castle at the top of a hill. Now go back on your tracks, returning to the asphalt road and continuing along the itinerary, riding for 2.5 km until you reach a crossroads, where you keep right following the road signs pointing to Lake Accesa. After covering 2 km, get ready for a steady, cyclable uphill stretch to la Pesta near Lake Accesa.

After getting back on the main road, ride up to a clear fork and turn right heading towards Massa Marittima. At this point, go downhill and reach (5 km) the road that starts at the foot of the **Massa Marittima** hill. This is where the last uphill stretch starts leading to the cathedral square.

ALTERNATIVE

You can shorten the rise of the itinerary by approximately 100 m, starting from the Esso petrol station situated south of Massa Marittima on the road to Follonica. In this case, start by following the wide ring road leading to Siena for about 5 km, up to the crossroads for Massa: turn right towards the town center, and immediately afterwards, take the by-road on your left towards Ghirlanda-Ribolla.

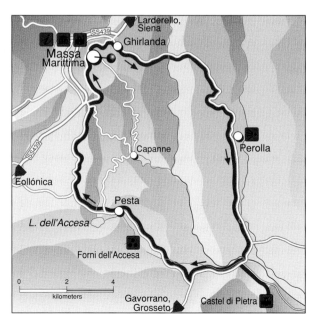

Maremma
The tuff cities
26 Km

An itinerary at the heart of the Tuscan Maremma, along roads that explore the fascinating world of the tuff of Sorano, Sovana and Pitigliano, a realm deeply rooted in the mysteries of the ancient Etruscan civilization.

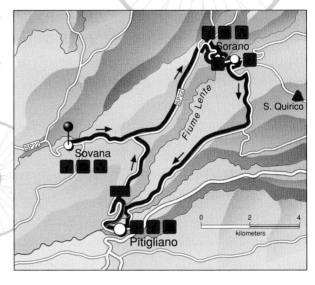

From the **Sovana** square, ride down towards the S.P. 22 provincial road, arriving near the Aldobrandesca fortress, where you continue heading towards Sorano-Pitigliano. Cycle for about 2 km on a not too challenging uphill stretch until you reach a crossroads where you follow the road signs pointing to Sorano. The road now continues on gentle rolling terrain for about 4.5 km. Cross pastures and cultivated fields on a plateau that overlooks the profiles of Mount Amiata, clearly visible on your left. At a bend on your right starts the downhill stretch (1.7 km), along a road cut between two imposing tuff walls, which passes near the San Rocco necropolis. At this point, we suggest a walk in the archaeological area to visit the natural balcony on Sorano and the Lente Valley,

Technical info

Route

26 Km: Sovana - Sorano - Pitigliano - Sovana.
On completely asphalt and lightly-trafficked roads.

Difficulty

A fairly challenging itinerary, with no particular difficulty in store. All in all, the route is really cyclable. The toughest stretch is the uphill part (short though) towards Sorano. Other uphill stretches are the one exiting Sovana and the initial stretch from the bridge over the Lente,

heading towards the crossroads for Sovana. In case of rain or humidity, pay great attention to the ride down to Sorano where the road surface can be quite slippery.

Cycling period

All year round.

Notes

The short route makes this itinerary coverable in about two hours, but it would be worthwhile to spend the whole day out since the three villages deserve a good visit.

Map

Atlante stradale d'Italia, Central volume, scale 1:200,000, TCI

Technical assistance

F.lli Brizzi, via Maddalena Ciacci 24, 58017 Pitigliano; t. 0564616038.

Tourist information

Information Office:
• Sorano, piazza Busati, t. 0564633099;
• Pitigliano, via Roma 6, t. 0564614433;
• Sovana, Palazzo Pretorio, t. 0564614074.

POINTS OF INTEREST

"Archeotrekking" at the heart of the Etruscan civilization, across necropoli and cave roads. We suggest the **Sorano-Vitozza route** *that starts from the San Rocco necropolis. No technical difficulties here, but orienteering yourself is quite a feat, so you should better be assisted by an expert guide: Enzo Cusumano qualified regional tourist guide and authorized for the province of Grosseto (t. 0564633591 and cell. 3393291035), or the "La Fortezza" Cooperative with offices in the Sovana Duomo, t. 0564616532 and 0564633402.*

and especially the fascinating cave road dating back to the Etruscan times. Now get back on your bicycle and continue the ride on the winding downhill stretch that ends at the bridge over the River Lente. At this point, start climbing: on your left you see the village of Sorano. Ride for just less than one kilometer following gentle switchbacks until you reach the heart of the town. After arriving in the square with a parking lot, you can proceed on your left towards the old town center that is certainly worth a visit. Otherwise, you can continue your ride leaving town and heading towards Pitigliano. After a short uphill section (up to the crossroads for San Quirico), proceed firstly on gentle ups and downs, then downhill along a smooth and pleasant road until you reach Pitigliano (9 km). The road, already in a built-up area, enters a sharp bend passing under a tuff bridge. On your right, enter town, riding straight ahead and down a series of hairpin bends for 600 m, until you reach the crossroads on your right for Sovana. Just when the downhill stretch starts, a magnificent view opens on the town of Pitigliano.

Ride at the foot of the tufaceous shelf upon which Pitigliano stands, reaching the bridge over the River Lente, where the last uphill part starts, up to the intersection on the S.P. 22 provincial road, where you turn left heading towards **Sovana**.

LEFT, grazing land between Sovana and Sorano.
ABOVE, the village of Pitigliano.

The land of Siena 1
The "Crete" area

27 Km

A journey along the hills and gravel roads that mark the territory south of Siena, in the rolling lands between San Giovanni and Torrenieri around the Asso Valley.

From the railroad station of **San Giovanni d'Asso**, after approximately 400 m, you reach a clear crossroads. Turn left towards Montisi, passing the level crossing, then cross the bridge over the Asso torrent, and after

Technical info

Route
27 Km: San Giovanni d'Asso - Lucignano d'Asso - Cosona - Torrenieri.

Difficulty
A very cyclable route, with two uphill stretches: the first from San Giovanni d'Asso (1.7 km) and the second towards Lucignano d'Asso (1.6 km). You ride mainly on gravel road, so we suggest a mountain bike or a good touring bike with medium-wide tires.

Cycling period
All year round.

Bicycle + Train
Only on the Treno Natura that leaves on fixed dates, on a line no longer used by ordinary railroad traffic.

Technical assistance
Real, via Roma 46/50, Asciano;
t. 0577719138;

Tourist information
• APT Siena,
via di Città 43,
Siena;
t. 0577280551.
www.terresiena.it
• San Giovanni d'Asso:
Municipal Information Office,
via XX Settembre 15;
t. 0577803101.

Notes
Detailed information and maps of the cyclable routes across the province of Siena can be found at the www.terresiena.it web site You can combine this route with other routes (by bike or on foot) you find along the Treno Natura stretch.

200 m, turn right on the uphill dirt road (road signs pointing to the Trove farm holidays). You ride on an uphill dirt stretch for 0.8 km up to a crossroads. Now turn right on a ridge following the path marked as n° 560 A (if you go straight, you ride down fast to the Trove concern). At the next crossroads (200 m), keep right, then reach a farm where the road continues to go downhill. After passing a sheep fence (close it) and a farming concern, you enter a wide gravel road. Turn left and ride uphill towards Lucignano d'Asso (1.6 km). This is where a spectacular ridge route starts on gravel road. Follow the road signs pointing to Montisi-Pienza

ABOVE, Lucignano d'Asso.
PAGE OPPOSITE, the "crete" landscape at Asciano.

POINTS OF INTEREST

For any information on the **Treno Natura**, *contact the Associazione di Volontariato Ferrovia Val d'Orcia t. 057 7207413 or 3388992577, trenonatura@katamail.com "Viaggio sul Treno Natura" is a great guide, with heaps of historical-environmental information, and a description of routes covered either on foot or by bicycle, directly connected to the places brushed by the Treno Natura.*

up to an intersection, where you keep right (keeping left takes you to Pienza). Follow the beautiful, wide gravel road, which curls, with gentle up and downhill stretches, along the typical landscape of the Siena "crete", marked by rolling pastures and scattered farms in the open countryside.

After reaching the farms at Cosona, continue on the main road that enters the asphalt road (6.5 km from the crossroads). Now ride downhill towards **Torrenieri** (2 km).

ALTERNATIVE

From this point, you can go back to San Giovanni d'Asso, riding for 9 km on a mainly level surface.

This itinerary can be combined with the Treno Natura route, a circle stretching for 140 km, with start and finish at Siena. The first stretch, Siena-Asciano-Monte Antico (84 km), is covered on tracks no longer used by the ordinary lines. The Monte Antico-Buonconvento-Siena stretch (56 km) is part of the Grosseto-Siena line, today still running. You can cover the entire circle only on certain fixed dates, usually on Sundays, when three passages are arranged: in the morning, half way through the day and in the afternoon. This logistics solution allows you to get off at a station, enjoy a short trek or ride, and catch the next train at the same or different station to finish off the circle.

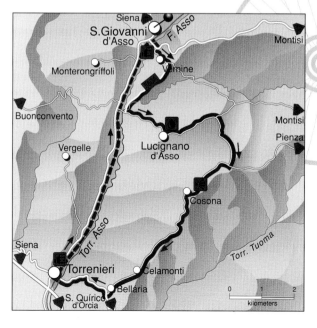

The land of Siena 2 — 21 Km
The Merse Valley

An itinerary across the "other side of Tuscany", at the heart of the Merse Valley, an oasis of ideal peace to discover while cycling.

Starting from **Rosia** (piazza Garibaldi), turn left towards Roccastrada, and after 300 m, turn left again towards Torri. After approximately 1 km along the S.P. 99 provincial road, at the crossroads with a tall cypress tree standing at the centre, turn right. Now climb along the tree-lined avenue left of a cemetery, up to the road sign at the start of the town. Continue on your right up to the gate that enters the village of Torri. Looking at the gate from outside the walls, climb up on your right on a dirt road, and after 250 m, turn left and get ready for a short spurt, then ride on up and downhill stretches for about 1 km. At the first V-junction, keep left, and at the next (after passing a curve on your left), take the path on your right that ends at the urban area of the Rancia. Now ride down to the intersection with the S.P. 99 provincial road and then turn right towards Stigliano (approximately 300 m). Just before the square, ride up along the asphalt road, above the sources, towards the Campalfi estate (don't ride towards it). At the end of the slope, the road becomes unsurfaced. Keep right at the two following crossroads. After a few hundred meters, climb along the "Viali", a rolling gravel road, just over 2 km long, bordered by two parallel rows of tall cypresses.

At the end of the "Viali", turn left, and after approximately 700 m, you arrive in front of the Montestigliano farm, on a hill dominating the entire Rosia plain. At this point, ride down on your right, paying due attention to the slope and the bends. After reaching the crossroads at the bottom of the downhill stretch, avoiding the road sign pointing to Brenna, ride along the S.P. 99 provincial road to Orgia. After about 1 km, turn right, and after crossing the iron bridge over the River Merse, climb up towards the village of Orgia. After reaching the road

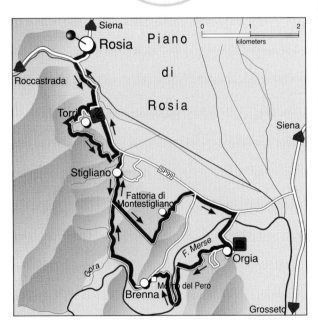

ABOVE, cycling between Stigliano and Rosia.
PAGE OPPOSITE, view of Torri.

POINTS OF INTEREST

An ideal reference spot for cycle tourists is **Palazzo a Merse**, *bed & breakfast service, specialized in accommodation and in special services for cycle tourists also with the family along: technical assistance, tips on local itineraries, guides on demand. Strategically positioned for itineraries in the Siena territory. Palazzo a Merse, at Palazzo a Merse, San Rocco a Pilli; t. and fax 0577342063; palazzo merse@tin.it.*

sign at the start of the village, ride down on your left along the dirt road and crossing the bar. At the end of the downhill stretch starts an electrified fence, against wild boars. Soon after, you reach a V-junction that you take on your right until you reach the edge of the River Merse. Now ride up the river on the country path that follows the margins of the wood, and after 600 m, at the following V-junction, turn right to reach the ford. After wading the river, keeping on your right, you reach the sports field and shortly after, Molino del Pero in the hamlet of Brenna. From the mill, turn left, and after crossing the small village, you reach the bridge over the Gora. Enter the dirt road between the bridge and the house, then continue on a track that enters the Nature Reserve of the Upper Merse. At the end of the track that runs along the Gora, climb up on dirt road on your right to Stigliano, emerging at the start of the "Viali" with the cypress trees, and continue on asphalt road along the S.P. 99 provincial road up to **Rosia**.

Technical info

Route
21 Km: Rosia - Torri - Montestigliano - Orgia - Brenna - Stigliano - Rosia. On mixed asphalt-dirt roads, we suggest using a mountain bike or a touring bike equipped with MTB-type gear and wide tires.
Difficulty
Short itinerary with a varied course. Ideal also for the peaceful cycle tourists.

Road map
Valdimerse in Bici, 11 itineraries in the area stretching from the Siena Montagnola and the Merse Valley, with maps of the routes. Available at the Municipal Tourist Office of Sovicille: c/o Pro Loco, via Roma 27, 53018 Sovicille; t. 0577314503.
prolocosovicille@jumpy.it
Map
Carta turistica e dei sentieri,

Itinerari nella Montagnola Senese, 1:50,000, Multigraphic - Florence (edited by CAI, Siena section).
Technical assistance
• Centro Bici, via Toselli 110, Siena; t. 0577282550.
• DF Bike, via M. Romana 54, Siena; t. 0577271905.
Tourist information
APT Siena, via di Città 43, Siena; t. 0577280551; www.terresiena.it

The Florentine Chianti   15.6 Km
San Polo and the Ema Valley

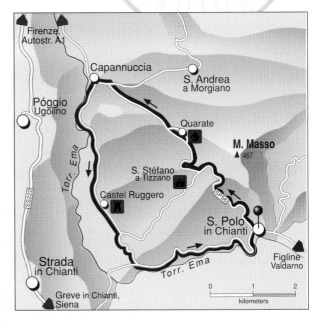

Chianti is a quite a harsh territory, not too easy to be challenged by bike, but this easy route in the San Polo area will suit even the less trained cyclist. San Polo in Chianti, situated in a strategic position along the road linking Ponte a Ema and Figline, was once a castle, although no traces remain today. Only some important documents have been gathered, dating back to the early years after the year 1000, and kept in the archives of the Montescalari and Passignano monasteries.

The itinerary starts from **San Polo in Chianti**, exactly from the square opposite the town church. Leave the town by taking the S.P. 56 provincial road to Florence, ignoring the by-roads that start from the main route.

Ride for 4.5 km, crossing Quarate where, near a crossroads on your right, you'll find a fountain, if you should need to fill up your flask. At this point, it would be worthwhile to focus your attention on an oddity: if you raise your eyes up to your right, at the built-up

POINTS OF INTEREST

*Near San Polo, you can visit the **Tizzano castle**, whose Romanesque tower appears to have been erected on the foundations of a building dating back to the late Imperial age, between 1580 and 1630. Close by, the **Church of Santo Stefano** at Tizzano, dating back to the year 1000, with its façade entirely covered by grapevine.*

area of Quarate, you'll be able to spot an olive tree that grows on the summit of a tower.

Now take the smooth ride on a mainly downhill stretch and reach Capannuccia. Once you enter the town, follow the second road on your left that starts just near a café and a fountain. Start riding towards Castel Ruggero, which you reach after a 3 km climb up the hydrographical right side of the Ema torrent.

Castel Ruggero is easily recognizable by the tower and the Renaissance elements of the house, surrounded by a large Italian-style garden. From Castel Ruggero, ride along the road that flanks on your left the homonymous lake and the farm, cycling straight ahead. After crossing a short uphill stretch, at the crossroads, keep left. After covering approximately 1.7 km, you reach a crossroads, marked by the pres-

ABOVE, the legendary Chianti vineyards. PAGE OPPOSITE, towards Castel Ruggero.

ence of a tabernacle, where you keep right. The track now stretches for approximately 700 m, accompanied by a double row of cypress trees, up to a crossroads with the main asphalt road. Now go straight ahead, climbing the valley of the Ema torrent, towards **San Polo in Chianti**, which, from this spot, is just over 3 km away.

Technical info

Route

15.6 Km: San Polo in Chianti - Quarate - Capannuccia - Castel Ruggero - San Polo in Chianti.

Difficulty

An easy itinerary, ideal also for families with children along, with 11.2 km of asphalt road and 4.4 km of wide and well-beaten dirt road. The altitude profile does

not present challenging stretches and the gradients of the ascents and descents are gentle and easily cyclable.

Cycling period

All year round.

Map

Carta turistica stradale, Chianti e colline senesi, scale 1:50,000 (CAI routes and itineraries for mountain bikes), Multigraphic - Florence.

Assistance and MTB rental

Marco Ramuzzi, via I. Stecchi 23, Greve in Chianti; t. 055853037.

Tourist information

Municipal Information Office, via Luca Cini 1, Greve in Chianti; t. 0558545243. www.greve-in-chianti.com

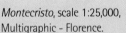

The Elba island
From Rio Marina to Cavo
23 Km

The Elba island offers magnificent opportunities for road and mountain bike enthusiasts, but the island roads require good legs. The itinerary has an average difficulty level and reveals the north-eastern tip of the island. This route crosses the iron soul of Elba, amid reddish rocks and industrial archaeological findings in the old mines mostly situated in the coastal stretch between Rio Marina and Cavo.

From **Rio Marina**, start riding along the coastal road towards Cavo. Just after the start, the road turns inland on a slight uphill stretch. After riding for 1.5 km, go down towards the canal of the Albano brook, then continue on a short ascent (0.6 km) and a slope of approximately 1 km up to the Telegrafo creek.

Now get ready for the pleasant, steady downhill ride that follows the coastal profile and ends at the Cavo seafront, an ideal spot for a short stop, an energetic snack and the chance to fill up your water-flask, before venturing on the mainly uphill part of this itinerary. In

Technical info

Route
23 Km: Rio Marina - Cavo - Rio nell'Elba - Rio Marina. The route stretches in the less busy area of the island and can be covered also in the middle-peak season, when on the other roads of Elba, motorized traffic is really heavy.

Difficulty
An itinerary with an average difficulty level. Technically speaking, there are no difficulties, but it's not a walkover either. The first part (4 km) has a few up and downhill stretches, while the Parata climb between Cavo and Rio nell'Elba, although with no challenging gradients, is 7 km long.

Bicycle + Boat
Hydrofoils and ferry boats travel every day to Elba, linking Portoferraio and Cavo to the ports of Piombino and Leghorn.

Map
• *Atlante stradale d'Italia*, Central volume, scale 1:200,000, TCI.
• *Carta Turistica e dei Sentieri, Isola d'Elba, Capraia,*
Montecristo, scale 1:25,000, Multigraphic - Florence.

Technical assistance
• Calamita Bike, via Pietro Gori 8, Capoliveri; t. and fax 0565967024. Also guide service and bicycle rental.
• Ciclo Sport, via Carducci 146, Portoferraio; t. 0565914346.

Tourist information
• APT dell'Arcipelago Toscano, Calata Italia 26, Portoferraio; t. 0565914671, fax 0565916350.

POINTS OF INTEREST

Rio nell'Elba is one of the most characteristic villages of the island. It would be worthwhile to stop and see some interesting spots, such as the old public wash-houses, and in a panoramic spot near the town center, the Sanctuary of Santa Caterina d'Alessandria, with the adjoining Orto dei Semplici Elbano and the endemic, medicinal and rare plants of the Tuscan archipelago (for information and visits, t. 056595316).

any case, before riding towards Rio nell'Elba, you should take a short detour. From the Cavo seafront, after crossing an area of residential villas, you reach the nearby Capo Castello. This is a wonderful panoramic view on the Topi island and on Capo Vita, the northern tip of the island.

To continue along the itinerary, ride back on the road you have already covered, up to the Cavo seafront, where the road to Rio nell'Elba starts. This is where the most challenging stretch of the route begins, the wonderful road called Parata.

It's a very cyclable uphill stretch, immersed in the undergrowth which, after about 7 km, reaches an altitude of 242 m on the Parata pass, between Mount Serra (on your right) and the Giove tower (on your left). The road climbs steadily upwards, with no tiring spurts, but pay due attention to the length. From the pass, just follow the road, and remember to touch the brakes now and then and to ride at a gentle pace to exercise your legs. This is where the spectacular descent towards Rio nell'Elba and **Rio Marina** begins.

RIGHT, cycling towards Rio nell'Elba. PAGE OPPOSITE, the coast near Cavo.

The Orbetello lagoon — 24.7 Km
Tombolo della Feniglia

A very smooth itinerary in the fascinating atmosphere of the Nature Reserve, which stretches from the Maremma coast to Mount Argentario, on the thin strip of land separating the lagoon waters from the sea.

From **Orbetello** to Porto Santo Stefano. Take the road built on the strip of land that separates the two lagoons of Ponente and Levante and ride on the cycle road. Once you cross the dam, after 1.9 km, at Terrarossa, turn left towards Porto Ercole, up to a crossroads (1.4 km), where you

turn left. Now cross a large parking lot and ride for approximately 300 m and turn left again, taking a dirt road that ends near a big gate. Pass the pedestrian crossing and continue on your right along a tree-lined avenue (approximately 300 m) that ends opposite the group of buildings belonging to State Forest Rangers.

At this point, turn left, following the dirt road heading at the heart of the Tombolo della Feniglia (sand-gravel causeway). After exactly 300 m, turn left on the path that leads straight to the lagoon. Cycle

for another 300 m up to an intersection, where you turn right on the track that follows the course of the sandy banks of the lagoon. You'll spot lots of roots emerging on the road surface, but only in the first stretch. Along this route, you meet, on your left, two pedestrian crossings that lead to observation huts to watch the lagoon birdlife.

Continue riding along the main road, avoiding the detours on your right. After approximately 5 km, the road enters the pinewood near a wide glade, where you can spot fallow deer

Technical info

Route

24.7 Km (10 Km on asphalt and 14.7 on dirt road):
Orbetello - Terrarossa - Tombolo della Feniglia - Tagliata Etrusca - Cosa - Tombolo della Feniglia - Feniglia beach - Terrarossa - Orbetello. Mainly on roads closed to motorized traffic. The stretch on the Tombolo that flanks the sandy banks of the lagoon is rough (roots and sand), but easily cyclable even with a normal touring bicycle.

Difficulty
This is an easy itinerary, ideal even for families with kids along. The Tombolo della Feniglia stretch is ideal also

for the whole family, and is interesting for birdwatching enthusiasts too. The only tough part is the uphill stretch (about 1 km) on the promontory of Cosa.

Cycling period
All year round.

Tips
Along the route on the margins of the Tombolo, there are lots of bicycle rental spots, but the bicycles are not too good. Better rely on the Atala Point at Orbetello.

Map
Atlante Stradale Toscana, scale 1:100,000, Multigraphic-Florence.

Technical assistance
Atala Point, via Vittorio Veneto, Orbetello; t. 0564867790. Sale and workshop; rental on demand (better phone first).

Tourist information
• Pro Loco Orbetello, piazza della Repubblica; t. 0564860447.
• APT Grosseto, viale Monterosa 206; t. 0564462611.
• Museo Archeologico Nazionale di Cosa, via delle Ginestre 35, Orbetello; t. 0564881421. Open every day, except Mondays, from 9 a.m. to 7 p.m.

POINTS OF INTEREST

*In the Tombolo della Feniglia, visit **Cosa**, founded by the Romans in 273 B.C., after the defeat of the allied Etruscan forces. The name comes from the more ancient name of "Cusi" or "Cusia", a small Etruscan center situated on the area where Orbetello stands today. Apart from the itinerary on foot (about 40 minutes) that brushes the Casa dello Scheletro, the Baths, the Forum, the Acropolis and the three entrance gates, visit the National Archaeological Museum with its many local findings.*

and wild boars. Once you reach the main road axis, turn left, passing in front of the group of buildings of the State Forest Rangers. Just outside the gate, get back on the asphalt road and keep left. After crossing the Tagliata Etrusca (a canal controlling the flow of waters between sea and lagoon) and the La Lampara restaurant, turn right along the uphill road that reaches the promontory with its ruins and the Archaeological Museum of Cosa (roughly 1 km). After visiting the interesting archaeological area, go back on the same road and reach the gates of the Duna di Feniglia Nature Reserve, then ride along the dirt road that crosses

lengthways the entire woodland. The wide dirt road is bordered on the right by landmarks.

After approximately 3.5 km, we suggest the detour (250 m) on your left to the wonderful beach of Feniglia. Now you're back on the main axis, take the easy

ride to the other station of the State Forest Rangers, and return on the road you have already covered. To get back to **Orbetello**, pass the gate riding up to the asphalt road. At this point, turn right, and after 1.4 km, right again, until you reach the starting point.

RIGHT, the Orbetello lagoon.

 # The Upper Valley of the Potenza   48 Km
Tour of Mount Gemmo

This itinerary unveils the unscathed territory lying between Matelica and Pioraco, an important wine production area (Verdicchio di Matelica DOC), with a time-honored tradition also in paper production.

From the town center of **Matelica** (piazza Enrico Mattei),

ride towards the S.S. 256 main road, following the road signs pointing to Castelraimondo-Camerino. After about 1 km, leave the rather busy S.S. 256 main road, turning right and following the signs for Castel Santa Maria-Santangelo-Brondoleto-Vasconi, on a by-road that crosses cultivated fields and farms. Initial-

ly gentle, then steeper and steeper, the track climbs up to the hamlet of Vasconi (3.5 km); after a short stretch, you reach the enchanting village of Castel Santa Maria, where you can shortly stop to fill up your water flask at the fountain situated at the entrance of the town. At Castel Santa Maria, the road branches off:

Technical info

Route
48 Km: Matelica - Castel Santa Maria - Sant'Angelo - Pioraco - Fiuminata - Palazzo - Matelica. Quiet by-roads to cover with a good touring bicycle or with a mountain bike, so you can challenge the tougher stretches at ease.

Difficulty
This is a route with quite a capricious altitude profile, requiring good basic physical conditions. The more challenging parts are the uphill stretches towards Castel Santa Maria and Sant'Angelo,

the short spurt towards the center of Pioraco and the climb up to the pass before the Trocche Valley. Ride with care along the steep downhill stretch (bumpy surface) to the paper mills of Pioraco.

Cycling period
All year round, but it may be chilly in the winter months and the roads slippery.

Map
Atlante stradale d'Italia, Central volume, 1:200,000, TCI.

Technical assistance
First Love, viale Cesare Battisti 40/42, Matelica; t. 073785699.

A center specialized in the sale of and assistance for mountain and road bikes; if you want to rent a bike, contact them some days in advance.

Tourist information
• Associazione Pro Matelica Tourist Information Office, piazza Enrico Mattei 3; t. and fax 073785671.

• La Valle dell'Arte - Cooperativa Arché (management of the museums of Matelica, Pioraco), via Morbiducci 39, 62100 Macerata; t. 0733232218; Matelica offices: t. 073784445.

POINTS OF INTEREST

Lovers of genuine tastes should not lose this grand opportunity to stop and visit the **Ossoli farm**, *at Pagliano, between Matelica and Esanatoglia; t. 0737 784777, to see the birth of cheese, from milking to maturing. You can buy ricotta, fresh and ripe pecorino, cheese aromatized with truffles and chilly pepper.*

ABOVE, towards Sant'Angelo. Background, Mount San Vicino.

if you go straight ahead, you ride down towards Brondoleto and Castelraimondo; if you keep right (yellow sign Il Giardino degli Ulivi farm holidays), you ride at the foot of Mount Gemmo, following the contour line up to the nearby Sant'Angelo, a village set in a wonderful natural environment. Continue on a gentle uphill dirt road for 1.6 km, until you reach a group of houses, and proceed on a steep descent, on asphalt, although bumpy surface. After 2.1 km, you get to the intersection and turn right up to the paper mill of Pioraco, situated in deep ravines formed by the upper course of the River Potenza. On your left starts the steep but short spurt (200 m) that enters the center of Pioraco. This is where the first paper mills in Italy were built, around the year 1300 (shortly after Fabriano), adopting Arab techniques. Stop and visit the Gualchiera Prolaquense (paper production) and the Paper and Watermark Museum, both housed in the town hall. After crossing the town, take the S.S. 361 main road that runs on a level stretch towards Fiuminata, where you turn right, following the road signs for Collamato-Palazzo. Shortly after starts the uphill stretch which, in 4 km (250 m rise), rises steadily up to the pass where the descent into the solitary Trocche Valley begins, passing near the small village of Palazzo. The itinerary continues downhill to the crossroads for Esanatoglia (on your left), where you go straight ahead until you smoothly reach **Matelica**.

ALTERNATIVE

You can make the itinerary easier by avoiding the ride up to Mount Gemmo. From Castel Santa Maria, ride down towards Brondoleto and Castelraimondo, from where you can go back by train to Matelica.

Mount Conero   18 Km
Balcony on the Adriatic

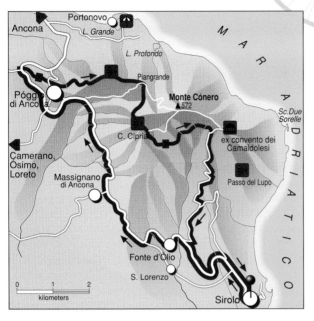

covered in this spot the geological layer known as "KT" (it stands for cretaceous and tertiary), indicating the boundary between the Eocene and Oligocene. The provincial road continues to climb with curves and up and downhill stretches for another 7 km up to the crossroads, where you turn right heading towards Poggio di Ancona. Once you enter the town, next to the Osteria del Poggio, turn right, taking the dirt road marked as trail mark n° 1 Conero Crossing. This is where a very tough stretch begins, so we suggest getting off the bike instead of sweat-

Riding along the roads and cart roads of Mount Conero requires some stamina, but the spectacular panoramas on the magnificent coast of Portonovo, Sirolo and the hills of the Marca of Ancona do really reward your effort.

From the old town center of **Sirolo**, exit the town northwards along via Giulietti, until you enter the Conero provincial road that climbs up to Ancona. Pass Fonte d'Olio and continue your climb up to a winding profile, until you reach the equipped area of the Massignano quarry (about 4 km from the start). This is a really important site, since expert researchers dis-

POINTS OF INTEREST

Two walks, with a spectacular dive into the sea if the season's right: one towards **Portonovo**, *with its beaches and the wonderful path between Forte Napoleonico, the defense tower and the small Romanesque Church of Santa Maria di Portonovo; the other towards the* **Passo del Lupo**, *a stunning panoramic spot towards the rocks of the Due Sorelle, which you can reach by taking a pretty tough track (in some points equipped with fixed ropes).*

station, which you skirt along a smooth dirt road.

After reaching the asphalt road accessing the station, ride down to a crossroads, where you turn left, and cycle uphill. Now ride along the last stretch of the asphalt road up to the former Camaldolesi convent. Stop here and visit the crypt and the interior of the Church of San Pietro al Conero. From this moment, no more grueling uphill stretches, so enjoy your exciting "landing" on the village of **Sirolo**, along hairpins that slope towards the sea.

ABOVE, towards Poggio di Ancona. PAGE OPPOSITE, the Portonovo beach.

ing on the pedals. Fortunately, the slope soon sweetens, and on your right, you'll see a wooden fence: from this spot, you can stop to enjoy the amazing panorama overlooking the sea and the promontory of Portonovo.

The road now skirts the western slopes of the mountain until reaching the crossroads of Piangrande, from where you continue your ride on a flat stretch, following trail mark n° 1. Once you get near a crossroads, keep left, following the road signs pointing to Pian dei Raggetti (white-green trail mark) and admire the great view on the inland and Loreto, Castelfidardo, Recanati and Osimo. Continue on a downhill stretch along a route still identified by trail mark n° 1. Shortly afterwards, ride up a short ascent, then down to the fence of a former military

Technical info

Route
18 Km: Sirolo - Fonte d'Olio - Massignano - Poggio di Ancona - Piangrande - Badia di San Pietro. Asphalt roads and an approximately 6 km dirt stretch.

Difficulty
The itinerary is short, but quite tough, due to a few uphill stretches that require some training.

Road signs
The dirt stretch (Poggio-Badia di San Pietro) is indicated by trail mark n° 1.

Cycling period
All year round, preferably in spring.

Map
• *Parco del Conero, Carta escursionistica,*1:20,000, Consorzio Parco del Conero.
• *Parco del Conero, Carta geologica con itinerari*

escursionistici, 1.20,000, Consorzio Parco del Conero.

Technical assistance
Bonifazi Centre Shop, via Litoranea 184, Marcelli di Numana; t. 0717390516.

Tourist information
• Consorzio Parco del Conero, via Vivaldi 1/3, 60020 Sirolo; t. 0719331161, 0719331518. parco.conero@regione. marche.it
• Centro Vsite del Parco, via Peschiera 30a, Sirolo; t. 0719331879.
Seasonal Information Offices:
• Sirolo, piazza Vittorio Veneto, t. 0719330611;
• Numana, piazza Santuario, t. 0719330612;
• Marcelli, via Litoranea, t. 0717390179.

The Upper Valley of the Metauro 25.2 Km
From Lamoli to the Alpe della Luna

A short itinerary, with a very interesting landscape, near the Bocca Trabaria pass, that plunges into the unspoilt nature of the Alpe della Luna and the small valley crossed by the Villa brook.

You start your ride from the San Benedetto di **Lamoli** Oasis, entering the S.S. 73 bis main road to Bocca Trabaria. After an easy start, the climb gets challenging, with hairpin bends leading to the pass. The first part of the itinerary holds the toughest stretches, so we suggest riding with great serenity and climbing up with an agile pace. After 4 km, a road sign indicates Lake Sole on your right, which you reach after a 1 km uphill ride; you are now at an altitude of 900 m, and the path keeps climbing up to the pass (1 km) at 1,000 m above sea level. At this point, after gaining height, comes a very spectacular stretch, where the road keeps running on the contour line, curling along the side of the mountain: on your left, a wooded ridge of the Alpe della Luna, on your

ABOVE, the Lamoli Abbey. PAGE OPPOSITE, on the Alpe della Luna.

Technical info

Route
25.2 Km (15.2 Km asphalt, 8.7 dirt road, 1.3 on track):
Lamoli – Lake Sole – Alpe della Luna - Villa - Parchiule - Borgo Pace - Lamoli. Mixed itinerary. A mountain bike is required.

Difficulty
This is a wonderful and challenging itinerary too, despite its being short. The first stretch of 6 km and 400 m rise (climb up to Lake Sole and subsequent pass) requires trained legs. The path near Vallepetra calls for good riding techniques but, given its shortness (1 km), it can be easily covered on foot.

Cycling period
From April to November.

Map
Alpe della Luna, Carta dei sentieri, 1:25,000, CAI Pesaro and Mountain Community of Urbania - Upper Middle Metauro; available at the more specialized local book shops and tobacconists.

Technical assistance
• Happy Bike,
via G. Leopardi 28,
Urbania;
t. 0722319010, 3298066622, 3382921709;
www.happybike.it.
Technical assistance, rental, sale, guided itineraries, advice: the most authoritative spot in the area.

• Guerra,
via XXVIII Luglio 14,
Mercatello sul Metauro;
t. 072289212.
Specialist sales point and assistance.

Tourist information
• L'Oasi San Benedetto,
Lamoli
t. 072280133,
fax 072280226
Nature-trekking centre, it organizes seasonal touring programs inspired on open-air life: trekking, cycle touring and orienteering.
• Pro Loco Casteldurante,
corso Vittorio Emanuele 27,
Urbania;
t. 0722317211.

POINTS OF INTEREST

The short walk from the center of **Borgo Pace** *to the point where the Meta and the Auro torrents flow into the same bed, giving birth to the Metauro, which starts its journey towards the waters of the Adriatic. A day to spend at* **Urbania**, *a very interesting center from a historic and artistical point of view, with its Ducal Palace (seat of the Town Museums) and its charming artisan workshops.*

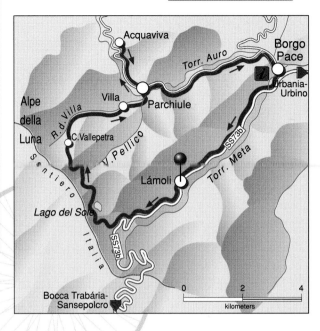

right, the green funnel of the Pellico Valley. For 4.1 km, continue your ride on the mid-coast cart road, ignoring the tracks dropping on your right (woodcutters' pathways), up to a hairpin bend that turns sharply left, where you ride down on your right (this point must be identified with great care). You enter the valley of the Villa brook, approaching a few abandoned country houses. The track passes near the ruins on your left. From this moment on, keep a constant eye on the white-red signs of track n° 90. Only the skilled cyclists stay on their saddle, while the others hop off and take a nice, peaceful walk up to the point where the road becomes rideable again, dropping steeply down towards the villages of Villa and Parchiule, where you meet the watercourse of the Auro torrent. From Parchiule, you

can take a short detour towards the abandoned village of Acquaviva. Parchiule is situated at 500 m above sea level; from this point the road, which is asphalt again, runs gently down to Borgo Pace. After covering 3.5 km, at Sant'Andrea, on your right, you can

clearly see a stone country house, a splendid example of rural architecture, which is certainly worth a stop. Another 2 km and you reach Borgo Pace, where you get back on the S.S. 73 bis main road that returns to **Lamoli**, on a 5.5 km gentle, rideable uphill stretch.

Between Gabicce and Pesaro 48 Km
Up and down the panoramic road

The panoramic road of Gabicce Mare is an ideal itinerary that unfolds the enchantment of the first rocks facing the Adriatic Sea. Gabicce offers the chance to ride on enthralling roads that roll between the sea and the inland; the up and downhill stretches are never too steep and allow you to ride smoothly along. There are some challenging parts, but altogether, the tour is enjoyable.

Starting from **Gabicce Mare**, take the road leading to Gradara, and after approximately 2.5 km, start the first uphill stretch of 2 km with very cycleable slopes. Once you get to the foot of the castle, leave the main road and turn left to climb up to the old town center and the castle, scene of the romance between Dante's Paolo and Francesca.

After a short stop in the vil-

ABOVE, stop along the panoramic road. PAGE OPPOSITE, view of Gabicce Mare.

Technical info

Route

48 Km on asphalt road:
Gabicce Mare - Gradara –
Monteluro di Tavullia -
Tre Ponti - Case Bruciate –
Pesaro Fiera - Baia Flaminia-
Santa Maria Alta - Fiorenzuola
di Focara - Casteldimezzo -
Gabicce Mare.

Difficulty

This is not a difficult route but, although there are no steep climbs, the rolling altitude profile requires good basic training. The more challenging stretches are the first 4 km along the panoramic road from the port of Pesaro, and the climb that reaches Gabicce Monte from Baia Vallugola (approximately 2 km).

Cycling period

All year round.

Bicycle + Train

The starting point and finish

and part of the itinerary develop along the Ancona-Rimini railroad line.

Technical assistance

Cicli Moroncelli,
via Verdi 6, Gabicce Mare;
t. 0541958056.
Sale, rental and specialized workshop.

Tourist information

• IAT Gabicce Mare,
viale della Vittoria 41,
Gabicce Mare; t. 0541954424,
fax 0541953500.
iat.gabicce@regione.marche.it

• Pro Loco Gradara,
piazza V Novembre 1,
Gradara;
t. 0541964115,
fax 0541823035.
proloco.gradara@provincia.ps.it

• Marche Turismo,
viale Trieste 164, Pesaro;
t. 072169341.
iat.pesaro@regione.marche.it

lage, get back on the main road and climb up towards Tavullia. The route now climbs steadily for about 5 km; the gradients are not too tough, although the last kilometer may be quite difficult. Just before the climb ends, at Monteluro, reach a crossroads, where you turn left following the road signs for Pesaro; this is where the descent starts towards the hamlets of Tre Ponti, Case Bruciate and Babbucce. Watch out on this stretch, since some sections of the asphalt road are quite bumpy. At the end of this stretch, you meet the main road in the Pesaro Fiera area, where you turn left towards the town center. You now enter the city of Pesaro: follow the road signs leading to the port or to Baia Flaminia. This stretch, up to Baia Flaminia, is the only part where you have to

POINTS OF INTEREST

*For people who adore spending their holidays on a bike, the right contact is **Bike & Sport Hotels Regione Marche** t. 0541 831838, www.bikesporthotels.com, an association formed by hotels and specialized in cycle touring. The associated facilities offer a broad range of services tailored to guests who spend their vacations on a saddle. There is also the possibility of going out on excursions together with expert guides, and receiving detailed information on the local routes.*

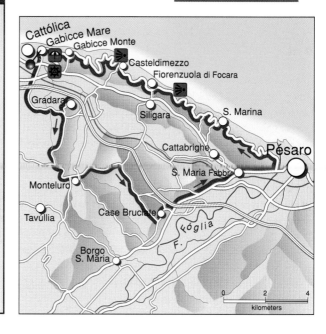

watch out for traffic. The panoramic road of Mount San Bartolo (approximately 25 km) starts from Baia Flaminia. This road ends exactly at Gabicce Monte, so it's easy to follow without taking the wrong directions. Now it's a rolling route, with never too challenging up and downhill stretches, crossing a magnificent natural environment. You ride immersed in nature, halfway between the green trees and the blue sea, crossing the small towns of Santa Maria Alta, Fiorenzuola and Casteldimezzo, where time has come to a standstill, with spectacular panoramic views high on the sea level.

At Casteldimezzo, the Bellavista restaurant is a traditional refreshment spot for local cyclists and cycle tourists. We also suggest a stop to visit the small old town center of Fiorenzuola di Focara, with its gardens overhanging the sea. Once you reach **Gabicce Monte**, the wonderful panoramic road is now behind you, so get ready for the pleasant downhill stretch towards the sea of the Riviera.

Umbria

 ## The Umbria Valley 24 Km
Along the water path

A nice ride along the course of the Marroggia torrent up to the Fonti del Clitunno.

Leave the town center of **Foligno** through Porta Firenze and continue along via XVI Giugno, heading towards the football pitch, up to the San Magno bridge.

After crossing the bridge, turn right, heading towards Montefalco, then cross the hamlet of Corvia and reach Torre di Montefalco (6.4 km from the starting point). Just before the bridge over the Marroggia torrent, take on your left the road that runs along the banks of the

river. After 3.4 km, turn left, leaving the river towards Casevecchie. Once you cross the bridge over the Clitunno, take on your right the dirt road that follows the watercourse. After passing by the trap shooting circle of Foligno and the hamlet of Casco dell'Acqua, continue

Technical info

Route
24 Km (18.5 Km asphalt, 5.5 Km dirt road): Foligno - Montefalco Tower - Borgo Trevi - Campello sul Clitunno. On by-roads.

Difficulty
Very easy, completely flat, ideal also for families with children along.

Bicycle + Train
The area is crossed by the Terontola-Foligno and Ancona-Rome stretches. You can go back by train from Campello sul Clitunno, catching the regional trains that also offer bicycle transport.

For information:
Foligno Railroad Station, t. 0742350730.

Cycling period
All year round.

Map
IGM map, 1:50,000 and/or 1:100,000, Foligno.

Road map
Daniele Poletti, *Foligno in mountain bike - 10 itinerari nei dintorni della città*, Edicit. Edited in conjunction with Azimut Mountain Biking, via dei Villini 24, Foligno; t. 074223168, 074340170.

Technical assistance
• Cicli Battistelli,

via XX Settembre 88, Foligno; t. 0742344059.
• Cicli Clementi, via XVI Giugno 36, Foligno; t. 074223085.
• Perfection Bikes Campana, via Verdi, Campello sul Clitunno; t. 0743521330.

Bicycle rental
Testi Cicli, strada Trasimeno Ovest 287, Perugia; t. 0755172123.

Tourist information
IAT Folignate, Porta Romana 126, Foligno; t. 0742781150.

POINTS OF INTEREST

*The **Azzano Tower** is an old rural structure, where you can admire a collection of farming tools used for the olive harvest and crushing (www.seeumbria.com). Also an interesting sight to see is the XVIII century mill where flour is made with artisan techniques: the old watermill with its millstone sets the wooden gears in motion. For information: Forno dell'Antico Mulino, at Torre di Azzano; t. 0743.521396.*

your ride, following the river along the cart-road.

Nearing a farm, get ready to ride on a cattle track, cycling along the river, until you cross the asphalt road at Pietrarossa. At the bridge, turn right, then continue for 400 m up to a road regularly closed to vehicle traffic, where you turn left, riding along the Marroggia torrent. After approximately 800 m, you reach another crossroads near Borgo Trevi. At this point, turn left, and after 500 m, after crossing the bridge over the Clitunno, leave the asphalt road again, turning right along the bank and reaching Faustana. Now ride near the Molino del Clitunno, the Cartiere di Trevi (paper mills) and the washhouses on the river, up to a crossroads (roughly 700 m). At this point, turn left, tak-

ing again the lightly-trafficked road running along the Marroggia torrent.
Follow the track for 3.7 km, without taking detours right up to the end, then turn left (if you turn right, you go towards the Azzano Tower), past the overbridge on the railroad, near the railroad station of Campello sul Clitunno. Continue your ride until you enter the S.S. Flaminia main road at Settecamini, where you turn left, until you reach the nearby Fonti del Clitunno. The itinerary ends near **Tempio del Clitunno**. The way back to Foligno can be covered either by train (from Campello sul Clitunno), or by bicycle: from Tempio, ignore the S.S. Flaminia main road and follow the road signs indicating the pedestrian crossing. After 500 m, near an antiquities shop, cycle downhill towards the right, passing by the Clitunno and taking the underpass that leads to the road you have already covered. To get back to Foligno, follow the bank of the Marroggia up to Montefalco Tower.

RIGHT, the Umbria Valley, the village of Trevi.

Mount Subasio   35 Km
Between Assisi and Spello

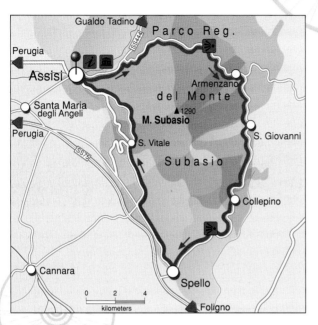

After a couple of kilometers, take the climb (roughly 2 km, average 10% gradient) that requires some effort, then make the hill crossing near the small village of Armenzano (9 km from Assisi). From Armenzano, continue riding at a high altitude, until you reach San Giovanni (3.9 km), where the road starts to gently slope towards the village of Collepino (4 km), a stone jewel and an ideal spot to snack and freshen up. From this moment, you ride along a panoramic downhill stretch immersed in green land, up to Spello (5 km). The place deserves a thorough visit. After the stop, return to the topmost part of the town where, near the Bastiglia hotel, you take the road leading to Assisi.

After crossing a tree-lined avenue on a downhill stretch (a few hundred meters), watch for the forthcoming detour. Take via degli Ulivi on your right, a by-road that

A highly interesting itinerary from a landscape point of view, which develops around the foot of Mount Subasio and penetrates the heart of the mystic side of Umbria, along roads and villages that live a magical solitude.

You start from **Assisi**, fleeing from the gridlock of buses and cars that jam the city of San Francesco. The starting point is the parking lot situated in piazza Matteotti, at the topmost part of Assisi. Leave the town, following the road signs pointing to Gualdo Tadino on the S.S. 444 main

RIGHT, along the Costa di Trek towards Collepino. PAGE OPPOSITE, the village of Spello.

road, and after approximately 1 km, turn right and head towards Collepino. The road climbs immediately and quite sharply, reaching the Costa di Trek (4 km), then stretches along mainly flat ground with slope sections, and follows the winding course of the contour lines.

POINTS OF INTEREST

crosses the foot of Mount Subasio. The road now remains high up. After riding for about 5 km, ignore the crossroads for Capodacqua di Assisi on your left, and continue up to the next crossroads (just before the Malvarina farm holidays), then turn right. Now climb up for 1 km on the steepish dirt road, until you enter another gravel road. Turn left (if you turn right, you reach the Villa Gabbiano farm holidays) and keep on this mid-coast track, ignoring other detours, until you reach the asphalt road for **Assisi** (4.5 km), which climbs up with wide hairpin bends, until you reach the parking lot situated in piazza Matteotti (2 km).

Technical info

Route

35 Km: Assisi - Costa di Trek - Armenzano - San Giovanni - Collepino - Spello - via degli Ulivi - Assisi. Almost entirely on asphalt road with some dirt stretches. It would be preferable to use a mountain bike to easily cross the more challenging stretches and ride better on the dirt roads.

Difficulty

An itinerary with an average difficulty level; some stretches have tough gradients: the first part to Costa di Trek, the uphill climb (1.8 km) to Armenzano

and the final stretch before Assisi. You don't need specific training, but the itinerary is barred to people who are not used to cycling at all.

Cycling period

All year round, although it may be chilly in the winter months.

Map

Atlante stradale d'Italia, Central volume, 1:200,000, TCI.

Technical assistance

• Testi Cicli,
via Trasimeno Ovest 287/289, Olmo;
t. and fax 0755172123.
Rental of MTBs and hybrids

equipped for cycle touring, home delivery and collection service of rented bikes, cycling road books, guides and tour leaders.

• Battistelli Carlo,
via XX settembre 88,
Foligno;
t. 0742344059.
Sale and assistance.

Tourist information

• Azienda Promozione Turistica, piazza del Comune; Assisi,
t. 075812534.

• Pro Loco of Spello,
piazza Matteotti 3;
t. 0742301009.

Between Todi and Orvieto   68 Km
Tour of Mount Peglia

An itinerary that crosses a fascinating landscape between Mount Peglia and the valley of the Faena torrent, brushing villages and places ignored by the great tourist waves.

From **Montecastello di Vibio**, follow the road signs pointing to Doglio: you reach the small village after 8 km and a short uphill stretch. From the village of Doglio, continue your ride towards the Vibio farm, a farm holidays concern marked by road signs. Shortly afterwards, ride on dirt road, and after 3.8 km, you reach the old Orvietana (79 bis), a very beautiful road with a highly varied course and very little motorized traf-

fic. At the crossroads with the old Orvietana, turn left and head towards Orvieto.

After 3.9 km, we suggest the detour on the left towards Titignano, a magnificent village you reach on a dirt road 3.4 km long. From the belvedere, you can admire Lake

Corbara from above. You can benefit from the stop by buying fresh pecorino cheese from Riccifontana, at the Fattoria di Titignano store. Once you're back on the Orvietana, continue riding towards Prodo (7 km), where the road drops and then climbs up shortly after towards Colonnetta (6.3 km). At this point, turn right following the road signs to Marsciano.

The road continues to constantly climb, without tough spurts though, and after 10.2 km, it crosses the hills near Mount Peglia, the highest spot of the itinerary (approximately 800 m).

At this point, ride down towards the hamlet of Ospedaletto (2.2 km). At the crossroads for Ripalvella, turn right and take the wonderful dirt road that drops sharply towards the valley of the Fae-

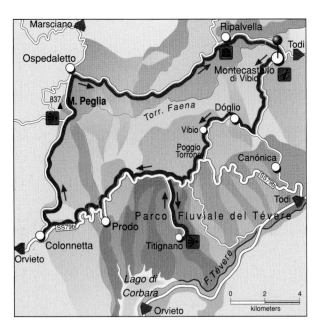

ABOVE, cycling at Doglio.
PAGE OPPOSITE, the Torrone estate at the foot of Mount Peglia.

POINTS OF INTEREST

A trip to Montecastello di Vibio to visit the **Teatro del-la Concordia,** *the smallest theatre in the world, featuring drama, opera, operetta, classical and jazz music concerts. In summer, you can visit the theatre every day (10-12.30 a.m., and 3.30-7 p.m.); from October to June, on Saturdays and Sundays, same timetables; on other days, prior to phone booking, contact the Società del Teatro della Concordia, t. 0758780737, 0758780307.*

Technical info

Route
68 Km: Montecastello di Vibio - Doglio - Titignano - Mount Peglia - Ospedaletto - Ripalvella - Montecastello di Vibio. A third of the route (22.6 km) is on dirt road, so a mountain bike would be the best vehicle, the whole itinerary develops along roads with very little traffic.

Difficulty
The length and rise (approximately 1.1 km) require a discrete physical condition and some basic training. In particular, you must consider the uphill stretch to Mount Peglia, which is never too steep, but pretty lengthy (approximately 13 km), the up and downhill stretches along the gravel road to Riparvella,

and the last challenging climb to Montecastello di Vibio.

Cycling period
All year round.

Map
Atlante stradale d'Italia, Central volume, 1:200,000, TCI.

Technical assistance
• Ruspolini Paolo,
via Cortesi 26, Todi;
t. 0758942030.
Sale and technical assistance.
• Saccarelli Lucio, via Tuderte, Marsciano; t. 0758743421.
Rental, sale and assistance.

Tourist information
• Pro Loco,
piazza del Popolo, Todi;
t. 0758943456, 0758942526.
• APT Tuderte, piazza Umberto I, Todi; t. 0758943395.
• Pro Loco Montecastello,
di Vibio; t. 0758780655.

na torrent. Continue on this downhill stretch for about 5 km, climb up for 900 m, then go mainly downhill for 4 km, before entering the asphalt road near the crossroads for Ripalvella, which you reach after a few meters. Cross the town, riding for about 400 m, and near the nursery school, turn sharply right, following the road signs for Montecastello di Vibio. Soon after, the asphalt road ends, and

after a steep descent, you reach, after about 2.5 km, the bottom of the Valley of the Faena torrent.
This is where the final stretch of the itinerary begins, riding

up on the last climb of 2.4 km, on gravel road, up to the crossroads for **Montecastello di Vibio,** which you reach after 1.3 km, closing the circle and your trip.

Colli Perugini DOC 48 Km
The cashmere and wine path

A small, though grand trip to discover the vineyards that blanket the hills south of Perugia, starting from Solomeo, an enchanting medieval village, recovered and transformed into a factory village, where the famous colored cashmere of Brunello Cucinelli are made.

From **Solomeo**, start your ride leaving the factory behind, along a pleasant downhill stretch towards via Pievolana (S.S. 220 Perugia-Città delle Pieve main road), reaching it after about 3 km. At the junction, turn left, crossing the built-up area of Capanne, then turn right heading towards

Castel del Piano. At this point, turn right, then immediately left to Pila, riding constantly uphill. Just after the built-up area (following the road signs for San Mar-

tino in Colle), we suggest stopping at the Goretti wine-cellars, situated on a natural balcony facing the vineyards of the Colli Perugini Doc and the city of Perugia. Now continue your ride, initially downhill, then upwards, on a not too challenging climb, until you reach San Martino in Colle. At the intersection on the S.S. 317 Perugia-Marsciano main road, turn left, then immediately right towards Torgiano, in the vast Tevere Valley.

At this point, cross the railroad line and the 4-lane S.S. 3 bis Perugia-Terni expressway. After crossing the bridge over the Tevere,

---

Technical info

Route

48 Km: Solomeo - Capanne - Castel del Piano - San Martino in Colle - Torgiano - San Martino in Colle - Sant'Enea - San Biagio della Valle - Capanne - Solomeo.
You can reach the starting point by leaving the Perugia - Bettolle expressway at the Corciano interchange, taking the S.S. 75 bis main road towards Ellera and then Solomeo. You can make the itinerary more interesting by following the "variante" to Deruta, a town famous all

over the world for its pottery and ceramics.

Difficulty

A route of average difficulty, on asphalt roads, no great rises, with a rolling profile, but never too challenging gradients.

Cycling period

All year round.

Map

Atlante stradale d'Italia, Central volume, 1:200,000, TCI.

Technical assistance

Punto Bici
via G. Brodolini 11,
Ellera di Perugia;

t. and fax 0755181293,
0755181295;
www.puntobici.com
Situated along the road to Solomeo just after the Corciano interchange. Technical assistance, sale, technical apparel and accessories, rental of personalized bicycles (road and mountain bikes).

Useful addresses

• Territorial Tourist Service of Perugia, via Mazzini 6, Perugia; t. 0755728937, 0755729842.
• Tourist information piazza IV Novembre 3, Perugia; t. 0755736458.

POINTS OF INTEREST

A visit to the outlet of the **Brunello Cucinelli** *factory of cashmere clothing t. 075827157.*

Visits and wine tasting *in the cellars you meet along the route may be arranged by contacting in advance the following concerns: Goretti at Pila t. 075607316, Lungarotti at Torgiano t. 0759880348, Chiorri at Sant'Enea t. 075607316. At Torgiano: Wine Museum, corso Vittorio Emanuele 11, t. 0759880200; 5,000 years of archaeology, techniques, history and the art of wine. Oil Museum, via Garibaldi 10; t. 0759880300: history, tools and production techniques.*

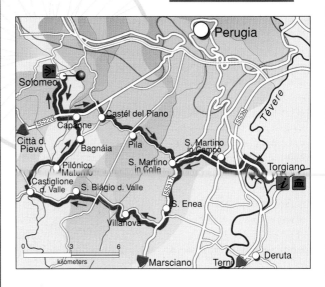

let, you reach an intersection, where you turn left, and immediately after, right, passing by San Biagio della Valle. At the next crossroads, keep right, until reaching Castiglione della Valle. From this point, continue up to Capanne, passing by Pilonico Materno and Bagnaia. At Capanne, go back on the Pievolana main road (S.S. 220), where you turn left, then immediately right, climbing back on the **Solomeo** hill.

you reach Torgiano: welcome to the Umbria capital of wine! A stop should be arranged here to visit the Lungarotti wine-cellars and the Wine and Oil Museums, a true journey to discover the culture of the Umbria territory.

From Torgiano, go back, following the same road up to San Martino in Colle. Continue following the road signs pointing to Marsciano. After approximately 4 km, cross the hamlet of Sant'Enea (Chiorri wine concern) and soon after, turn right on the road leading to Villanova. After crossing the ham-

RIGHT, the countryside at San Martino in Colle. PAGE OPPOSITE, the village of Solomeo.

The Nera river park   12 Km
Between Arrone and Ferentillo

The Nera river park covers the middle-lower section of the river, exactly from the border with the province of Terni, to the confluence with the River Velino, better known as the Marmore Waterfall.

After parking your car at **Arrone**, at the rest area with camper service, start riding on the carriageable road. Just shortly ahead, ride along a crook of the river where the stream is more peaceful. When the season's nice, you can have a refreshing swim here. The road starts climbing, and you'll have to cycle on asphalt road for about 1 km before reaching Palombare. At this point, take a brief stop to freshen up, then turn right, 20 m before the fountain (if in doubt, ask for information from a local villager). After taking the detour, the road becomes a mid-coast carriageable track, curling along cultivated fields, olives and copses, until reaching a crossroads of four gravel roads (2.8 km from the starting point). Here comes the technical stretch of the itinerary, a bumpy descent, cut lengthways by an awkward drainage canal,

Technical info

Route
12 Km: Arrone (rest area) - Palombare - Precetto - Ferentillo - Arrone.
On mixed asphalt and dirt roads. You can reach the starting point by taking the S.S. 209 Valnerina main road from Terni. After the Marmore Waterfall, continue up to km 12 and turn right, following the road signs pointing to Arrone. After crossing the bridge over the River Nera, the first bend on your left (via delle Palombare) takes you to the Trekking Center - Off-Road Cycling School.

Difficulty
The short route makes this itinerary easy and needs no specific training, even though some stretches require quite an effort and some ability when using the mountain bike derailleur.

Cycling period
All year round, preferably in spring in fall.

Map
IGM 138 *Terni serie M691*, edition 5.

Technical assistance
Voglia di Bici di Massarucci, via Oberdan 12, Terni;
t. 0744409769.
Mechanical assistance, sale also of personalized bicycles, cycling apparel and accessories.

Tourist information
• Consorzio Parco Fluviale del Nera, via del Convento 2, Montefranco;
t. 0744389966.
• APT Terni - Tourist territorial service, viale C. Battisti 7, Terni;
t. 0744423047.

where it would be wise to ride with caution, or better still, to get off your bike. After 200 m, the downhill stretch ends crossing a smoother gravel road. Now turn right, riding amid cultivated expanses of land. Short uphill stretches alternate with as many downhill parts. Continue riding with no detours among cultivated fields and irrigation canals at the heart of the Nera river park,

POINTS OF INTEREST

Trekking Center – Off-Road Cycling School, *via delle Palombare, Arrone; t. 0744 287686, cell. 380 3088533; www.cuoreverde.com/blob/.* *The Blob Service association provides information on path conditions, weather forecasts, route cards, guided outings, bicycle rental, MTB school, summer camps for children from eight years old onwards, tourist packages for the weekend or for the whole week.*

where you can spot pheasants, greenfinches, hawks, squirrels, weasels and badgers. Shortly after, get back on asphalt road on a gentle ascent to the drinking trough at Precetto, a typical medieval village that is worth a visit. Return on the carriageable road opposite the drinking trough that leads to the Ferentillo cemetery. The road initially drops, then constantly climbs. At the top of the climb, leave the carriageable road and take the level cart-road on your right in a panoramic spot.

The road covered by vegetation shortly ahead branches off: take the right side downhill and continue down to the house of the "Inglesi", where the road ends. Now turn right on a very steep and bumpy downhill stretch for a

short leg (100 m), which perhaps you should better cover on foot. At the end of the descent, on your right, take the cart-road that ends at a crossroads. Turn left, continuing on the main road with no detours. Now get back on

the dirt road you have already covered, up to the crossroads with the carriageable road leading to Palombare. Proceed downhill on your right, and after passing the crook of the river, reach the starting point at **Arrone**.

ABOVE, cycling towards Ferentillo.
PAGE OPPOSITE, the Valnerina.

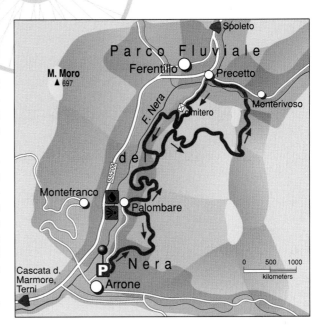

🚴 Via Appia Antica   16 Km
🚆 Cycling at the heart of Rome

A journey into the history of Rome along the "regina viarum", riding amid mausoleums, sepulchers, villas, marble stelae, all traces of a far-off past. This is an out-of-town trip (without crossing the beltway), near in space, though distant in time, immersed in the wealth of an exceptional monumental road and its remarkable landscape and archaeological value.

You start your tour from **porta San Sebastiano**, riding along the via Appia Antica, whose urban stretch corresponds to the present-day Terme di Caracalla and porta San Sebastiano roads. After cycling under the bridges of the ring road and railroad, pass by the Quo Vadis Church, opposite the crossroads with the Ardeatina, and further ahead, the entrance to the San Callisto catacombs. After leaving the Appia Pignatelli on your left, start riding on a straight stretch, along which you can admire the San Sebastiano

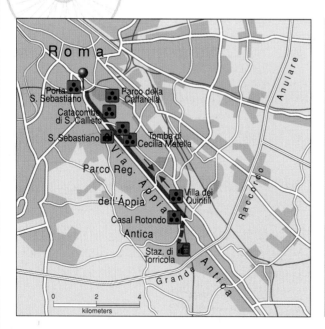

POINTS OF INTEREST

The itinerary offers many opportunities to visit places that are very important from a historical-archaeological point of view. Like the **San Callisto catacombs** *(open 9 -12 a.m. and 2.30- 5.00 p.m., closed on Wednesday). The* **San Sebastiano catacombs** *(9-12 a.m. and 2.30-5.00 p.m., closed on Thursday). The* **Massenzio circus**, *which can be visited upon request, t. 066710 2070. The* **Cecilia Metella mausoleum** *(9.00 a.m.-1.30 p.m., closed on Monday).*

Technical info

Route

16 Km: porta San Sebastiano - via delle Terme di Caracalla - San Callisto catacombs - San Sebastiano catacombs - Massenzio circus - Cecilia Metella mausoleum - Villa dei Quintili - Casal Rotondo. The starting point is situated near the Aurelia walls and the San Sebastiano gate in via Cristoforo Colombo.

Difficulty

The rise is irrelevant and the itinerary may be covered also by families with children along. The basalt surface of some stretches is not suitable for road or touring bikes with narrow tires.

Cycling period

All year round, preferably during the holidays to avoid heavier traffic. Wednesday must be ruled out when the San Callisto catacombs are closed.

Map

Atlante stradale d'Italia, Central volume, 1:200,000, TCI: with map of Rome 1:80,000.

Bicycle + Train

Roughly two kilometers from Casal Rotondo, you meet the Torricola railroad station along the Rome-Nettuno line.

Technical assistance

F.lli Lazzaretti, via Bergamo 3/A-B, Rome; t. 068553828.

Tourist information

• Parco Regionale dell'Appia Antica, via Appia Antica 42, Rome; t. 0051203014, 0051300082. www.parks.it/parco.appia.antica/

• APT, Municipality of Rome, via Parigi 11, Rome; t. 0648899214. www.romaturismo.com

• Municipality of Rome, Call Center; t. 06421381.

---

basilica and catacombs. This is where the most interesting part of the itinerary starts. On your left, the Massenzio circus, one of the most important circuses in ancient Rome, once the scene of chariot races. Its visit offers peculiar views of walls and hay bales on the great arena. After a short climb, you reach the tomb of Cecilia Metella, a cylindrical mausoleum, one of the most famous in the Roman world, built to preserve the mortal remains of the noble Cecilia, daughter-in-law of Crassus, who formed the famous Triumvirate with Caesar and Pompey (don't be surprised by the odd posthumous battlements, subsequently added by the Caetani family to transform the mausoleum into a castle). Flanked by secular pines and cypress trees, the road continues its elegant course with sepulchers, marble stelae, sarcophagi, buildings once luxurious, whose sumptuousness can be vaguely made out today in the sections of walls and the scattered architectural fragments. The recent mushrooming of villas, built extensively near the historical road, does not outshine the attractions offered by this ride in time. At the edges of the road, humbled today by the bustle of cars, you can still spot the "crepidines", sidewalks once used by pedestrians. After passing the Curiazi Tomb and the monumental Villa dei Quintili, you reach the great sepulcher called Casal Rotondo, where the most interesting stretch of the road comes to an end and you ride back to return to **porta San Sebastiano**.

LEFT, a stretch of the Via Appia Antica.

The Circeo Park 37 Km
Sand dune crossing

A typical nature ride at the heart of the Circeo National Park, crossing the littoral dune system and the wetlands with their coastal ponds and lakes, the ideal environments for wintering or for the nesting of many a species of migratory birdlife.

From the houses of **Borgo Grappa**, which you easily reach from Sabaudia and Latina, start your ride, following the road signs pointing to the sea. After reaching the crossroads that spans the course of the Martino brook, keep right, riding along the canal where numerous vessels are berthed. Once you reach the sea, follow the

*The Melacotogna Cooperative runs the **Park Visit Center** and organizes guided visits such as the one to the Capre caves and the Villa Fogliano botanical garden. During the summer months, it organizes a baby center at the seat of the Park.*

For information: Melacotogna Cooperative, via Carlo Alberto, Sabaudia; t. 0773511206, 0773691695. A sight to see at Sabaudia is the Sea and Coast Museum, t. 0773511340 and the Nature Museum at the Park Visit Center.

Technical info

Route
37 Km: Borgo Grappa - bridge over the Martino brook - Lake Fogliano - Lido di Capo Portiere - Borgo Grappa - Capo d'Omo roadman's house – Lake Caprolace – Lake Monaci - bridge over the Martino brook - Borgo Grappa.
Route on asphalt roads, part of them closed to motorized traffic.
The starting point is 10 km away from Latina and 13.5 km from Sabaudia.
Difficulty
No difficulties and virtually no rise, therefore suitable also for cyclists

with little practice and for families.
Cycling period
All year round, preferably in the intermediate seasons, fall and spring and the mild winter days.
Map
Atlante stradale d'Italia, Central volume, 1:200,000, TCI.
Technical assistance
• Cicli Torre,
via G. Antonelli 71, Terracina;
t. 0773724611.
Also rental at Sabaudia by:
• Mauro Zicchieri,
corso Vittorio Emanuele II;
t. 0773517383, 3392788502.
• L'Angolo della Bici,

via Emanuele Filiberto 5;
t. 0773517336.
• Giuseppe Aquino,
via Duca della Vittoria 43;
t. 0773510489.
• CG 67,
corso Vittorio Emanuele II
t. 0773515290.
Tourist information
• Centro Visite del Parco Nazionale del Circeo,
via Carlo Alberto, Sabaudia;
t. 0773511385-6
www.parks.it/parco.nazionale.circeo/
• APT Latina,
via Duca del Mare 19, Latina;
t. 0773695404-7.
www.aptlatinaturismo.it

coastal road that stretches between the coast and Lake Fogliano, the biggest lake in the Circeo (over 395 hectares). Just beyond a few palms, the brackish waters host fish farming activities, especially for mullets and eels. The birds you can easily spot the most are cormorants that flock by the hundreds in the area and perch on the wooden stakes emerging from the waters. Ride along the last strip of the lake, along the road that turns right towards Latina, then right again to pass on the other side of the river. From this road, the lake is no longer visible since your ride takes you far away from the bank.

If you wish, you can reach the lake by taking a detour on your right and following the road that takes you to Villa Fogliano, near a buffalo farming.

Once you're back on the coastal road, ride for approximately 12 km, passing by Borgo Grappa, until you reach the detour on your right, at the Capo d'Omo roadman's house. Just before the sea and a double curve, ride along the Pantani dell'Inferno wetlands, a highly interesting birdlife spot. Get your binoculars out, because this is the most interesting birdwatching place in the entire Circeo Park, where you can easily spot stilt-birds, glossy ibises, storks, spoonbills, purple herons and mullets.

After reaching the coast, on your right, pass the car ring-fence and start riding at ease on the dunes, amid juniper bushes and the green patterns of the sour figs. On your right, Lake Caprolace still offers you the opportunity to birdwatch. The final stretch of the itinerary develops along the small (95 hectares) Lake Monaci. The road then crosses the car ring-fence and turns right, where you follow the Martino brook, then shortly get back to the bridge, closing the circle and your tour at **Borgo Grappa**.

LEFT, the Park's information board.
PAGE OPPOSITE, buffalo farming at Villa Fogliano.

The Ponza island
From the port to Punta d'Incenso

17 Km

Isola di Ponza

Cala Fonte
Piana d'Incenso
Isolotto di Gavi
Punta d'Incenso
Cala del Gaetano
Forna Chiesa
Forna Grande
Campo Inglese
Faraglioni di Lucia Rosa
Conti
Santa Maria
Giancos
Punta C.Bianco
Guarini
Baia di Chiaia di Luna
S.Antonio
Gli Scotti
Ponza
Mad. d. Civita
Scarrupata
Faraglioni del Calzone Muto
Punta della Guardia

I. Palmarola   I. Zannone
Isole Ponziane
I. di Ponza
Mar Tirreno   I. Ventotene

0   1   2
kilometers

A magnificent ride on the ridge of the largest of the Ponza islands, which becomes an oasis of peace during the off-seasons, to explore entirely by bicycle.

From the **port of Ponza**, follow the coast up to the Sant'Antonio beach. After the news-stand, take the first curve on your left. The road starts gently climbing, and shortly afterwards, you reach the belvedere that faces the majestic tuff wall of the bay of Chiaia di Luna. At this point, ride along the wonderful road known as the "Panoramica" (scenic road) which, after passing Guarini and after a wide

hairpin bend on your left, overlooks Chiaia di Luna again from up above. The "Panoramica" continues on the western side of the island reaching, after 3.6 km, the junction with the Ponza-

Le Forna direct route. After a good 1 km, you reach the highest spot of the itinerary near Campo Inglese. From this point, you can enjoy a superb view on the Palmarola island and on the Lucia Rosa stacks. From Campo Inglese, the road drops, and after 1.8 km, you reach Le Forna, a built-up area with a scrambled layout, developing up to the end of the road that finishes just after the sports field, at the Gaetano creek. Besides a possible detour at the Fonte creek, the itinerary can be completed with a short walk (about 30 minutes) in one of the most panoramic spots on the island.

The excursion starts at the end of the carriageable road, approximately 500 m after the sports field and the Da Angelino restaurant. The track starts climbing up

Technical info

Route

17 Km: Ponza Porto - Sant'Antonio beach - Campo Inglese - Le Forna - I Conti - Santa Maria - Giancos - Sant'Antonio - Ponza Porto.
Entirely on asphalt roads that cut the island lengthways. Besides the ride, the itinerary is integrated with short walks (Cala Fonte and Incenso plain).

Difficulty

Itinerary with no particular difficulty. The most challenging stretches are the "Panoramica" road between Ponza and Campo Inglese (4.9 km and 174 m rise), and on the way back, the climb from Le Forna to Campo Inglese

(2.2 km and 175 m rise); anyhow, if you cover these climbs with an MTB or touring bike with triple gear ratio, you can pull it off easily.

Cycling period

All year round, except for the peak summer months (July and August), when the island is really crowded and the roads are busier. Ideal in spring and late fall.

Bicycle + Boat

You can reach the island from Anzio: hydrofoils and motorships with car transport (only in summer); from Formia by ferry boat and hydrofoil; from Terracina by ferry boat and from San Felice Circeo (only in summer) by ferry boat.

Technical assistance

Tuttociclo, via Tacito 13, Formia;
t. 0771267608.

Tourist information

• Pro Loco,
Ponza Porto;
t. 077180031.
• Agenzia Helios, Anzio: information and reservation for ferry boats and hydrofoils from the port of Anzio;
t. 069845085, 069848320.
• Caremar, port of Formia;
t. 0771461600, 0771800780.
• Traghetti Mazzella Terracina;
t. 0773723979.
• Linee Lauro,
San Felice Circeo;
t. 0773661493, 064828579.

---

the terraced hill appearing opposite.

Actually, there are two tracks (the one on the left is less steep) and both lead, after 15 minutes, to the Incenso plain. After reaching

the plain, continue riding high up, until reaching Punta d'Incenso, clearly visible from up above with the Gavi islet.

Go back on foot up to the road, following the same track, and once you're back on your bike, ride back, following the same road you have already covered, up to the Campo Inglese area: after reaching the crossroads with the "Panoramica", turn left and go downhill, passing by I Conti, up to Santa Maria and the Giancos beach.

Now continue riding towards Sant'Antonio, just a stone's throw away from the **port**.

POINTS OF INTEREST

The ramble to the **Guardia Lighthouse**, *which can be reached from the port along the path that climbs up to the Scotti. After 600 m, at the crossroads, turn left towards the Madonna della Civita, then continue on the path (1 km) along the Scarrupata, a tuff wall covered with maquis facing the stacks of the Calzone Muto, up to Punta della Guardia with its lighthouse. Go back to the port by following the same track.*

LEFT, the small port of Cala Fonte. PAGE OPPOSITE, stop at Punta d'Incenso.

Lake Bracciano   36 Km
Classic ride along the banks

The tour of Lake Bracciano is a classic ride that allows you, especially during the off-season, to spend a day immersed in the peaceful villages and countryside facing the great spaces of the old volcano that fell asleep 100,000 years ago. Contrary to common belief, its basin was never a real crater, but formed itself after a series of faults (fractures of the earth crust with horizontal, in this case vertical, displacement of the two surfaces) that caused its cave-in. The lake has a virtually circular shape and its diameter, between the two banks, measures up to 9 km.

Your circumnavigation starts from **Bracciano**, the largest and most important town facing the lake. The place is surely worth a visit. Between the alleys and the houses stuck one to the other, magnificent panoramic views open up on the lake. After riding down to the bank, start cycling towards Anguillara Sabazia (approximately 10 km), passing by Vigna di Valle. Anguillara appears after a few kilometers, amid the trees of the lakefront, lying on a promontory that emerges beyond a small quay. The origin of the name seems to be foregone, given the overflowing quantity of eels populating the waters of the lake; instead historians believe that the name comes from the position of the built-up area in a "corner" of the bank. Atop, you can clearly spot the profile of the collegiate Church of the Assunta, dating back to the XVIII century, and at its foot, the usual web of alleys and houses, now increasingly inhabited by foreigners.

The road now continues with a series of curves towards Trevignano (12 km). Before reaching the village,

Technical info

Route
36 Km: Bracciano - Vigna di Valle - Anguillara Sabazia - Trevignano Romano - Vicarello spa - Bracciano.
Entirely on asphalt roads.
The difficulty
The route is quite easy and ideal for everyone.
Cycling period
All year round. During the summer season, especially during weekends, the roads may be busier, so keep a closer eye on the road when cycling.
Bicycle + Train
The Bracciano railroad station is situated along the Rome-Viterbo line.
Map
Atlante stradale d'Italia, Central volume, 1:200,000, TCI.
Technical assistance
Tecnobike, via Anguillarese 22,

Anguillara Sabazia;
t. 069996741.
Tourist information
• Municipal Tourist Office, piazza IV Novembre 5, Bracciano:
Tuesday-Saturday 9 a.m.-1.00 p.m. and 3-5 p.m., Sunday 10-12 a.m.;
t. 0699840062, 0699840085.
www.comunedibracciano.it
• Parco dei Laghi di Bracciano e Martignano, via A. Saffi 4/A, Bracciano;
t. 0699806261-2.
www.parks.it/parco.bracciano.martignano/
• Motonave Sabazia, Bracciano: trip around he lake in the summer period, with berthing at Bracciano, Anguillara and Trevignano;
t. 0699805462, 0667667115.

POINTS OF INTEREST

The visit to the **Orsini-Odescalchi castle**, *dominating, with its cylindrical towers, the trachyte cliff on which Bracciano lies. Inside you can visit the courtyards, armories and halls decorated with important period furnishings; visits: 9 a.m.-1 p.m. and 3-6 p.m. (winter 9-12 a.m. and 3-5 p.m.), closed on Monday; t. 0690 24451.* **Historical Museum of the Air Force**, *at Vigna di Valle: set up in three hangars on the banks of Lake Bracciano, it hosts 60 aircraft and engines, interesting relics from the origins up to the present day; visits: 9 a.m.-6 p.m. (winter 9 a.m.-3 p.m.), closed on Monday; t. 069023975.*

ride along a small strip of bank overgrown with canes, protected by a nature reserve run by the municipality and the province. The village's main feature is the XVI century Church of the Assunta, situated just under the ruins of the fortress of the Orsini, once masters of these lands. After Bracciano, often surrounded by fog on the opposite bank, your next and final stage is the Vicarello spa, which you reach after riding along the wooded elevation of Mount Rocca Romana. In this point and in other points of the bank, such as the one that follows Anguillara Sabazia, it's easier to spot the volplane of red kites, birds of prey with a dark profile and forked tail that usually populate the lake.

The last stretch of the circle still continues by crossing a wonderful section of countryside, firstly downhill, then uphill, until you complete the tour that ends at **Bracciano**, starting point of your nice ride.

Above, the Orsini castle.
Page opposite, Bracciano Park, Martignano. Lake Bracciano.

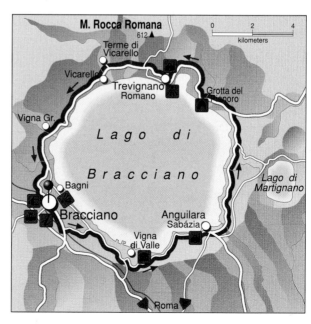

Lake Vico
Cycling through the woods

30 Km

This ride offers you the charms of Nature around Lake Vico, virtually surrounded by beech-tree, oak and chestnut woods. The lake expanse occupies the old crater of the Cimino volcano, active already 4.5 million years ago and still today the source of energy of the numerous thermomineral springs existing in the area. The lake has a horseshoe shape due to the formation of a small volcanic cone (Mount Venere) emerging after the volcano's last eruptive phase on the northern bank. Legend has it that Lake Vico originated from the club that Hercules drove into the ground to challenge the local inhabitants; nobody managed to eradicate it. When Hercules did, out came a deluge of water that filled the valley, thus forming the lake.

The itinerary starts from the small village of **Ronciglione**. Ride uphill and reach the edge of the crater, then ride down on a steep descent along the banks of the lake, where you turn

right, reaching the Bella Venere restaurant. From this point, on your right, starts a track that leads you to the Fontanile Grande, where you can continue on foot, following a path in the wood until you reach the top of Mount Venere (approximately one and a half hours there and back).

Once you're back on your bicycle, return on the bank of the lake, riding on level ground near the camping area of the Nature Reserve and of the Horse Center. Now ride along the Pantanacce marsh, an ideal spot for some interesting birdwatching through the slits of a reed hide looking directly onto the lake, a wonderful opportunity to watch mallards, teals, herons and marsh harriers. Just further

ahead, ride in the shade of chestnut trees, and after passing a crossroads, proceed uphill reaching the edge of the crater. At this point, turn left, following the ridge along the wide dirt road that offers beautiful panoramic views, curling amid lush beech trees along the shaded slopes of Mount Fogliano.

At the end of the downhill stretch, go back on asphalt road to the hamlet of Casaletto. Turn left, and at the next crossroads, left again to emerge back on the lake. Now ride, following the bank and passing Punta del Lago up to the crossroads on your right towards **Ronciglione**, which you reach after crossing the edge of the crater.

The circumnavigation of

ABOVE, Ronciglione, view.
PAGE OPPOSITE, Lake Vico, birdwatching at the Pantanacce.

the lake crosses most of the Regional Nature Reserve, created in 1982 and stretching over 3,240 hectares. The southern side of the basin is not included in the protected area, where anthropization is greater.

Technical info

Route
30 Km: Ronciglione – Lake Vico - Camping Natura - Pantanacce marsh – Mount Fogliano - Casaletto - Punta del Lago - Ronciglione. Mixed asphalt, dirt terrain (easily rideable).

Difficulty
Not too many difficulties on this itinerary. The only challenge is the uphill climb to Mount Fogliano, but this can be avoided by following the tour of the lake and riding along the perimeter, instead of riding up the road that crosses the ridge of the crater.

Bicycle + Train
Ronciglione, starting point and destination of the itinerary, is situated along the railroad axis that connects Orte to the Rome-Viterbo line.

Map
Atlante Stradale d'Italia, Central volume, 1:200,000, TCI.

Technical assistance
• Ranaldi, via Garbini 66, Viterbo;
t. 0761340865, 0761346626.
• Tomi, piazza Vittorio Veneto 8, Viterbo; t. 0761220169.

Tourist information
•Riserva Naturale Lago di Vico,

viale Regina Margherita 2, Caprarola.
Guided trips on foot, by bicycle and on horseback; rental of bicycles, canoes and sailing boats; school camps for children; t. 0761647444, 0761647864.
www.parks.it/riserva.lago.vico/
• Camping Natura, c/o Riserva Naturale Lago di Vico;
t. 0761612347, 335377572, 3356527123.
• APT Viterbo,
piazza Oratorio 1,
San Martino al Cimino;
t. 0761573455.

Tuscia: from Selva del Lamone to the Castro ruins   25 Km

The Castro territory, in the Tuscia area, is a corner of Upper Latium where Nature and the environment are still virtually unspoilt.

After leaving your car in the parking lot outside the castle walls of **Farnese**, perched high up on a tufa spur, the itinerary starts with a gentle uphill stretch towards the north-east and towards Ischia di Castro. Just outside the town, after approximately 500 m, you reach a fork, near which stands a small old church; now take the road on your left, following the road signs pointing to Latera. The road drops gently for 2 km and must be covered right up to the end, where you take a gravel road on your left. A road sign indicates Il Voltone: this path leads you directly into the heart of the Selva del Lamone.

After about 3 km, once you reach the edge of the wood, you find the road signs of the nature reserve that stretches on a plateau of volcanic origin. Entering the reserve, ride on a track about 10 km long, which crosses the entire Selva del Lamone on a constant gentle downhill stretch. After exiting the Selva, take the asphalt road linking Farnese and Pitigliano, then turn right. After approximately 2 km, you reach an intersection, where you turn left to Manciano; after 500 m, the road sign indicates the Castro ruins.

Now take the path on your left and arrive in front of a church with a crucifix. You continue along the path that leads to the Castro ruins. The lush vegetation fortunately does not entirely conceal the capitals and architraves of the XVI century town. After getting back to the crucifix, a gravel path facing south leads directly to the necropolis of the Etruscan Castro. This is the site where a chariot was discovered in a magnificent tomb, and close by, outside the "dromos" (passage), the bones of the two horses that used to pull it. Along the track, you pass near a "colombaio" (a differ-

POINTS OF INTEREST

The **Valentano Museum** *in the Farnese fortress, t. 0761 420018, dedicated to the prehistoric times of Tuscia and of the Castro territory. The museum has an interesting collection of ceramics dating back to the XIV-XV centuries, gathered in an appropriate room. The* **Ischia di Castro Museum,** *t. 0761 425400, with frescoes of the Poggio Conte hermitage and the numerous findings of both the Etruscan necropolis and of the medieval city of Castro. The* **Farnese Museum,** *t. 0761458741: currently hosted in the town hall, gathers relics from the archaeological site at the Sorgenti della Nova and the ceramics of the wells inside the Farnese Palace.*

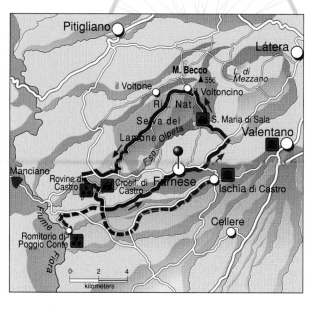

50 m). This fascinating landscape is connected to a route which is marked and well-kept. After one kilometer, you reach a crossroads, where you turn left and return to **Farnese** (6 km).

ALTERNATIVE

At the last abovementioned crossroads, you can continue straight ahead to Ischia di Castro (10 km).

Otherwise, you can go right towards the hermitage of Poggio Conte along the River Fiora, then continue towards Ponte San Pietro and go back on asphalt road (12 km) to Farnese.

Technical info

Route

Approximately 25 Km

(35 Km with the alternative towards Ponte San Pietro):
Farnese - Selva del Lamone - Castro - La Via Cava - Farnese. On mixed asphalt, dirt route to be covered by mountain bike.

Difficulty

Rolling route with an average difficulty level, plus a few short stretches on foot (50 m): the cave road and the Poggio Conte hermitage.

Cycling period

All year round.

Notes

During the summer season, it would be wise for you to start the ride with plenty of water in your flask, given the difficulty in finding places where you can top off your water supply; also bring gadfly repellents along.

Tourist information

• Archeobike di Ennio Soldini, via Valverde 80, Tarquinia; t. 0766840123, cell. 3392409689. www.archeobike.it
Bicycle outings along the most beautiful and undiscovered roads of Tuscia; Ennio Soldini, the expert guide, organizes great itineraries where it's virtually impossible to find your bearings alone.

• APT Viterbo, Palazzo Doria Pamphili, piazza dell'Oratorio 1, San Martino al Cimino; t. 07613751.

• Information Office, piazza San Carluccio, Viterbo; t. 0761304795.

ent kind of tomb). After reaching the Olpeta torrent, pass the remains of a medieval bridge (an easy ford on tufaceous surface) and follow a flagstone road up to a trail of a quarry dug in the tuff (you go on foot for

ABOVE, Etruscan ruins in the Selva del Lamone.
PAGE OPPOSITE, near the Voltone.

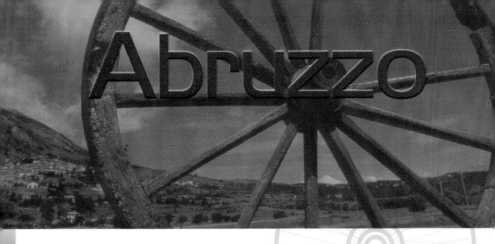

The National Park of Abruzzo   17.5 Km
A trip around Lake Barrea

This ride takes place entirely in one of the most beautiful areas of the National Park of Abruzzo, the first Italian park established in 1922. Lake Barrea is an artificial lake (created in 1950), but in a distant past, it was a natural basin that discharged its waters, opening a gap between the rocks that today form a canyon known as La Foce di Barrea.

The itinerary starts from **Civitella Alfedena**, where it would be worthwhile to stop and visit the Wolf Museum. Nearby, a path leads to the faunal area, where you can have the chance to view different pairs of wolves in their natural habitat. Now follow the road signs pointing to Villetta Barrea, which you easily reach along a downhill stretch of approximately 2.5 km. Cross the town and go right (road signs for Barrea) along the S.S. 83 Marsicana main road that flanks the lake. After approximately 5 km, pass

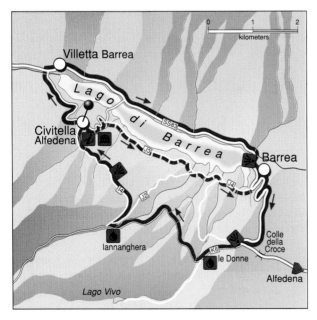

ABOVE, Abruzzo Park, view of the lake from the K6 road.

POINTS OF INTEREST

In Barrea lives **Pasetta**, *aka Tommaso D'Amico*, an expert on this land and descendant of a generation of "lupari", mountain people specialized in defending the flocks from the attack of wolves and of other wild animals. Today he manages the La Genziana di Barrea camping site (t. 086488101, www.cam pinglagenziana-pasetta.it), specialized in the accommodation of cyclists and trekkers.

Technical info

Route
17 Km (10 km on asphalt, 7 Km on dirt road): Civitella Alfedena - Villetta Barrea - Barrea - Strada K6 - Iannanghera spring - Strada I4 - Civitella Alfedena.

Difficulty
The road is short, but you need a mountain bike to cover the dirt stretch that has a short, but challenging climb (start of the K6), and winds along a trail that may be difficult after heavy showers. The climbs on asphalt road (total of 3.2 km) are rideable.

Cycling period
From May to October.

Map
Parco Nazionale d'Abruzzo, tourist map, 1:50,000, Ente Parco Nazionale d'Abruzzo.

Road map
Duilio Roggero, *Mountain Bike nel Parco Nazionale d'Abruzzo*, Il Lupo & Co. 20 itineraries and bicycle-trekking with maps and altitudes.

Technical assistance
Neri Sport House

via Prato delle Corte 1, Pescasseroli; t. 0863910796. Bicycle rental.

Tourist information
• Centro Visitatori Parco Nazionale d'Abruzzo, via S. Lucia, Civitella Alfedena; t. 0864890141. www.parks.it/parco.nazionale. abruzzo
• Agenzia Wolf, via Nazionale, Civitella Alfedena; t. 0864890360. Booking and tourist service.
• Pinus Nigra, via Virgilio 145, Civitella Alfedena; t. 086489141. Tourist service.
• La Betulla piazza Plebiscito, Civitella Alfedena; t. 0864890215. Tourist service cooperative.
• Ecotur, via Piave 7, Pescasseroli; t. 0863912760. www.ecotur.org Tourist service, trekking.

---

the Diavolo bridge, riding on the dam facing the deep narrow valley of the Foce. From the bridge, start climbing on switchbacks, reaching Barrea after 2 km (1,066 m above sea level). Continue riding towards Colle della Croce-Alfedena, up to a narrow hairpin bend on your left (1.2 km from Barrea). At this point, the K6 dirt road starts on your right. The first stretch (1 km) has a very tough ascent. Soon after, you meet the Donne spring (at the edge of the road) and the path on your left (K5) that climbs up to Lake Vivo. Another 3 km along the K6 and you reach the Iannanghera spring. After fording the stream and covering 300 m uphill, take the I4 path that runs high up, and be careful not to take the J2 that drops down steeply towards the lake. The road now narrows and becomes an easily rideable path that

follows the profile of a natural balcony with a stunning view on the lake. The final kilometer to **Civitella Alfedena** has a bumpy surface, so we suggest covering it on foot, due to the presence of shifted stones that may cause problems to tire grip.

ALTERNATIVE
For dirt road enthusiasts, you

can ride along the lake by avoiding the asphalt road. From Civitella Alfedena, ride down towards the lake (not towards Villetta Barrea), and shortly before the bridge that crosses the lake, turn right on the J3 dirt road (after 2.3 km, it becomes J4) that follows the lake bank up to Barrea.

🚲 The National Park of Sirente Velino 21.3 Km
The Rocche Plateau

At the heart of Abruzzo, the Velino and Sirente massifs border a vast expanse named the Rocche plateau, famous for its karstic tableland, rocky ridges, beechwoods and stone villages.

The itinerary starts from the built-up area of **Rovere**, at 1,432 m, the oldest village in the plateau, at the foot of the Sirente mountain range. Exit the town, following the road signs pointing to L'Aquila. After the first 700 m downhill with wide bends, you reach a more rectilinear stretch of road on apparently flat ground that allows you to enjoy the enchanting scenario: an expanse of grassland surrounded by a crown of mountains. After 2.3 km, you reach the centre

BELOW, the village of Rovere in sunset light. PAGE OPPOSITE, road sign in the Park.

of the built-up area of Rocca di Mezzo (1,329 m above sea level). At the bottom of the main square, take the street on your right and follow the signs for Terranera, passing in front of a church and the cemetery to enter the level provincial road. Just after 4 km, a short spurt of about 100 meters takes you to the town of Terranera.

Continue following the road signs for L'Aquila. At this stage of the itinerary, you have two options. First option: turn left and head towards Rocca di Cambio, along a rectilinear road on apparently flat ground that offers you a panoramic spot with benches on the plateau; after 4 km, you reach the S.S. 5 bis main road at Rocca di Cambio. The second is a

good option for the more trained cyclists. After Terranera, follow the road signs indicating L'Aquila, and on a good road surface and gentle uphill climb, pass near Fontavignone, then with a series of narrow bends, reach San Martino d'Ocre. In this stretch of the itinerary, the panorama changes: the view sweeps the Aterno Valley, with the profiles of the majestic Gran Sasso massif clearly visible on the background.

After crossing the built-up area of San Martino d'Ocre, ride uphill for about 4 km, with two final hairpin bends and an average 8% gradient, riding along a road lined with holms and oaks. On an excellent road surface, reach the pass of Rocca di Cambio and enter the S.S. 5 bis main road. The two itineraries join up at this point, and immediately on your right, you

Technical info

Route
21.3 Km: Rovere - Rocca di Mezzo - Terranera - Rocca di Cambio - Rocca di Mezzo - Rovere. On asphalt roads.
36 Km, long alternative:
from Terranera – Fontavignone - San Martino d'Ocre - Rocca di Cambio.
Difficulty
No sweat on this short itinerary, with asphalt roads in good conditions. On the long alternative, the most challenging part is the uphill climb of 4 km, from San Martino d'Ocre to Rocca di Cambio.
Cycling period
From May to October.

Map
Atlante stradale d'Italia, Central volume, 1:200,000, TCI.
Technical assistance
• Capulli Center Bike, Piazza Principe di Piemonte, Rocca di Mezzo; t. 0862917363.
• Marco Sport, Ovindoli; t. 0863705484.
Tourist information
• Pro Loco of Rocca di Mezzo, Largo IV Novembre, Rocca di Mezzo; t. 0862916125. www.roccadimezzo.org
• Ente Parco Sirente-Velino, via degli Orti di Santa Maria, Rocca di Mezzo; t. 0862916343 www.parks.it/ parco.sirente.velino

can see the crossroads to reach the town centre of Rocca di Cambio, at 1,434 m above sea level, one of the highest towns in the entire Apennine.

Cross the built-up area of Rocca di Cambio, passing by via Duca degli Abruzzi, squeezed between the houses and paved with "sampietrini" stones. After a short downhill stretch, enter again, on your right, the S.S. 5 bis main road, following the road signs for Avezzano. A long rectilinear stretch running in the middle of the plateau, after about 2 km, leads you to Rocca di Mezzo, then back to **Rovere**, to close the circle and your ride.

POINTS OF INTEREST

The Rocche plateau is part of the **National Park of Sirente Velino.** *We suggest stopping for a few days to have the opportunity of going on nature excursions to the plains of Pezza, to the Prati or to the Sirente beechwood.* **Rovere** *is the oldest and most suggestive village of the plateau, Rocca di Cambio dates back to the XII century. At Rocca di Mezzo, every year, on the last Sunday of May, the town celebrates the* **Festa del Narciso:** *a parade of floats completely decorated with narcissuses that grow on the plateau.*

Molise

North of Isernia: from 48 Km
Pescolanciano to Agnone

The Upper Molise is a "mountain island" situated in the northern part of the Isernia province. This territory, heart of the Samnite civilization, was a very important part of the millennial tradition of the transhumance, and is today an area of exceptional environmental, historical and artisan value. Agnone,

capital of the upper Molise, is a center known worldwide for bell casting.

You start your ride from **Pescolanciano**, a town situated at 819 m above sea level, and dominated from the year 1000 by the castle of the d'Alessandro dukes. After leaving the built-up area from the

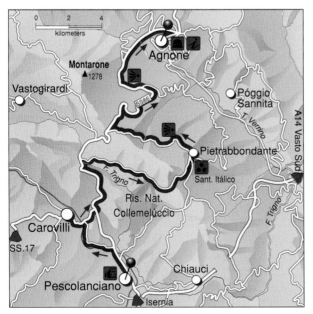

north-western side, just after the La Cona restaurant, you can clearly see the big Castel di Sangro-Lucera cattle road, a grassy trail 111 m wide! A true "green freeway", initially 127 km long, it is one of the most famous roads once used by shepherds for the old transhumance practice. At this point, the track is in perfect conditions and is a well-kept archaeological heritage, as all the cattle roads in Molise. From Pescolanciano, take the S.S. 85 main road towards

Technical info

Route

48 Km: Pescolanciano - Carovilli - Ponte San Mauro - Collemeluccio forest - Pietrabbondante - Agnone. On asphalt roads. You can easily reach the starting point from Isernia (about 15 km). To get back to the starting point, you can go either by bus (Agnone-Pescolanciano line) or you can organize the way back by contacting in advance the Agnone Tourist Center. Special service for cycle tourists is offered by the Masseria Mastronardi dei Maranconi farm holidays (see "tourist information") of Agnone, which organizes the trip back to the starting point for its guests.

Difficulty

A rolling and not too challenging route, requiring a minimum of staying power due to its length.

Cycling period

From April to November, preferably in May and September.

Bicycle + Train

Pescolanciano station along the Isernia-Lanciano line.

Map

Atlante stradale d'Italia, Central volume, 1:200,000, TCI.

Technical assistance

Orlando Antonio, via Aquilonia, Agnone; t. 086578502.

Tourist information

• Presidio Turistico Agnone, piazza Plebiscito 8, Agnone; t. 086577722.
• Pro Loco, corso Vittorio Emanuele 78, Agnone; t. 086577249.
• Busico Car Rental, via Aquilonia, Agnone; t. 086577564.
• Masserie dell'Alto Molise (tourist service and rural accommodation), Agnone; t. 0865770361. www.masseriealtomolise.it

---

Agnone for about 1.5 km. At the first crossroads, turn left towards Carovilli, then after 3 km, reach the junction with the S.S. 86 main road, where you turn left heading towards the town. From Carovilli (832 m above sea level), continue your ride on the S.S. 86 main road to Agnone.

The gentle uphill stretch amid woods and meadows, after 6 km, leads to the San Mauro bridge, over the River Trigno. From this point, go right on the provincial road to Pietrabbondante (1,050 m above sea level), a town you reach after crossing the MAB Forest of Collemeluccio (protected by UNESCO), with an asphalt route of about 12 km on a constant, gentle climb. The theatre and the temple of Pietrabbondante are some of the main archaeological traces of the Samnite civilization. Apart from the visit to the archaeological diggings, we suggest the easy climb to the Morgia, a rock that dominates the old town center, from where you can enjoy a view on the entire region of Molise.

After leaving Pietrabbondante, take the provincial road towards Agnone, up to the Tre Termini crossroads (6.7 km). Now continue your ride, heading towards **Agnone**, reaching it after about 18 km on a mainly downhill stretch. In the small old town center, there are 17 churches, but Agnone is famous all over the world for the Pontificia Fonderia di Campane of the Marinelli family, the oldest bell casting foundry in the world, which you can visit together with the Historical Bell Museum, t. 086578235.

RIGHT: cycling in the center of Agnone.

Campania

The Amalfi Coast · 37 Km
From Vietri sul Mare to Positano

Welcome to one of the most beautiful roads in the world. The tarmac running along the Amalfi coastal strip, stretches halfway between sea and sky, performing spectacular acrobatics in the imposing rocky wall of the southern side of the Lattari mountains.

You start your ride from **Vietri sul Mare**, a town famous for its artistic ceramics and gateway to the Amalfi Coast. As soon as you start, the road has a twisting course and reaches the village of Cetara, which deserves a stop. Now ride towards Capo d'Orso, the first breathtaking balcony overlooking the Amalfi coast. Irregular and spectacular trajectories follow the coast up to Maiori.

The road gets wider and smoother between Maiori and Minori, but alas, this is

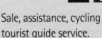

Technical info

Route
37 Km: Vietri sul Mare - Cetara - Maiori - Minori - Atrani - Amalfi - Conca dei Marini - Praiano - Positano.
Vietri sul Mare is easily reachable from Salerno (5 km).

Difficulty
Rolling and varied route, with no particularly challenging climbs. Ideal for people with average training in their legs.

Cycling period
All year round, thanks to the climate. Rule out the peak periods (July and August) and the weekends from May to September. The midweek days are ideal.

Bicycle + Bus
To get back to the starting point, you can catch the scheduled SITA buses; t. 089871016.

Map
• *Atlante stradale d'Italia*, Southern volume, 1:200,000, TCI.
• Club Alpino Italiano - Comunità Montana "Penisola Amalfitana", *Monti Lattari - Penisola Sorrentina e Costiera Amalfitana*, map of the routes 1:30,000, SELCA Florence.

Assistance and bicycle rental
• Sorrento Bici, corso Italia 258/c, Sorrento; t. 0818075561.

Sale, assistance, cycling tourist guide service.
• It's Bicycle Time, via Palma 44, Massa Lubrense; t. 081.8789157.
• Tuttobici Sport, via L. Conforti 13, Salerno; t. 089790707.

Tourist information
Local tourist boards:
• Sorrento, via L. De Maio 35; t. 0818074033.
• Positano, via del Saracino 4; t. 089875067.
• Amalfi, corso Repubbliche Marinare 15; t. 089871107.

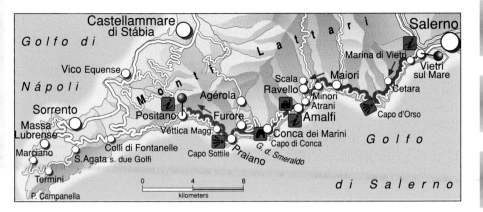

just an illusion that lasts a couple of kilometers. In fact, just before reaching the village of Atrani (19 km from Vietri) the road narrows again, wedging itself in the rock.

Shortly after, you reach Amalfi, the old Maritime Republic, which still maintains all the charm of a sea capital. After a short detour towards the Duomo, which deserves a thorough visit, ride back to the sea, continuing the nice ride towards Conca dei Marini and its magnificent bay. You can stop here and visit the

POINTS OF INTEREST

*Another possible circular route is the one that starts from **Sorrento** and continues on a gentle ascent to Massa Lubrense, discovering the "Neapolitan" side of the peninsula.*

From here, you climb up towards Marciano and Termini and continue your ride to Sant'Agata sui due Golfi. This is where the descent towards Colli di Fontanelle and Sorrento starts (31 km, 400 m rise, not too challenging).

Smeraldo cave (information and timetables available at the local tourist board of Amalfi). After passing Capo di Conca, ride along one of the most beautiful stretches on the coast. The passage over the bridge facing the Furore fjord, a tiny fishermen's village clinging to the vertical walls of the gully, is one of the treats on the entire route.

The road now runs smoothly, with no great rises, up to Praiano. You have to pass a few short tunnels before skirting Capo Sottile, yet another balcony on the final part of the peninsula. From here, you can enjoy the view on the village of Positano, Punta della Campanella and the island of Capri, with the unmistakable profile of the "faraglioni".

Another 6 km of curves accompany you along the final stretch of this rectilinear itinerary up to **Positano**.

LEFT, the Amalfi Coast, stop along the road to Positano.

179

Cilento   44 Km
From Palinuro to the Inferno Valley

This itinerary unveils the magnificent coast between Palinuro and Marina di Camerota, and the wild inland scenery that opens out between Camerota and the Inferno Valley, indicating the route to cycle along the roads of one of the most beautiful and unpredictable coasts in the Mediterranean.

You start from **Palinuro**, following the road signs pointing to Marina di Camerota. The road initially stretches inland, passing near the Molpa hill, whose summit can be reached on foot (15-20 minutes). The place offers a magnificent view on Capo Palinuro, the Marinel-

la beach and the Arco Naturale. The road then continues on level ground, passing by a few camping sites, then reaching the coastline. Before reaching Marina di Camerota, you can enjoy stunning views on the rocky coast, alternated now and then by splendid beaches (at this point, you're near the TCI Holiday Resort). After covering 11.5 km, you reach Marina di Camerota, where you turn towards the inland, heading for Camerota. The road now constantly rises for 3.5 km, up to a belvedere facing the small town perched up above. Now that you're high up, continue on a smooth route

that leads (2 km) to the medieval village, at 320 meters above sea level. After a visit to the old town center of Camerota, ride downhill to Licusati (approximately 3 km), a small hamlet where you can fill up your water flask before challenging the second tough stretch of the itinerary. A climb with hairpin bends curls along magnificent secular olive trees, up to the hill crossing you make after 2.4 km. Right near the pass, you can take a short detour on your right leading you to the nearby small Church of the Annunziata (415 m above sea level). From the pass, the road drops for 7.5 km along a spectacular descent that penetrates the impressive

Salerno
S.Nicola
Caprioli
Severino
Valle dell'Inferno
Mingardo
l'Annunziata
Licusati
La Molpa
Palinuro
Capo Palinuro
Grotta Azzurra
Camerota
Sapri
Lentiscosa
MAR TIRRENO
0   2   4
kilometers
Marina di Camerota

Inferno Valley, crossed by the River Mingardo. The long descent has clearly sloping rectilinear stretches interrupted now and then by narrow hairpin bends. This road reaches the bottom of the valley, where you turn right, taking the Mingardina, set in imposing rocky walls. Ride for 1.2 km, up to the crossroads for San Severino, where you keep left, riding for 900 m up to a wide hairpin bend. You can leave your bicycle here and walk along the track that climbs up to the abandoned village of San Severino, which dates back to the XI century and is situated on a spectacular ridge that dominates the In-

ferno Valley and the western spurs of Mount Bulgheria. From San Severino, ride back up to the River Mingardo, following it along the road on the bottom of the valley, until you reach the

plain near the Molpa hill (7 km). After reaching a big intersection, turn right and reach **Palinuro** (3.3 km).

ABOVE, the "Finestrella", with the "Semaforo" at Capo Palinuro.

Technical info

Route
44 Km: Palinuro - Marina di Camerota - Camerota - Licusati - San Severino - Palinuro.
A route with a wide assortment of habitats: sea, olive groves, medieval villages and wild areas such as the Inferno Valley.

Difficulty
The most difficult stretches are the climb up to Camerota (3.5 km) and the Annunziata pass (2.4 km), though with no tough gradients. For this tour, we suggest a bicycle equipped with triple gear (MTB type). If you want to challenge this route with a road bike, you should be in fairly good shape.

Bicycle + Train
The nearest railroad station is Pisciotta-Palinuro (approximately 9 km from Palinuro) and is situated along the Reggio Calabria-Naples line.

Cycling period
All year round

Map
• *Cartoguida, Dal Golfo di Napoli al Cilento*, 1:175,000, TCI.
• *Capo Palinuro e Costiera di Camerota*, tourist map, scale 1:20,500; Litografia Artistica Cartografica - Florence.

Boat outings and diving
Boat outings to Capo Palinuro with its caves and Porto Infreschi, with spaghetti feeds

on the beach, are organized in the summer period and during weekends in spring by Palinuri Travel, contrada Valle Di Marco 18, Caprioli; t. 0974976154.

Tourist information
• Parco Nazionale del Cilento e Vallo di Diano, via O. de Marsilio, Vallo della Lucania; t. 0974719911, fax 09747199217. www.parks.it/parco.nazionale.cilento/
• Pro Loco, via Porto, Marina di Camerota; t. 0974932900.
• Pro Loco, piazza Virgilio 1, Palinuro; t. 0974938144.

The Cilento Coast 50 Km
From Agropoli to Punta Licosa

Welcome to one of the most fascinating coast stretches of the Peninsula, situated in the huge territory (180,000 hectares) of the National Park of Cilento, just a stone's throw away from the Sele plain and the archaeological area of Paestum. Agropoli is the gateway to the coastal strip of the Park that stretches for over 100 km. Your destination is Punta Licosa, the old, legendary "Leucosia", home and sepulcher of the mermaids, enchantresses of Ulysses. Here, history lies at the bottom of the sea, where the walls belonging to a Ro-

man villa and to a fish-pond, remains of columns and tombs witness settlements dating probably back to the XI-X century B.C.

From the **Agropoli** railroad station, to the northern border of the Cilento National Park, you ride along a short uphill stretch to reach the main square of the town, now a pedestrian precinct. From this point, turn left towards the S.S. 267 main road for Santa Maria di Castellabate, approximately 12 km away. Cover a rectilinear stretch leading you inland,

along the valley of the River Alento. Riding along a few small promontories, on a route that gradually climbs up to Case San Pietro (100 m above sea level), then

Technical info

Route
50 Km: Agropoli - Case San Pietro - Santa Maria di Castellabate - San Marco di Castellabate - Punta Licosa - Ogliastro Marina. Including the way back, on asphalt and dirt roads. You can reach the starting point by taking the A3 Salerno-Reggio Calabria freeway, Battipaglia exit, and further stretch on the S.S. 18 main road up to Agropoli Nord.
Difficulty
The itinerary has no particular difficulties in store: this is a mainly rolling route with no challenging climbs.
Bicycle + Train
Agropoli, starting point of the

itinerary, is situated along the Salerno-Reggio Calabria railroad line.
Map
Salerno, Map of the Province, 1:150,000, Litografia Artistica Cartografica - Florence.
Technical assistance
Domini Antonio, via Dante Alighieri 136, Agropoli; t. 0974826618. Sale and repair of bicycles, information for cyclists on the local routes.
Useful addresses
• Cicoloverdi, largo Proprio d'Avellino 8, Napoli; t. 081.291184, cell. 3384286399 (Gino Aji, secretary), cell. 3337188318

(Antonio Daniele, president) www. cicloverdi.it Information and ride along the Cilento coast and in Campania.
• Pro Loco San Marco di Castellabate - Ogliastro Marina, c/o Giulio Passaro, via De Angelis, San Marco di Castellabate.
• Associazione Leucosia, c/o Luigi Giovanni Durazzo, via Matarazzo 100, Santa Maria di Castellabate.
• Parco Nazionale del Cilento e Vallo di Diano, via O. de Marsilio, Vallo della Lucania; t. 0974719911, fax 09747199217, www.parks.it/parco.nazionale. cilento/

The **archaeological diggings of Paestum,** *with three Doric temples facing the east (Basilica, Cerere and Nettuno). The National Archaeological Museum, t. 082 8811023, is one of the most important in the world. Many relics are still brought to light in the area, and still await cataloguing, among these, worth mentioning are: the Tomb of the Diver, according to its discoverer, dating to 480 B.C., and the fictile metopes of the "Heraion" of Foce Sele, terracotta decorations from the temple dedicated to Hera.*

drops down again towards the sea, you reach the town of Santa Maria di Castellabate. From this point, the road continues for about 4.5 km on up and downhill stretches along the coast, to the next town, San Marco di Castellabate, where you leave the main road and ride down towards the quaint tourist and fishing port.

A short climb on your left leads you quickly from the port of San Marco to a dirt track, which runs along the marine area below Mount Licosa (326 m above sea level) and reaches the homonymous cape. You now enter a poorly populated area, touching both the sea and the maquis. Along this stretch of the route, you can plan pleas-

ant stops near the beaches, inlets and rocks, which can be reached with simple detours right of the track.

After nearing the cape, you can spot a small port and a church nearby. Now get back on the road that flanks a large private estate, which immediately after becomes gravel road, with large tree-lined rectilinear stretches that lead, after about 4 km, to Ogliastro Marina, with a coast rich in large sandy beaches.

To get back to the starting point, you can cover the same route backwards, avoiding busy roads, or you can get back on the S.S. 267 main road to **Agropoli** about 25 km away.

LEFT, Punta Licosa, the small port. PAGE OPPOSITE, cycling along the coastal strip towards Punta Licosa.

🚲 Irpinia   52 Km
◼ DOC itinerary along the Taurasi hills

A trip to discover the Campania hinterland, along hills and villages of the green Irpinia, across very suggestive roads. In particular, the itinerary stretches across the DOC vineyards of Taurasi, probably the finest wine (DOCG) in southern Italy.

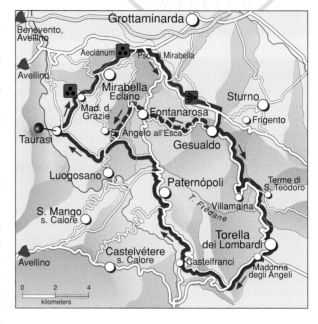

From **Taurasi**, start on a constant downhill stretch, until you reach Madonna delle Grazie (approximately 3.5 km), where the road starts to climb up to Mirabella Eclano (370 m above sea level). After crossing the town, continue riding towards the Mirabella pass. A final spurt leads you to the entrance with an intersection on the road linking Benevento and Grottaminarda. Turn left, and shortly after, you reach the ruins of "Aeclanum", a

Roman city dating back to the V century B.C., situated along the via Appia. You can recognize the remains of a spa complex and a big build-

ing, with walls built according to the typical "opus reticolatum" geometries.

Now you're back on the main road, continue your ride up

Technical info

Route
52 Km: Taurasi - Mirabella Eclano - Gesualdo - Villamaina - Torella dei Lombardi - Castelfranci - Paternopoli - Taurasi. On asphalt roads with little traffic.

Difficulty
The itinerary has a quite irregular altitude profile; you need good legs and discrete training to challenge this varied trip with peace of mind, in the trajectories and on the rises. The ideal vehicle would be a road or touring bicycle.

Cycling period
All year round. In the winter season, the area may have chilly temperatures, and the roads, especially in the early hours of the day, may have slippery stretches.

Map
Atlante stradale d'Italia, Southern volume, 1:200,000, TCI.

Technical assistance
Bicyclery, via Francesco Tedesco 19, 83030 Taurasi; t. 082774189, fax 0827770900. www.bicyclery.com Specialized workshop, sale of bicycles and accessories, bicycle rental upon reservation.

Tourist information
EPT Avellino, via dei Due Principati 5, Avellino; t. 082574731, 082574695, fax 082574757. www.eptavellino.it

POINTS OF INTEREST

A visit with the tasting of the fine Taurasi wine, produced with Aglianico vine. The wine cellars are really beautiful for their architectural features; the Taurasi is an excellent wine and can be bought at the farming concern of Antonio Caggiano, contrada Sala, Taurasi; t. and fax 082774043; www.cantinecaggiano.com. As early as 1932, Arturo Marescalchi, Minister of Agriculture, once said: «Under the coat of mail of my coarse Piedmontese nature, I must sincerely declare, may my Barbera and Barolo forgive me, that your Taurasi is their elder brother!».

to Gesualdo. Cross the old town center, dominated by the castle, in the words of Igor Stravinskij «residence of some hens, a heifer and a browsing goat, as well as a human population numbering, in that still pill-less decade, a great many *bambini*».
The itinerary continues up to Villamaina, the old "Villa Magna", situated on a territory warmed by the presence of hydrothermal springs, as witnessed by the nearby San Teodoro spa.
From Villamaina (23.5 km from the starting point), ride

ABOVE, bicycle "on the ground", detail.
PAGE OPPOSITE, the archaeological diggings at Mirabella Eclano.

down into the valley of the Fredane torrent, and climb up to Torella dei Lombardi. After crossing the town, you reach an intersection at Madonna degli Angeli. At this point, turn right and ride towards Castelfranci and Pa-

ternopoli, where the final part of the itinerary starts.
Ride on the S.P. 164 provincial road, crossing the Fredane torrent. Just after the bridge, turn left and ride towards Sant'Angelo all'Esca. At the next crossroads, instead of going straight towards the town, keep left and follow the road signs to **Taurasi**, less than 5 km away.

ALTERNATIVE
The itinerary can become much simpler, therefore suitable even for the less trained cyclists, shortening the circle to a 34 km trip. After reaching Gesualdo, you can continue riding towards Fontanarosa, Sant'Angelo all'Esca, then Taurasi.

The Procida island   14 Km
In the fishermen's villages

Procida is the smallest of the Parthenopean islands, but for various reasons, it is truly the most genuine. Less mundane of the elder sisters Capri and Ischia, it preserves the soul and traditions of its fishermen.

After landing at **Marina del Sancio Cattolico**, you can stop and briefly visit the port, then take via Libertà, which starts climbing. Shortly after, near a wide hairpin bend, take the path on your right that leads to

the Starza area. At the next intersection, keep right and enter the narrow street that leads to the cemetery (1 km), where you can make a short detour towards the Pozzo Vecchio beach. If you continue, instead, on the

Technical info

Route
14 Km: Marina del Sancio Cattolico - Starza - L'Olmo - Chiaiolella - Punta Solchiaro - Punta Pizzaco - Corricella - Terra Murata - Marina del Sancio Cattolico.
Mainly on asphalt or paved road (only 5% of the itinerary is on dirt road).

Difficulty
The route is ideal for everyone and does not require much effort; we suggest a mountain bike or a bicycle with wide tires, due to the irregular road surface.

Bicycle + ferryboat
Procida can be reached by ferryboat from the port of Pozzuoli, by hydrofoil and by ferryboat from the ports of Naples (Mergellina and Molo Beverello). You can check the timetables on the local dailies ("Il Mattino", "La Repubblica", "Corriere della Sera").

Cycling period
All year round. It would be advisable to avoid the summer period (July and August) and the traditional dates (May 1°, April 25, Easter Monday), to dodge crowded ferryboats and riding on very busy roads.

Map
Ischia e Procida, Nuova Pianta Topografica 1:15:150, Lozzi, Rome.

Boat rental
From April to September, you can contact:
La Nautica dei Procidani via Roma 2, t. 0818101934, or directly the fishermen who run this service in the ports of Corricella and Chiaiolella.

Tourist information
Azienda Autonoma di Soggiorno e Turismo, via Roma; t. 0818101968.

main road, you turn left reaching the camping site of Punta Serra, then turn left again on the pathway that enters, after 1.1 km, via Vittorio Emanuele at L'Olmo. After reaching the main artery of the island, turn right on via Giovanni da Procida and ride down to the Chiaiolella port (1.2 km). From the quay, continue on your left, skirting the characteristic fishermen's houses, and after 600 m, turn right (ignoring the two previous side-streets, first left, then right) towards Punta Solchiaro. After 200 m and a steep but short climb, turn right and start covering the circle on the small peninsula. After 800 m, you meet a crossroads where a dirt stretch starts: turn left and continue for 600 m until you close the circle on the small peninsula.

Now you're back on asphalt road, keep riding on the main road, and after 400 m, turn right, riding on

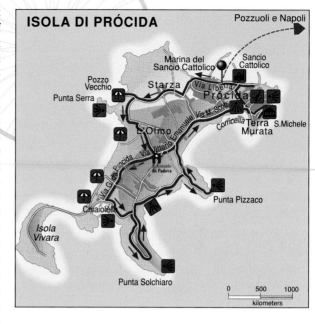

ISOLA DI PRÓCIDA

a gentle ascent along the panoramic road towards Punta Pizzaco.

After covering nearly 1 km, near small gardens, turn right until the road comes to an end. Now continue (10 minutes) on foot up to Punta Pizzaco, a magnificent panoramic spot. Go back up to the asphalt road, and

after reaching a large crossroads, keep right and reach via Vittorio Emanuele.

From this point, on your right, take via Marcello Scotti up to the widening-belvedere overlooking the splendid Marina della Corricella. From piazza dei Martiri, the road rises up to the summit of Terra Murata, near the San Michele Abbey. The return trip to the **Marina del Sancio Cattolico** is very simple. Go back to piazza dei Martiri and continue downhill along via Principe Umberto (approximately 300 m) that enters via Vittorio Emanuele. You end the descent on the port quay, near the Sancio Cattolico Church.

LEFT, towards Punta Serra.
PAGE OPPOSITE, the Chiaiolella marina.

Apulia

 Salento   55 Km
From Gallipoli to Santa Maria di Leuca

Where the blue waters of the Ionian and Adriatic seas meet, a white and calcareous strip of Italy juts out towards the East, a land not far from here. The Salento peninsula is caressed by the sun that follows clear horizons. On the last strip of the Italic peninsula lies the Sanctuary of Santa Maria di Finibus Terrae. This is where land ends, where one enters a dimension made of sea and imagination: the view stops where sky and sea meet, but fantasy pushes further beyond.
Today the heel of the Peninsula is a piece of Italy where you can still feel the charm

of a world made of dry walls and tiny streets that seem to have been made to ride in great spaces. If it's true that the Salento is a "land of passage", it is surely worth a bicycle trip.

The itinerary starts from **Gallipoli**, the old "Kalè polis" (the wonderful city), which juts out into the waters of the Ionian Sea, on a small island surrounded by fortified walls and linked to the mainland by a bridge. Go immediately southwards, riding along the lido San Giovanni, then the Baia Verde. The road turns towards the inland and re-

POINTS OF INTEREST

A guided visit to the old town center of **Gallipoli**, *with the Sant'Agata Cathedral, the hypogean oil mills, the palaces, bulwarks, paved streets, the clear tufa churches and the white houses that herald the nearby East. Caroli Hotels and Mamo Services promote and organize "Invito a palazzo", walks in the old city to discover the historical palaces.*
For reservation and information, t. 0833261831 and 0832720004.

PAGE OPPOSITE, cycling at Torre Vado.

Technical info

Route
55 Km: Gallipoli - Marina di Mancaversa - Torre San Giovanni (Ausentum) - Marina di Leuca - Capo Santa Maria di Leuca - Gagliano del Capo. On lightly-trafficked roads.

Difficulty
This is a very smooth route, with virtually no significant altitude difficulties. Your main foe in this area is wind, which can give you many a problem and can thwart your smooth, constant pace. For the round trip, we suggest planning a whole day out (3-4 hours cycling).

Cycling period
All year round; in the summer season (August) the impact of traffic on these roads is clearly greater.

Bicycle + Train
The route includes the return to Gallipoli by train, departing from the Gagliano Leuca railroad station situated along the Casarano (change trains) - Melissano - Taviano line in approximately one hour's trip.

Map
Atlante stradale d'Italia, Southern volume, 1:200,000, TCI.

Technical assistance
• Bicisport,
via Principedi Napoli,
Racale;
t. 0833552552.
• Mariano Matino,
Via Firenze 15,
Melissano;
t. 0833597759.
• Colaci Enrico,
via Rovigo 40,
Ugento;
t. 0833555895.

Tourist information
• Ruotalibera,
via Bonazzi 35,
Bari; t. 0805236674.
• Associazione Biciclando:
su due ruote tra due mari,
Lungomare Colombo 59,
Santa Maria di Leuca;
t. 0833758242.
(manager: Vito Maruccia).
• APT Lecce, via Monte
San Michele 20,
Lecce;
t. 0832314117.
www.pugliaturismo.com
• IAT Gallipoli,
via Aldo Moro,
Gallipoli;
t. 0833262529.

turns near the coast at Marina di Mancaversa.

As far as orienteering is concerned, this itinerary humbly "asks" you to keep riding along the coast to reach, after 23 km from the starting point, the old "Ausentum" (archaeological ruins) and Torre San Giovanni.

At this point, leave the coast and turn towards the inland: after 1.2 km, go right, along the road that points straight to Santa Maria di Leuca. From this moment, the road runs parallel to the coast, but to reach the coastline, which becomes rocky near the

Cape, you must make short detours towards Torre Mozza, Marini, Marina di Pescoluse, Torre Vado and Torre San Gregorio.

After reaching Marina di Leuca (approximately 25 km from Ausentum), continue skirting the Cape, then cycle along the coastal

road with its imposing sea-cliffs (beautiful sight when spurges blossom) facing the Adriatic.

Ride for 7 km up to the crossroads for Gagliano del Capo, where you turn left, cross the built-up area up to the station, and then catch the train to **Gallipoli**.

Murgia: from Trani to Castel del Monte — 63 Km

POINTS OF INTEREST

Before starting your ride, go and visit the extraordinary **Trani Cathedral** *(1094), one of the finest examples of Romanesque architecture in Italy. Also worth visiting is the bronze portal (1175) by Barisano da Trani, who introduced relief sculpture, departing from the Byzantine concept of engraving. The portal weighs 25 quintals and is formed by 32 bronze panels that represent saints, dragons, wrestlers and archers.*

A journey into the great spaces of the Bari Murgia area, amid dry walls, "trulli" and country paths, riding towards the alluring elevation of the Federico II of Hoenstaufen castle.

From the **Trani** railroad station, 40 minutes away from Bari, turn left and enter corso Imbriani. After approximately 200 m, near a school, turn left on a road that passes a level crossing. From here, follow the road signs pointing to the Associazione Sportiva Centro Libero, leading you out of the built-up area up to the San Luca vicinal road. Continue on this road until you cross the Bisceglie-Andria provincial road and pass the A 14. Go straight to the first crossroads, turn left at the second, then reach another crossroads with two pillars on your right.

At this point, turn left and continue without changing direction, until you reach the S.S. 378 main road, where you turn right and head towards Corato. To avoid traffic, turn right after the IX/8 kilometer sign, and after approximately 100 m, at a crossroads, take the first bend on your left that leads you to Corato. From here, following the road signs for Castel del Monte, pass over the S.S. 98 main road and reach a crossroads, which you recognize by an oil mill on your right: continue on your left, riding towards San Magno.

Cross the S.S. 170 main road, and after approximately 1 km, turn right, following the road signs indicating the Pedale farm. After leaving the farm on your left, at the foot of the hill-step of the Murge, pass the junction with the S.S. 170 main road. Now continue straight ahead towards Femmina Morta and reach the road connecting Andria-Castel del Monte, where you turn left. Climb up for a few kilometers, and towards your right, you reach the castle. The castle appears like a perfect white stone sculpture: an octagon rounded at the corners by eight octagonal turret masts. The rooms inside are eight too on each

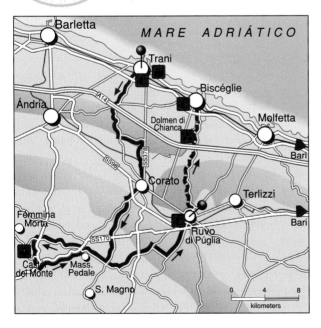

MARE ADRIÁTICO

Barletta
Trani
Biscéglie
Ándria
Dolmen di Chianca
Molfetta
Barì
Corato
Terlizzi
Femmina Morta
Bari
Ruvo di Púglia
Cast. del Monte
Mass. Pedale
S. Magno

0   4   8
kilometers

Technical info

Route

63 Km: Trani - Corato -
Castel del Monte - Ruvo.
All on by-roads.

Difficulty

The route is really cyclable;
the only tough stretch is the
climb to Castel del Monte:
approximately 3.5 km uphill,
with no grueling spurts.

Cycling period

All year round; bear in mind
that the Murge area has a
continental climate, with hot
summers and cold winters
(especially due to the winds

blowing from the Balkans).

Bicycle + Train

This itinerary implies the
train plus bicycle integrated
transport, with departure
and arrival at Bari. You reach the
starting point (Trani) in
40 minutes' time, on the Bari-
Foggia line; you return to Bari,
again catching the train at
Ruvo di Puglia on the Terlizzi-
Bitonto-Bari line, or at Bisceglie,
towards Bari.

Map

Atlante stradale d'Italia,
Southern volume, 1:200,000, TCI.

Technical assistance

Saverio De Marzo,
via Conte Giusso 13/E, Bari;
t. 0805481856.

Tourist information

• Ruotalibera, via Bonazzi 35,
Bari; t. and fax 0805236674.
Cycle-environmental association.

• Azienda Autonoma
Soggiorno e Turismo,
via Cavour 140, Trani;
t. and fax 0883588830.
www.pugliaturismo.com

• Information Office,
Piazza della Repubblica, Trani;
t. 088343295.

---

floor, all with the same size. Built between 1240 and 1246, the castle was once a hunting residence and astronomical observatory of Federico II.

After a stop in this extraordinary spot, continue your ride turning right, then left on the S.S. 170 main road towards Ruvo. After reaching the crossroads for Corato, turn right, heading towards the Pedale farm, riding along a stretch already covered on the outward trip.

Don't change direction and cross the road for San Magno. After 1 km, you reach a crossroads, where you turn left for Ruvo. After passing Caledano and crossing the Corato-Altamura main road, continue straight ahead for approximately 1 km, until

you reach a large villa on your left. At this point, turn right on a country path and emerge on another road that takes you, on your left, to **Ruvo**. You can now catch the

train to get back to Bari. The more trained cyclists can continue riding up to the Bisceglie railroad station along the road that skirts the Chianca Dolmen.

RIGHT, around Castel del Monte.

The Itria Valley: the white magic of the "trulli" and the "masserie"   45 Km

Ride on this itinerary to discover the Itria Valley, to observe the most original, spontaneous architecture in Italy: from the simple, though ingenious " trulli" to the more typical "masserie" that bear witness to an old rural civilization that is gradually dying out.

Leave the old town center of **Martina Franca**, riding towards Noci-Alberobello. After about 3 km, you arrive near a crossroads: keep left, cycling towards Noci and ignoring the road on your right leading to Alberobello. After 300 m, you reach the masseria (farm) Luco , one of the finest "masserie", recognizable by its monumental aspect. Once you're back on the provincial road for Noci,

ABOVE, across the Martina countryside.

after riding for 1 km, at the crossroads, keep left (road sign for Noci), and after 5.3 km, you reach the masseria Masella, the only masseria that preserves its original bucolic functions. Continue cycling on the provincial road for 300 m, up to the crossroads, where you turn right, following the road signs for Alberobello. After 2.5 km, you can take a detour on your left, and then take the dirt road leading, after 1.3 km, to the masseria Galeone, that hosts a horse centre of the State Forest Rangers.

Now that you're back on the asphalt road, continue up to a crossroads (500 m), where you turn right and reach the masseria Caravuzzo (1.3 km). At this point, ride along the Mangiatello provincial road which, after 3 km, enters the Martina Franca-Alberobello road. Now turn left, keeping on the provincial road, until you get to the junction (4 km) on the S.S. 172 main road that reaches Alberobello. After a visit to the Monti and Aia Piccola districts, continue your ride towards Locorotondo, avoiding the S.S. 172 main road.

From the coach parking area, ask for the road that leads to the sports field: 700 m on your left, 200 m on your left again towards Monopoli, 1.4 km on your right towards the Capitolo district. Follow the Alberobello-Capitolo provincial road up to the center of Locorotondo (10 km).

To get back to Martina Franca (6 km), ignore the S.S. 172 main road (narrow and busy): the Rampone parallel road would be a better option. At the 44th km of the main road,

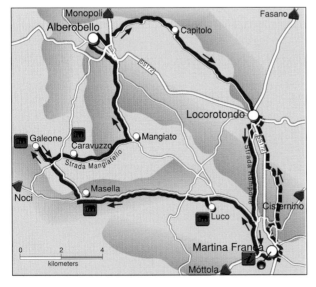

LEFT, "trulli" between Locorotondo and Alberobello.

turn right, following for 500 m the path that enters the Rampone road. Now continue for 5 km up to the junction with the road leading to Mottola, where you turn left towards **Martina Franca**.

ALTERNATIVE

Very simple, only 16 km: from Martina Franca, take the S.S. 172 main road, turning at the first crossroads on your right towards Cisternino, and soon after, on your left, taking the road running parallel to the S.S. 172 main road that stretches northwards. After 2.8 km, at a crossroads, keep left, until you reach another crossroads (1 km), where you turn left towards Locorotondo. Get back to Martina Franca along the Rampone road (see main itinerary).

Technical info

Route
Approximately 45 Km:
Martina Franca – Masseria Luco - Masseria Masella - Strada Mangiatello - Alberobello - Locorotondo - Martina Franca.
All on country paths.

Difficulty
This is not a difficult itinerary. Except for a few never too challenging up and downhill stretches, the altitude profile is virtually flat. The long distance, however, requires a minimum of training.

Cycling period
All year round. It may be really cold in winter.

Bicycle + Train
All the centers of the Itria Valley are well linked also to the main cities nearby: Brindisi, Bari, Taranto and Altamura.

Map
• *Atlante stradale d'Italia*, Southern volume, 1:200,000, TCI.
• *Martina Franca*, topographical and road map of the urban territory and of the countryside, 1:40,000, ed. CEDEC (available at the Martina Franca Tourist Office).

Technical assistance
De Carlo Angelo, via Rascaporta 2, Alberobello; t. 0804324047.

Tourist information
•Azienda Autonoma Soggiorno e Turismo, piazza Roma 37, Martina Franca; t. 080705702.
www.pugliaturismo.com
• G.S. Bici2000Bike Martina, viale Europa 80, Martina Franca; t. 0804801940.
www.bici2000bike.org

POINTS OF INTEREST

It's an interesting and exciting experience *to lodge in a* "trullo" *or in an old "masseria"; simply phone the Valle dei Trulli Cooperative, tel. 0804311825, www.valledei trulli.it. A visit to the* **Locorotondo Wine-Producers' Cooperative**, *via Madonna della Catena 99, Locorotondo; t. 080431164, www.locorotondodoc.com. Founded in 1932, it's the ideal place to truly discover the secrets of the different stages of winemaking and production of the Locorotondo Doc.*

Gargano
Discovering the Umbra Forest

25 Km

Apulia, known as being a sun-baked and scorched land, has a green heart: the Umbra Forest. Situated on the Gargano promontory, this enormous lung, rich in a lush and varied arboreal vegetation, stretches for over 10,000 hectares. The summit part of the Gargano promontory is not anthropized. Thanks to a well-organized forest administration, the environment is unspoilt and facilitates trekking on foot and by bicycle.

The itinerary starts from the **Villaggio Foresta Umbra**, where the S.S. 528 main road and the S.P. 53 bis provincial road meet. The Villaggio is formed by the facilities of the Rangers' Station, by the fallow deer compound and by the Centro Natura Ecogargano. Start riding along the S.S. 528 main road, heading towards Vico del Gargano, and after 5.2 km (first stretch downhill, then uphill), after crossing an imposing beechwood, you reach the Sfilzi station.
From the parking lot, the Sfilzi-Caritate stations forest path branches off towards the valley, running entirely along the slope of the Carpinosa Valley, which includes the Sfilzi integral nature reserve.
Enter the dirt road below the Sfilzi station (597 m), and

BELOW, a lush view of the extraordinary Gargano Coast.

shaded by majestic beech trees, ride down along the hydrographical right side of the Carpinosa Valley. After the first series of hairpin bends, the forest dirt road cuts the bottom of side gorges. After covering over half of the itinerary, at the last clear hairpin bend on your right, you'll spot a small wooden castle that crosses the fence of the integral reserve. On the other side, a path leads, after a few minutes' ride, to Fontana Sfilzi, the highest (419 m) perennial spring in the Gargano.
Now that you're back on the forest road, continue down-

POINTS OF INTEREST

A visit to the Centro Natura Ecogargano, at the Villaggio Foresta Umbra, tel. 088 4565444, open every day from Easter to October. This is the ideal starting point to grasp the extraordinary environmental variety of this park: from sea rocks, to wetlands and beechwoods. Special mention must be made of the so-called "low-lying beechwoods", found at the unusual altitude of 270 m above sea level. Another interesting feature, associated with these particular climate conditions, is the gigantism of several arboreal and shrubby species. Aleppo pines, yews, beech trees, holms and hollies reach unusual sizes.

ABOVE, the thick scrub near the Caritate station.

hill, past the lower limit of the beech trees, initially on a steep slope, then on a wide ridge, at the bottom of which you can see the Caritate station (272 m above sea level), a former hunting fortalice owned by the Forquet family. Between the station and the nearby S.P. 53 bis provincial road, lies an arboretum with every species of oak present in Apulia. After reaching the 53 bis provincial road, turn left and ride up the Tesoro Valley on asphalt road. A mainly uphill 12 km stretch is the final part of the itinerary that goes back to the **Villaggio Foresta Umbra**.

Technical info

Route
Approximately 25 Km (6 Km on dirt road):
Villaggio Foresta Umbra - Sfilzi station - Caritate station - Tesoro Valley - Villaggio Foresta Umbra.

Difficulty
Itinerary with an average difficulty level, including a stretch on dirt road. The distance is short, but the altitude profile, although with no great climbs, is pretty rough. Feasible for every cycle tourist with some training in his/her legs.

Cycling period
From April to November. Also in winter, but clad yourself against the cold.

Map
• *Atlante stradale d'Italia*, Southern volume, 1:200,000, TCI.
• *Carta d'Italia*, 1:50,000, sheet 385, IGM.

Tourist information
• Ente Provinciale del Turismo, via Perrone 17, Foggia; t. 0881723141.
• Ruotalibera, via Arpaia 25, Foggia; t. 0881665388.

• Ente Parco Nazionale del Gargano, via Sant'Antonio Abate 121, Monte Sant'Angelo; t. 0884568911. www.parks.it/parco.nazionale.gargano
• Cooperativa Ecogargano, largo Roberto Guiscardo 2, Monte Sant'Angelo; t. 0884565444.
• Azienda Autonoma Soggiorno e Turismo, corso L. Fazzini 8, Vieste; t. 0884707495.
• Information Office, piazza Kennedy, Vieste; t. 0884707130.

Basilicata

The Ionian Coast   46 Km
At the mouths of the Basento

The itinerary stretches between the beaches of the Metaponto plain and the inland south of the River Basento. The main feature of this strip of Ionian coast is the settlement of the Greek colony of "Metapontum" (VIII century B.C.), witnessed by the archaeological area situated in the alluvial Basento plain.

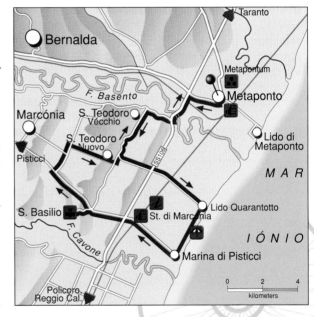

From the town center of **Metaponto**, ride towards Bernalda, and after 2.5 km, you reach the S.S. 106 Ionica main road, where you turn left, following the road signs pointing to Reggio Calabria and Policoro. Follow the usually heavily-trafficked road for a couple of kilometers, and after passing the bridge over the River Basento, turn right, following the Destra Basento road signs. At this point, ride up the hydrographical right side of the Basento for 1.8 km.
Near the crossroads for San Teodoro, turn left, riding on a gentle ascent amid cultivated fields, until you reach the country village of Iazzo San Teodoro, a group of abandoned houses and animal shelter constructions. At the next crossroads, after approximately 3 km, turn left and follow the road signs for Lido Quarantotto. After crossing the S.S. 106 Ionica main road, ride along a road immersed in the pinewood up to the opening on the coast near the beach. The route continues turning right towards the San Basilio lido, and running parallel to the coastline. After reaching the lido, turn inland, crossing the railroad and getting back on the S.S. 106 main road (approximately 4 km

POINTS OF INTEREST

The **Metaponto Archaeological Park,** *which you can reach by taking the road to the railroad station, comprises the remains of the Apollo Licio Sanctuary and the Agorà. The sacred area encloses four temples: the most ancient dedicated to Athena; the Doric temples of Apollo and Hera and the Ionic temple of Aphrodite. To the east, you can spot the remains of the altars, while to the south, you can see the ample colonnade; the precinct of the sacred area* temenos *separates the sanctuary from the Agorà, with the theatre dating back to the IV century B.C.*

ABOVE, Metaponto, the Palatine Tables.

from the coast), which you cross to reach the monastery-castle of San Basilio. From the junction with the S.S. 106 Ionica main road, ride for 2.5 km up to the crossroads on your left towards San Basilio (0.7 km), built on the foundations of an edifice dating back to the V century A.D. by Basilian monks, and subsequently transformed into a castle-fortress by the Normans.

After leaving San Basilio, continue riding towards the main road, where you turn left for Pisticci. After approximately 3 km, you reach a crossroads: turn right, following the road signs indicating Destra Basento. After 1.2 km, turn right again for San Teodoro Nuovo, on a by-road that crosses cultivated fields up to Iazzo San Teodoro. Now continue up to Metaponto along the road you have already covered: at the crossroads for the Lido Quarantotto, go straight ahead; after 3.2 km, turn right, until you reach the S.S. 106 main road where you turn left, crossing the Basento. Finally, turn right again and head towards **Metaponto**.

Technical info

Route
46 Km: Metaponto - Iazzo San Teodoro - Lido Quarantotto - Lido San Basilio - San Basilio castle - San Teodoro Nuovo - Metaponto. On by-roads.

Difficulty
This is an ideal itinerary for everyone, with no altitude difficulties, since it stretches along an almost completely flat territory. Due to its length, this itinerary is not recommendable for people who aren't used to cycling at all, since the ride lasts at least over 2 hours. The ideal two-wheelers are a touring or road bike.

Road map
• *Cicloturismo in Basilicata* – Eight itineraries to discover Basilicata, from the Ionian beaches to the Tyrrhenian coast, from the Pollino Park to the Matera "Sassi", APT Basilicata (available at APT Basilicata).
• *Atlante stradale d'Italia,* Southern volume, 1:200,000, TCI.

Information for cyclists
Marconia A.S. Bici Sport, via San Giovanni Bosco, Marconia, Pisticci; t. 0835411089.

Technical assistance
Antonio Pellegrino and Vittorio Melfi, via San Giovanni Bosco, Marconia, Pisticci.

Tourist information
• APT Basilicata, via Alianelli 4, Potenza; t. 097121812.
• APT Basilicata, via De Viti De Marco 9, Matera; t. 0835331983.

Between the Agri and Sinni rivers 38.5 Km
From Bosco Pantano to Santa Maria d'Anglona

A historical-environmental trip, from Bosco Pantano of Policoro to the Greek city of "Eraclea" and the old "Pandosia". Ride from the coast and turn inland, discovering a strip of Basilicata between the Agri and Sinni rivers.

(7.8 km from the starting point). Visit the museum area with its splendid material dating back to the Greek ages, or cover the archaeological site of the excavations of the old "Eraclea". Now enter via Colombo, riding towards An-

glona and crossing, after 2 km, the village of Cerchiarita; with small hairpin bends and gentle uphill stretches, you reach the Troili plateau. After covering a few kilometers and a short slope, you reach the foot of the hill of the Basilica Minor of Anglona, the old "Pandosia", where you turn right (about 700 m of uphill hairpin bends) and reach the equipped area at 263 m above sea level. Once you're back at the crossroads at the foot of the Anglona hill (towards Policoro), ride for

Start from the **Bosco Pantano Visiting Center of Policoro**, cycling for a short stretch along viale Mascagni before turning right for via Trieste and heading towards Policoro with a left detour at the next intersection. Continue your ride towards Policoro, and after about 500 m, after crossing a hump-backed railroad overbridge, pass a roundabout sign, then the flyover on the S.S. 106 main road, reaching the gates of the town. Leave the sports field on your right, and cross via Puglia, cycling towards the right and passing two crossroads with traffic lights, until you cross viale Salerno. From this point, proceed for 100 m to the right to via Colombo, riding towards the National Museum of Siritide

Technical info

Route
38.5 Km: Policoro, WWF Oasis - Policoro - Eraclea - Santa Maria d'Anglona - Pane e Vino - Bosco Pantano - Policoro, WWF Oasis. On lightly-trafficked roads.

Difficulty
An average-easy itinerary, with just one not too challenging climb on the Santa Maria d'Anglona hill.

Cycling period
All year round.

Bicycle + Train
The Policoro-Tursi railroad station is situated along the Taranto-Roccella Jonica line.

Map
• *Atlante stradale d'Italia*, Central volume, 1:200,000, TCI.
• *Foce Sinni*, 1:50,000, sheet

524, IGM. Policoro, 1:25,000, sheet 212, IGM.

Technical assistance
Cyclo Planet,
via Zanardelli 21,
Policoro;
t. 0835981332.

Tourist information
• WWF of Policoro,
piazza Eraclea;
t. 0835980535, 0835981360, 3470367692.
To book guided visits, you should contact the guides in advance; otherwise you can personally go the Centro Visite at Idrovora, Policoro.
• APT Basilicata,
via De Viti De Marco 9,
Matera; t. 0835331983.
• Information Office;
t. 0835333541.

POINTS OF INTEREST

The WWF Policoro-Herakleia Natural Oasis, *founded in 1995, with its 21 hectares, an integrating part of the Bosco Pantano, and since 1999 a regional reserve, is situated on the hydrographical left side of the mouth of the Sinni and Policoro rivers. The Bosco Pantano Regional Reserve is the last strip of wet plain forest (a few meters away from the sea) existing in southern Italy. The diversity of the habitats, the numerous ecological niches, and the great biodiversity, make this reserve an extraordinarily interesting biotope.*

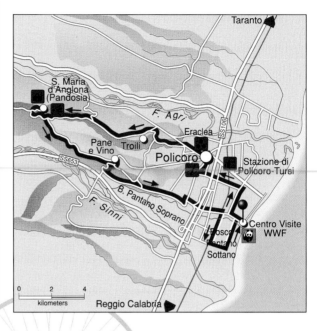

about 6 km on the provincial road that leads from Tursi to Policoro up to the village of Pane e Vino; cross the village, then with short downhill hairpin bends, you reach the hydrographical left side of the River Sinni. Follow, towards your left, the farm road you passed at the end of the hairpin bends, and ride towards the sea, until you pass a second flyover on the S.S.106 main road. At the crossroads with the eucalyptus-lined viale Mascagni, turn left and pass the level crossing on the Taranto-Reggio Calabria railroad line. Once you've passed (after 100 m) the reclamation canal on your right, cross a small bridge and proceed by approaching the Bosco

Pantano, crossing a second small bridge over the overflow channel which, after approximately 2 km, flows into the waters of the Ionian Sea. Take the path immediately right of the canal, until you cross a third bridge immersed in the vegetation. Following the path on the margins of the canal, you reach the sea following the dirt paths across the back of the dunes. The itinerary proceeds by turning right and crossing the

wooden gates that lead to the thicker wood. From this point, various paths have circular routes that return to the overflow channel. Cross the third bridge set in the vegetation, then ride along the path passing in front of the WWF Oasis board, until you reach the group of buildings of the draining pump on viale Mascagni. From this point, towards the right, return to the parking lot near the WWF Visiting Center of **Policoro**.

RIGHT, olive grove in the Sinni Valley. PAGE OPPOSITE, at the mouth of the Basento.

Calabria

Aspromonte   32 Km
At the top of Montalto

At the tip of the Italic Peninsula, mountain ridges cut by deep ravines slope towards the crystal-clear waters of the Ionian and Tyrrhenian seas, creating an exceptional place from an environmental and natural point of view.

The itinerary reaches the summit of Montalto, covering a dirt road immersed in lush woods.

You start from piazza Mangeruca in **Gambarie** (1,300 m above sea level), riding northwards. Follow the S.S. 183 main road on a 2.5 km asphalt stretch, and once you reach Pidima, near the Rumia lakelet, turn right. After 100 m, enter a thick wood, where the dirt road leading to Montalto starts.
Now ride on level road for about 1 km, and after reaching the glade called Piani di

POINTS OF INTEREST

The **Maesano, Forgiarelle** *and* **Palmarello waterfalls,** *respectively on the Menta-Amendolea, Ferraina and Aposcipo torrents, are surely worth a walk.*

Quarti, turn right. This is where a shaded 7 km ascent starts. After approximately 3 km from the start of the climb and a sharp bend on your left, go right (if you go straight, the track ends after a couple of kilometers). Ride southwards along the path crossing the new ski slopes, at the top of the built-up area of Gambarie (pass

PAGE OPPOSITE, the Compass Rose at the summit of Montalto.

under the new ski-lift). You now reach Acqua della Face, where we suggest a stop to fill your water flask.
Ride for a further kilometer on dirt road and reach the asphalt stretch (1,700 m above sea level) which takes you from Gambarie to Montalto. Go left and ride uphill, crossing Nardello, Menta Cavaliere and Materazzelli. After approximately 5 km, you reach the foot of Montalto (1,850 m above sea level). To get to the summit, you have to cover, firstly on foot, then by bike, a narrow pathway flanked by a wooden fence that leads to the foot of the statue of the Savior, erected there in 1900. From the top of Montalto, in good

conditions of visibility, you can stop to admire the Ionian and Tyrrhenian seas, and the Etna and Aeolian islands. At the top of the summit, next to the statue of the Savior, the bronze Compass Rose designed by the GEA (Aspromont Trekking Group) displays all its charm.
The return trip follows the asphalt downhill stretch leading to Gambarie d'Aspromonte. Pro bikers in search of thrills can take the path on the right which, after 200 m and the former radar base, leads to a TV transmitter and then drops sharply along the ski slope that ends in piazza Mangeruca at **Gambarie**.

Technical info

Route
32 Km: Gambarie - Pidima - Piani di Quarti - Acqua della Face - Nardello I - Nardello II - Menta Cavaliere - Materazzelli - Montalto - Gambarie.
On mixed asphalt and dirt route. You can reach Gambarie from Reggio di Calabria by taking the S.S. 184 (34 km) main road from Villa San Giovanni; from Melito Porto Salvo by taking the S.S. 183 main road and from the north by taking the A3, Bagnara Calabra exit, further stretch towards Santa Eufemia d'Aspromonte and the S.S. 183 main road.
Difficulty
The route has a roughly 550 m rise, the climbs are quite

challenging, but alternated by stretches where you can recuperate energy. You ride for most of the time in shaded areas. Fill your water flask at the starting point.
Cycling period
All year round, except for the snow-making periods.
Map
• *Motta San Giovanni,* 1:50,000, IGM sheet n° 602.
• *Mappa dei Sentieri,* 1:25,000, GEA.
Technical assistance
Sportime, Gambarie d'Aspromonte; t. 0965743010.
Tourist information
• Parco Nazionale d'Aspromonte via Aurora, Gambarie di Santo

Stefano in Aspromonte; t. 0965743060. www.parks.it/parco.nazionale. aspromonte/
• Aspromontebike, Gambarie d'Aspromonte; t. 3331191383. www.aspromontebike.it MTB trekking, information on the routes.
• GEA - Gruppo Escursionisti Aspromonte, via Castello 2, Reggio di Calabria; t. 0965332822, cell. 3474872105 (Giuseppe Trovato).
• Hotel Centrale, Gambarie d'Aspromonte; t. 0965743133. Hotel-restaurant working on an agreed basis with "puntobike".

Sicily

The Etna Park　　　　40 Km
On the back of the volcano

The Etna Park was created in 1987 on the largest volcano in Europe, situated north-west of Catania. In the past few years, the Etna, over 3,300 meters high, has had very strong eruptive episodes.

Take the Altomontana path at the **Brunek refuge**, up to the Pitarrone station, where you keep left. Cross an iron bar and continue uphill along a stretch that alternates beech and birch woods and old and recent lava flows. At the crossroads at km 6 of the itinerary, go left and uphill (Gelo cave, Mount Spagnolo), then on a level stretch crossing a pinewood and a bare lava slope. A long rectilinear stretch takes you near formations of roped lava. Just shortly ahead, you can spot a marked crossroads from where the path leading to the Lamponi cave branches off. The Altomontana path continues on your right towards the Dammusi pass (1,710 m, 8 km, wooden refuge), and

PAGE OPPOSITE, view of the snow-capped Etna.

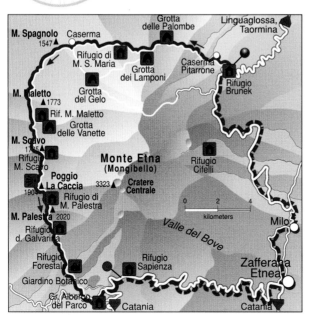

then goes back into the wood, passing the refuge of Mount Santa Maria. The road now drops down to 1,450 m and to km 13; at a hairpin bend on your right, take a marked cart road (Integral Reserve - Zone A), avoiding the descent and the climb up to the path, remaining high up and cutting a recent lava flow. Once you're back on the Altomontana path, cross a beech wood, passing the ruins of the station of Mount Spagnolo. The road now winds its way southwards along the vast western slope. At km 17, pass a wooden gate, continuing your ride crossing the oak woods, up to the fork on your right for the La Nave wood

(ignore it), and going straight towards Mount Maletto, which remains on your left like the homonymous refuge. Once you're out of the pinewood on a vast lava field at the foot of the smooth, black slope of the Bronte, go up to the refuge of Mount Scavo, as the other refuges, left unattended, but open. After skirting the La Caccia hillock from the right, pass the ref-

uge of Mount Palestra and climb up to the homonymous pass (1,985 m), the maximum altitude. Now ride down scattered and spectacular larch trees to the refuge of the Galvarina, then on a level stretch across the Galvarina plateau. Go downhill again in the sweet-scented larch wood, and back on asphalt road (33 km); keep right until you reach the big green gate of the State Property Administration that blocks the road. Past the gate, go left, climbing up to the confluence with the S.P. 92 provincial road from Nicolosi reaching the Sapienza refuge, where you can stop or continue on asphalt road along the eastern side up to the **Brunek refuge**.

Technical info

Route
40 Km: Rifugio Brunek - Dammusi pass - Rifugio Monte Santa Maria – ruins of the station - Rifugio Monte Scavo - Mount Palestra pass - Galvarina plateau - Rifugio Sapienza. On dirt roads along the southern slope, with constant up and downhill stretches. You can reach the starting point from the Fiumefreddo exit of the A18 Messina-Catania with the S.S.120 main road up to Linguaglossa, then with the Mareneve. From the Sapienza refuge, go back to the Brunek refuge on asphalt road, touching the centers of Zafferana Etnea and Milo (42 km).

Difficulty
A few stretches, cut in recent lava flows, require some effort and practice on an MTB; the rest is wide dirt roads with hard surfaces; the length of the route and the overall rise require good training.

Cycling period
Spring and fall.

Map
Parco dell'Etna, scale 1:50,000, TCI.

Technical assistance
• Le Due Ruote di F. Salvatore, via N. Martoglio 93/m, Santa Venerina.
• Salvatrice Carcatizzo, via Roma 265 A/B, Belpasso; t. 0957912802, 0957912577.

Tourist information
Local Tourist Boards:
• Catania, via Cimarosa 10, t. 0957306211.
• Linguaglossa, piazza Annunziata 7; t. 095643094.
• Nicolosi, via Garibaldi 63; t. 095911505.
• Ente Parco dell'Etna, via Etnea 107, Nicolosi; t. 095914588. www.parks.it/parco.etna/
• Etna Free Bike MTB Club, via Lanzerotti 33, Catania; t. 3473554381, 368663031.
• Museo Vulcanologico, via delle Querce 5, Nicolosi; t. 095914722.
• Alpine Rescue; t. 095914142.

ITINERARIES

Sicily

The Pantelleria island: in the 34 Km Mediterranean, amid spas and dammusi

In the blue heart of the Mediterranean, Pantelleria offers, at times, conditions of hard life, but it provides the traveler with landscapes and intense emotions, just like its wine.

From the **Pantelleria port**, ride westwards along the seafront (via Borgo Italia), until you reach a crossroads, after which, continue straight ahead on the side road that exits the town on a level stretch. After approximate-ly 2 km, the road steadily climbs until it crosses the Sesi Neolithic necropolis. A road sign indicates on your left the short path that takes you to the Sese Grande. Continue cycling along the side road on up and downhill stretches, and after approximately 5 km, at the bottom of a short descent, you find, on your right, the access stairway to the Sateria cave, where you can have a swim in the thermal waters. Now continue along the coast reaching Scauri (3 km) on a tough uphill stretch. At this point, leave the side road. After crossing the town center, you meet a double cross-roads, where you turn first left and then right, following the road signs pointing to Rekhale and taking a long rectilinear road running gently uphill. Once you reach Rekhale, instead of entering the town, continue climbing along the asphalt road up to the Serraglio pass, where a road sign indicates, on your

Technical info

Route

34 Km: Pantelleria - Sesi necropolis - Sateria cave - Scauri - Rekhale - Tracino - Khamma - Cala Cinque Denti - Campobello - Pantelleria. These roads must be covered with a mountain bike or touring bike equipped with good gears and wide tires.

Difficulty

This is a rolling route with frequent changes in gradients; no particular climbing qualities are required, but the route must be covered with a cool mind. Pay due attention to your riding techniques on the paved descent from the Serraglio pass to the Ghirlanda.

Bicycle + Ferryboat

You can reach the island by boat from Trapani with Siremar, t. 199123199 and 0923911120; or by airplane with Alitalia t. 848865643, Gandalf t. 848800858, Airone t. 8488488800.

Cycling period

All year round.

Technical assistance

Policardo, via Messina 31, Pantelleria; t. 0923912844 and 0923911741. Bicycle rental (also cars and mopeds).

Useful addresses

• Pro Loco Pantelleria, piazza Cavour; t. 0923911838. www.pantelleria.it/proloco.
• Agenzia Gira l'Isola, vicolo Messina 21, Pantelleria; t. and fax 0923913254 www.pantelleriatravel.com/agenziagiralisola

left, the road that leads to le Favare and Mount Gibele. Continue your ride down-hill, past the pass on the road that shortly after becomes paved and tough. After covering about 1 km from the pass, you reach a clear bend near a "dammuso" (typical Pantelleria con-struction) stuck against the rock on your right. Nearby, a

A trip to the lake known as **Specchio di Venere**, *which the locals call "u vagno i l'acqua" (bath of the water). It's a peculiar lake with salty mineral waters and extraordinary shades ranging from the exceptionally clear transparency to cobalt blue. The lake is surrounded by the typical terraces and is situated just a stone's throw from the Bugeber district. Try a swim in the thermal waters of the Sateria cave on the western coast.*

few terraces ("tanche") are surrounded by a small holm-oak wood. Leave your bike, and climbing down along three terraces, approach several Byzantine tombs (on your right) cut in the rock. After getting back on your bike, follow the descending road until it crosses, with a long rectilinear stretch, the Ghirlanda plain, the most fertile countryside expanse in the island, until reaching the village of Tracino with a short climb. In piazza Perugia, opposite the new church, turn right and ride down towards the sea; after covering approximately 100 m, take the first road on your left that crosses the town among the old houses and then climbs up to Khamma. Now proceed straight ahead for about 3 km on a gentle downhill stretch and then reconnect to the side road that you take towards your left, crossing the magnificent landscape of the Kaggiar lavas and touching Cala Cinque Denti. From this point, follow the Kattibugal coast: the road climbs up with two hairpin bends, leaving on your left the detour for Lake Venere and starting the descent towards Campobello.

After a 500 m downhill ride, leave the side road taking, on your left, a path (closed to motorized vehicles) that proceeds in the same direction with less gradient; continue riding straight ahead, ignoring the detours, until you emerge on an asphalt road, where you turn left, and at the next crossroads, turn right, riding down towards the centre of **Pantelleria**.

ABOVE, stop near the Serraglio pass. PAGE OPPOSITE, the coast near Scauri.

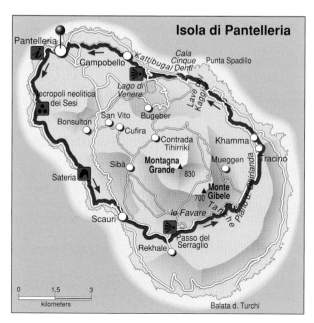

Isola di Pantelleria

Pantelleria
Campobello
Cala Cinque Denti
Punta Spadillo
Kattibugal
Lago di Venere
Necropoli neolitica dei Sesi
San Vito
Bugeber
Bonsulton
Cufira
Lave di Kaggiar
Contrada Tihirriki
Khamma
Sibà
Montagna Grande ▲ 830
Mueggen
Tracino
Piano di Ghirlanda
Sateria
Monte ▲ 700 Gibele
le Favare
Tane
Scauri
Passo del Serraglio
Rekhale
Balata d. Turchi

0   1,5   3
kilometers

🚲 The Madonie Park   40 Km
From Polizzi Generosa towards Mount Fanusi

Roads and paths invite the strong and well practiced bikers in the wild, spectacular heart of these mountains, to rediscover the taste of adventure immersed in Mother Nature.

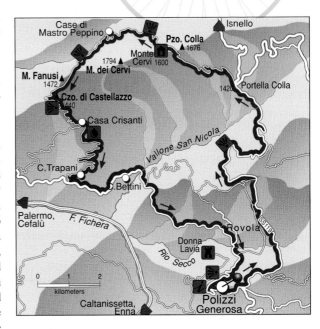

You start your trip from **Polizzi Generosa** on the S.P. 119 provincial road (towards Piano Battaglia) that gently rises for the first 6 km, then gets steeper for the second 6 km up to the Portella Colla pass (1,420 m). At this point, leave the main asphalt road and take dirt road n° 11 on your left, following the road signs pointing to the refuge of Mount Cervi and the Case di (houses of) Mastro Peppino. After 1.5 km, path n° 11 leaves the road: continue on the dirt road that climbs up more softly and meets again with the path further ahead.

Climb for 0.7 km, then descend for 0.8 km, where a very pleasant uphill stretch

Technical info

Route
40 Km (21 Km asphalt + 19 Km dirt road): Polizzi Generosa - Portella Colla - Rifugio Monte Cervi – Case di Mastro Peppino - Casa Crisanti - Polizzi Generosa.
Mixed route, where a mountain bike with shock-absorbing fork is really needed.

Difficulty
You must be in good shape to cover this route, owing to the rise (1,200 m). There are no technical difficulties; the fairly challenging part is the ride down towards the Crisanti house, due to the stony surface of the road (not very busy).

Cycling period
All year round, except in the chilly months.

Map
Carta dei sentieri e del paesaggio, Cefalù- Madonie, scale 1:50,000, table V: required to ramble on foot or by bike on the Madonie; available at tourist-accommodation facilities or at the local offices of the Madonie Park.

Technical assistance
Bici & Moto Shop,
largo Zingari 10/11,
Polizzi Generosa;
t. 3805034532, 3284020453.
Accessories, spare parts, apparel.

Tourist information
• Parco delle Madonie,
corso Paolo Agliata 16,
Petralia Sottana;
t. 0921684011,
fax 0921680478.
www.parks.it/parco.madonie/
• Club Alpino Italiano,
Polizzi Generosa chapter;
t. 0921688521, fax 0921649314.

starts, immersed in a wonderful beechwood, up to the pass of the Mount Cervi refuge (1,600 m).
Ride along an easy up and downhill stretch, and after 1.9 km, a magnificent view on Isnello opens up on your right. On sunny days, the archipelago of the Aeolian islands can be clearly seen. A further 1.5 km along the stony, but smooth panoramic descent, and you reach the Case di Mastro Peppino. From here, continue on your left, riding at mid coast on the mountain slope up to the spectacular passage in the rock where the dirt road starts following the ridge of Mount Fanusi (1,472 m). This is one of the most stunning spots of the itinerary.

PAGE OPPOSITE, the ride down from Mount Fanusi.

POINTS OF INTEREST

*An unforgettable **gastronomical itinerary** at Polizzi Generosa. With delicious ricotta cakes at the Al Castello confectioner's. Typical salumi at the Sausa butcher's and superb cuisine at the Giardino Donna Lavia farm holidays, contrada Donna Laura, S.S. 643 - km 8; t. 0921551037, cell. 339 6947829. Also available, car pick-up or drop service for cycling guests.*

After covering the ridge, start descending with a series of narrow hairpin bends to Casa Crisanti (approximately 5 km), where you can see a typical Madonita hut for shepherds.
At this stage, leave on your right the road that continues to drop, cross the bar near the house and continue on your left (the house remains on the right) towards the mountain. After 4.2 km, pass by the cattle sheds of the Ficile family (cheese producers) and a little further ahead, keeping on the main road, pass a group of country edifices. The descent ends by entering the asphalt road, where you turn left towards **Polizzi Generosa** (9 km) on a constant ascent with no tough spurts.

ALTERNATIVE
Since this is a very challenging itinerary, the less practiced cyclists may reach the Portella Colla pass directly by car and cycle up to the Case di Mastro Peppino, or they can reach the Portella of Mount Fanusi and go back, thus avoiding the long uphill stretches.

Between Palermo and Trapani 70 Km
From Scopello to the temple of Segesta

Western Sicily is a land of great charm, where your bicycle becomes the ideal fellow traveler to discover a spectacular coast and a hilly landscape made of old villages rich in monumental traces. Welcome to the Sicily that watches the sunset light, not far from the salt coast (Trapani-Marsala) and from the Erice belvedere.

The itinerary starts from Scopello, an old marine village and a well acclaimed sea resort, famous also for its "tonnara" (chambered nets to catch tuna fish), still active some years ago, and ends at Segesta, the city of the Elimi, a population who fought together with the Romans during the Punic war, and bitter rivals of Selinunte.

ABOVE AND BELOW, the spectacular coast near Scopello.
PAGE OPPOSITE, the Doric temple of Segesta.

Leave **Scopello**, following the road signs pointing to the Zingaro Nature Reserve, and turn right after approximately 700 m on a downhill stretch. After 1 km, on your left, you can see the old tonnara of Scopello opening on the view of amazing "faraglioni", and the workshops of pottery artisans. Ride for another 900 m and turn left, taking a long rectilinear stretch, then a series of hairpin bends up to the white beach of the Giudaloca bay.

The itinerary continues on the small bridge you see on your left, and then climbs up on your right towards Castellammare del Golfo. Once you get on the S.S. 187 main road, turn left towards Palermo, paying great attention when crossing the road. At the second traffic light, take the road on your right, continuing up to the Segesta Baths. From here, follow the road signs indicating Segesta. At the top of the climb, turn left and pass under the railroad and freeway

The archaeological area and the Segesta Baths. Of the old city, sacked by the Saracens around the year 1000, there remain the V century Doric temple and the Hellenistic theatre (III-II century B.C.). The Baths, built in 1958 and extended In 1990 on the ancient, legendary Acquae Segestanae, are famous for the therapeutic action of the radioactive, hyperthermal and highly mineralized springs. The waters gush out at a temperature of 46-47 °C, and are rich in sulphuretted hydrogen and many other sulphurous compounds.

bridges and follow the signs for Segesta. Now reach the railroad station, a refreshment spot and the archaeological site.

From the station, after passing under the railroad, continue for 2.7 km up to the crossroads, where you turn right, heading towards Buseto Palizzolo, crossing the village of Bruca. At this stage, the road runs along the Bosco di Scorace Nature Reserve and then continues towards the town center of Buseto, brushing Lake Rubino.

Continue towards the S.S. 187 main road to Palermo. Exit the main road at the interchange for Balata di Baida, and once you reach the small village, follow the road signs for the XIV century castle.

The final stretch of the itinerary curls towards Visicari and then **Scopello**, where the circle and your trip end.

Technical info

Route
70 Km: Scopello - Giudaloca bay - Terme di Segesta - Bruca - Buseto - Balata di Baida - Visicari - Scopello. Entirely on asphalt roads.

Difficulty
This route is, on average, challenging and requires some basic training. We suggest a road bicycle or a good touring bicycle with slick tires.

Bicycle + Train
The route crosses the railroad line between Castellammare del Golfo and Trapani near the Segesta and Bruca stations.

Map
Atlante stradale d'Italia, Central volume, 1:200,000, TCI.

Technical assistance
Ciclomania Pizzitola, corso G. Medici 41/A, Alcamo; t. and fax 092426392.

Information and organized trips
Siciclando, via M.T. Cicerone 19, Bagheria;

t. and fax 091495065
www.siciclando.com
Tour operator specialized in organizing bicycle holidays and itinerant trips in Sicily through various formulas, from support vehicles to guides, and autonomous trips with the provision of a personalized road book.

Useful addresses
• Tourist Information Office, piazzetta Saturno, Trapani;
t. 092329000, fax 092324004.

Sardinia

 ## Alghero, kingdom of the maestrale 30 Km
Between Lake Baratz and Porto Ferro

A magnificent ride in the lush maquis of the coral Riviera.

From the **Santa Maria la Palma** square, leaving the church behind, take the first road on your right (one-way street) that exits the town, and ride along a eucalyptus-lined path for 2.4 km, up to an intersection, where you turn right, then (1.2 km) left, following the road signs pointing to Lake Baratz. After 1.4 km, you reach a big fork, where you keep right and continue cycling up to the parking lot (1.1 km) bounded by a wooden fence. Near the square, stop to admire Lake Baratz, the only natural lake in Sardinia.

From the left corner at the end of the square starts the dirt road that runs right of the pinewood on constant ups and downs and reaches the Aragonese tower (1.7 km) overlooking the Porto Ferro bay. Go back to the square and continue along the asphalt road for 800 m, up to the detour on your right that drops and enters a pinewood.

Ignore the detour on your left, which you meet after 1.3 km, and continue towards a big crossroads (700 m); turning left, after 300 m, you get back on asphalt road near a crossroads, where you turn right and rapidly reach (400 m) the parking lot on Porto Ferro. Once you're back on the asphalt road, reach the crossroads and keep right; a further 50 m, then turn right until you reach the big parking lot, within sight of the Bantine Sale tower, a magnificent panoramic spot on the Gulf of Porto Ferro. Cover the 400 m up to the

LEFT, Alghero, Cala Viola and the Porticciolo tower.

POINTS OF INTEREST

*The nice ride from Alghero to the remarkable sea-cliffs of **Capo Caccia**, a spectacular arm of clear rock where griffins nest, cycling past the nuragic village of Palmavera, the Bombarde and Lazzaretto beaches and the Porto Conte bay.*

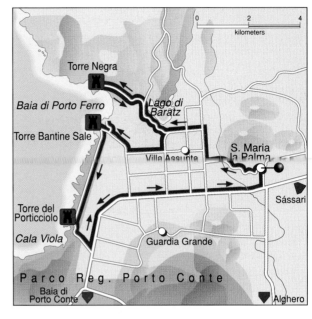

crossroads, where you turn right on the wide dirt road that cuts the undergrowth and follows the wild stretch of coast between Porto Ferro and the Porticciolo tower, on constant up and downhill stretches. Many detours on the right lead towards the sea.

The dirt road ends after 4.6 km with an intersection on the asphalt road: on your right, reach (200 m) the square and the belvedere facing the Porticciolo tower and Cala Viola, while on your left, continue up to a crossroads (700 m), where you turn left towards Sassari. After 600 m, take a detour on your right on the asphalt path that continues in the fields for 1.4 km up to an intersection.

At this point, turn left reaching the crossroads opposite a fish shop; proceed on your right for 4.1 km up to the entrance on the big asphalt road. Go left up to the traffic lights (1.9 km) and then straight ahead up to the **Santa Maria la Palma** square.

Technical info

Route
30 Km: Santa Maria la Palma – Lake Baratz - Porto Ferro - Cala Viola - Santa Maria la Palma.

Difficulty
The route is mainly asphalt, with a few stretches of easy dirt road. There are no difficulties in store, except for the section between Porto Ferro and the Porticciolo tower, on constant up and downhill stretches with a rather bumpy surface in several spots.

Cycling period
All year round; it may be really scorching in mid summer.

Notes
This is a very interesting itinerary from a natural viewpoint, which deserves a whole day out, stopping at the magnificent Porto Ferro beaches. The Bantine Sale and Porticciolo towers are two excellent spots where you can admire the sunset.

Map
Atlante stradale d'Italia, Central volume, 1:200,000, TCI.

Technical assistance
Velosport di Mario e Patricia Oppes, via Vittorio Veneto 90/92, Santa Maria la Palma; t. 079977182.

Tourist information
• Azienda Soggiorno e Turismo, piazza Porta Terra 9, Santa Maria la Palma; t. 079979054.

The Nuraghi Valley
From Rebeccu to Santu Antine

34.5 Km

A true journey back in time, crossing the Sardinian inland amid the monumental millenary stones of the Nuraghi Valley, between Bonorva, Sant'Andrea Priu and the nuragic palace of Santu Antine.

From the **Rebeccu** square, ride down towards the main road (1.2 km), where you turn right (for Bono) and continue for 1.8 km up to a crossroads where a road sign indicates, on your right, the archaeological site of Domus de Janas of Sant'Andrea Priu. After 2 km, near the small Church of Santa Lucia, proceed on a smooth dirt road for 500 m up to Sant'Andrea Priu. Stop at the archaeological

Technical info

Route
34.5 Km: Rebeccu - Torralba station - Santu Antine nuragh - Rebeccu. You can easily reach the starting point from Bonorva (5.5 km).

Difficulty
The route has no difficulties, but in late spring and summer, avoid the central hours of the day when it gets really hot. You ride along a level and asphalt road with only 3.2 km of dirt road that can be covered by any bike.

Cycling period
All year round, preferably in spring and fall.

Map
Atlante stradale d'Italia,

Central volume, 1:200,000, TCI.

Technical assistance
Società Ciclistica Santa Barbara, corso Umberto, Bonorva; t. 3486525801.

Tourist information
• Pro Loco, corso Umberto, Bonorva; t. 079687987.
• Azienda Autonoma di Soggiorno, via Roma 62, Sassari; t. 079231777.
• Information Office, Alghero Fertilia Airport; t. 079935124.

POINTS OF INTEREST

The hypogean necropolis of Sant'Andrea Priu, *close to Rebeccu, where you can visit one of the most beautiful Domus de janas of the island. The Domus de janas are the so-called "houses of the fairies", funereal structures of the recent Neolithic period (III millennium B.C.). Visits to the necropolis: 10.30 a.m.-1.00 p.m. and 3.00-6.30 p.m.; continuous working day during summer. Information: t. 079867205, 3485642611.*

site and continue on the same road, up to the provincial road n. 43, where you turn right and ride for 2.7 km up to a crossroads. On your left, take the provincial road n° 21 and follow the road signs pointing to Torralba and the S.S. 131 main road. After 3.1 km, turn right for Torralba, where you

ABOVE, the Nuragh Valley, nuraghs of Santu Antine. PAGE OPPOSITE, the Nuragh Valley at Torralba.

can see the clear volcanic cone of Mount Cujaru. Shortly ahead (2 km), the road gets rough, although the surface is still hard enough to be covered even with a normal touring bike for about 1 km. Once you're back on the asphalt road, after 2.6 km, pass near the Tomba dei Giganti (Giants' Tomb) - right of the road - and after 2 km, cross the railroad. Just after the level crossing (100 m), take the path on your left (dirt path for 1.2 km) towards the Torralba station (2.1 km). Opposite the station, turn right, following the road signs for the S.S. 131 main road. On your left, you can see the Oes nuragh, a rare example of construction without the typical "tolos" cover. You shortly (1.1 km) reach the Santu Antine nuragh that is worth a visit; you can fill your water flask here or have a snack at the bar.

The itinerary continues turning back to the railroad. After passing the level crossing, after 1.4 km, turn left on the road winding along the edges of the valley, passing under the town of Giave (visible on the upper right corner) and near a small hill (at a sharp curve on your right) dominated by the Poltolu nuragh (5.3 km).
Continue on this road for 1 km up to a big crossroads, where you turn left (again on the S.P. 43 provincial road) up to the crossroads (2.7 km) for **Rebeccu**.
Now take the last kilometer uphill with the small Romanesque Church (XII century) of San Lorenzo clearly visible on your right.
ALTERNATIVE
From the Santu Antine nuragh, you can continue towards Torralba (4 km), seat of an interesting archaeological museum.

The Sinis peninsula 1   34 Km
Tharros and the quartz beaches

The route stretches in the southern part of the peninsula, with white quartz beaches on very cyclable roads.

From **San Salvatore**, start riding towards Is Arutas along the S.P. 59 provincial road. Take the gentle ascent and cross the Su Pianu hills, and after 5.8 km, you reach the parking lot bounded by a dry wall, next to the Is Arutas beach, an

Technical info

Route
34 Km: San Salvatore - Is Arutas - Funtana Meiga - San Giovanni - Tharros - Capo San Marco - San Giovanni - San Salvatore. You can reach the starting point from Cabras (approximately 4 km).
Difficulty
This is an ideal itinerary for everyone, mainly level, with 14.6 km of lightly-trafficked dirt roads.
Cycling period
All year round.
Map
Carta Topografica d'Italia, 1:50,000, sheets 514 and 528 IGM.
Notes
We suggest planning the entire day out on this itinerary, with highly suggestive places such as the Is Aruttas beach, the village of San Salvatore,

the municipal park of Seu, the archaeological ruins and the Tharros beaches.
Technical assistance
• F.lli Cemedda, via Tharros 61/63, Cabras; t. 0783290804.
• Ciclosport Cabella, via Busacchi 2, Oristano; t. and fax 078372714.
Tourist information
• Sinis Peninsula guides, Cabras; t. 0783370019. Archaeological excursions and nature walks (including the protected area of Pauli e' Sali).
• Ente Provinciale Turismo via Cagliari, Oristano, t. 078336831.
• Pro Loco, via Vittorio Emanuele 8, Oristano; t. 078370621.

ideal spot to have a swim. From the parking lot facing the sea, turn sharply towards the left and follow the gentle uphill dirt road that runs for a short stretch (50 m) along a fenced wall, then turn right and follow the coastline. After less than 5 km, ride on your right along the municipal park of Seu, whose gates are just shortly ahead (6.2 km from Is Aruttas).
We suggest riding on the easy tracks that reach the tower and the coast through the thick maquis and a small colony of twisted Aleppo pines.
After 1.4 km, you reach a crossroads: ride down towards the left between the houses of Funtana Meiga,

ABOVE, the beach at San Giovanni di Sinis.
PAGE OPPOSITE, the village of San Salvatore.

POINTS OF INTEREST

The archaeological area of **Tharros,** *situated near the spectacular Capo San Marco, where the old Phoenician city founded in the VI millennium B.C. lies.*
At **Cabras,** *the XV century Pontis fish pond, where you can still fish mullets that assemble in the "lavorieri" (fish barriers). A place also worth seeing is the village of San Salvatore, with its small houses named* cumbessias, *gathered round the Church of* **San Salvatore** *(XVII century), built on a hypogean sanctuary where the ancients used to worship the waters.*

up to the asphalt road near the sea (intersection).
At this point, turn left, following the road that be-comes a dirt road after 400 m and enters the main road. Now turn right, and after crossing San Giovanni (1 km) with its beautiful early Christian church, you reach Tharros and its ruins facing the sea. From the archaeological excavations, continue on the dirt road leaving on your right the San Giovanni tower. Now ride on the ridge of the peninsula. The road continues uphill for a short, though steep stretch (250 m) and penetrates the thick undergrowth up to Capo San Marco (700 m).
In the vicinity, on a highly suggestive and extremely panoramic promontory, you can see a lighthouse. Once back at Tharros on the same road (1.7 km), continue your ride on asphalt road, passing by San Giovanni (800 m), then continue riding on level road; after 2.4 km, near the Angioa Corruda nuragh, the road turns towards the right up to the crossroads for Putzu Idu, where you follow the road signs pointing to **San Salvatore**.

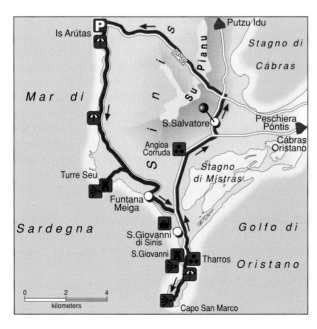

The Sinis peninsula 2
Towards the promontory of Capo Mannu

14.6 Km

An easy ride with extensive views along the coast and spectacular landscapes in the greater flamingo ponds.

Exit the **Orte & Corru Ranch** near the Sale Porcus Oasis (horses and Greater Flamingo Museum) and follow, on your right, the dirt road across a field for 1.1 km, until you reach a crossroads, where you turn left, then immediately right, riding along the eucalyptus wood. After reaching the asphalt road, turn right, and after 20 m, left. Once you reach an intersection on dirt road, turn right. After cover-

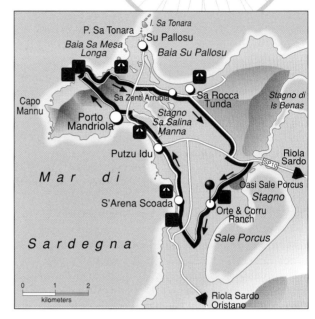

Technical info

Route
14.6 Km (10.6 Km on dirt road, 4 Km on asphalt):
San Vero Milis (Sale Porcus Oasis - Orte & Corru Ranch) - S'Arena Scoada - Putzu Idu - Sa Salina Manna - Capo Mannu - Sa Mesa Longa beach - Sa Rocca Tunda - Sale Porcus Oasis. You can easily reach the starting point from Cabras or Riola following the road leading to the Sale Porcus pond, where you meet the road signs for the Museo del Fenicottero Rosa (Greater Flamingo Museum).
Difficulty
The only tough, but not really challenging part, is the climb

up to Capo Mannu. We suggest using a mountain bike.
Map
Carta Topografica d'Italia, 1:50,000, sheets 514 (Cuglieri) and 528 (Oristano), IGM.
Technical assistance
• F.lli Cemedda, via Tharros 61/63, Cabras; t. 0783290804.
• Ciclosport Cabella, via Busacchi 2, Oristano; t. and fax 078372714.
Horse trekking
The Orte & Corru Ranch (t. 078352200) organizes outings and trips on horseback,

nature camps to watch the symbol of this area, the greater flamingo, to which an interesting museum has been dedicated in the center.
Tourist information
• Sinis Peninsula guides, Cabras; t. 0783370019. Archaeological excursions and nature walks (including the protected area of Pauli e' Sali).
• Ente Provinciale Turismo, via Cagliari, Oristano, t. 078336831.
• Pro Loco, via Vittorio Emanuele 8, Oristano; t. 078370621.

POINTS OF INTEREST

Extension towards the Falesie (14 km). From the S'Arena Scoada beach, a dirt path follows the coast southwards, winding on a balcony about 7.5 km long, along the panoramic spots of Roia de su Cantaru, Rocca de su Tingiosu and Capo Sa Sturaggia, up to the ponds of Mari Ermi.
To get back to S'Arena Scoada, cover the same road. The entire itinerary is 30 km long.

ing 200 m, reach the crossroads and turn right, then ride for a further 200 m and reach another crossroads, where you turn right again, up to a panoramic spot on the sea cliffs (starting point for the suggested extension). Now continue towards the S'Arena Scoada beach; after 100 m, the road passes between the houses of S'Arena Scoada and then crosses the built-up area of Putzu Idu. After reaching the asphalt stretch, at an intersection, go left on the road passing between the beach and the pond of Sa Salina Manna. After passing the crossroads for Mandriola, take the third gravel bend turning left (1.1 km from the start of the asphalt stretch) and entering a large widening: keep left and take the road opposite that climbs up to the promontory of Capo Mannu.

RIGHT, cycling at Capo Mannu.

After 1.4 km, after reaching the promontory summit, keep right, until you get to the tower overlooking the bay of Sa Mesa Longa, Punta Sa Tonara, with the homonymous islet and, at the back, the bay of Su Pallosu.
You're now at the northernmost point of the Sinis peninsula, from where you can distinctly see, on very clear days, Capo Caccia, 66 km away.
From the tower, ride down for 1.1 km on a bumpy track, with the Sa Salina Manna pond opposite. At the end of the descent, continue straight ahead on the main path towards the Sa Mesa Longa beach (200 m), keeping right (all the detours on your left lead to the beach). After reaching the asphalt road (600 m), at an intersection, turn right, up to the first

crossroads (200 m), where you turn left on a wide dirt road.
Ride for 400 m up to a crossroads, where you turn right on the road brushing the Sa Zenti Arrubia farm holidays (400 m) at Sa Rocca Tunda. After covering 800 m, take the asphalt road on your right that enters, after 2 km, the S.P. 10 provincial road for Riola Sardo (on your left). Ride for 600 m up to the gates of the Sale Porcus Oasis situated near a big dirt widening opposite the pond. From here, follow the central road, with the wooden telephone poles and the pond on your left, up to a crossroads (1 km), where you keep left, following the road signs pointing to the Greater Flamingo Center and the **Orte & Corru Ranch** (600 m).

The Giara Nature Park 5.5 Km
Between Pauli Maiori and Zepparedda

The Giara is an extensive plateau, rich in basaltic lava that was hurled into the air 2.5 million years ago from the craters of Zepparedda (609 m above sea level) and Zeppara Manna (580 m above sea level), today harmless elevations dominating the vast tableland blanketed by strawberry trees, mock privets, myrtles, mastic trees and rock roses. Space expands at the paulis, depressions that fill with water in winter, while in spring they dress up with the white colors of the buttercups. As far as the eye can see, shaped horizontally, you can see the flag trees, the cork oaks that can't grow upwards because

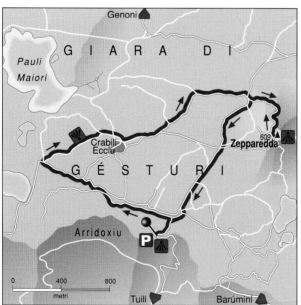

this is the land of the "maestrale" the north-west wind that loves to blow freely, with nothing in its way. As free as the "Cavallini della Giara", the last small wild horses in Europe and symbol of this mysterious land placed between land and sky.

At **Tuili**, exit the Madau parking lot and take the level dirt road that turns right after a few meters (on your left you would ride towards the small Church of Santa Luisa). Crossing a holm-oak

ABOVE, the Giara, panorama on the Marmilla. PAGE OPPOSITE, the Pauli Maiori pond.

POINTS OF INTEREST

A visit to the park *with expert guides from the Jara Service Center. Besides the nature visits to the park, you can book a traditional Sardinian meal: boiled sheep, roast piglet and lamb are just some of the specialties awaiting you.*

wood, you emerge on tableland dominated by an old pylon; now ride towards another wood (keeping right) in the presence of a few low dry walls. The track ends on a narrow passage on your right through the wall: after crossing this passage, follow, on your left, the road that stretches straight ahead, skirting the wall up to a circular courtyard (Bruncu 'e Sulas), once used to round up the small horses (1.8 km).

Now proceed on your right up to a widening (500 m) overlooking the Pauli Maiori pond. Two paths start on your right: the left one runs along the pond reaching the Salamessi spring (450 m), while the itinerary proceeds on the right one. The small road gradually narrows until it becomes a pathway. After reaching a clear widening, keep right, and after 30 m, take the path that turns right heading towards Crabili Ecciu, with the "su masoni" hut and the typical local "caprili" (stone huts for shepherds).

Now that you're back on the path (30 m behind), continue for a short distance, until you enter a clear cart road, where you turn left. At the first crossroads (150 m), keep right, continuing on the main

trail up to an intersection, where you turn right towards the Zepparedda hillside (500 m), passing two crossroads: the first on your left, the second on your right. Zepparedda is the crater that erupted the lava (two million years ago) that forms today the basaltic cover of this plateau. From this point, turn back up to the previous intersection, where you turn left, with the hillside at your back, riding for 1 km on the main track up to a small cork wood near a crossroads. Now turn left, following the road that leads to the wooden gate within sight of the Madau parking lot at **Tuili**.

ALTERNATIVE

The more practiced cyclists can extend their ride by riding down the plateau towards Genoni and continuing towards Nuragus, Gesturi, Barumini and Tuili. In this case, the route is longer (36 km), so we suggest you ask detailed information (see box aside).

Technical info

Route
5.5 Km: Tuili (Madau parking lot) - Bruncu 'e Sulas - Pauli Maiori - Crabili Ecciu - Zepparedda. You can reach the starting point from Tuili by taking the road leading to La Giara (5.5 km).

Difficulty
No difficulties on this route, which is mostly level, entirely on well-beaten dirt surface.

Cycling period
All year round, with some difficulties in case of heavy showers.

Map
Carta del Parco, scale 1:10,000, provided by the guides from the Centro Servizi Jara.

Technical assistance and tourist information
• Centro Servizi Jara,
via G.B. Tuveri 16, 09029 Tuili;
t. 0709373022,
fax 0709301569,
cell. 3482924983. www.jara.it,
info@jara.it
Bicycle rental, guided visits on foot or by bike.
• Cooperativa Sa Jara Manna,
via V. Emanuele III 72, Gesturi;
t. 0709368170.

The San Pietro island: towards Punta delle Colonne and Capo Sandalo 45 Km

This is not the usual circular route, since there is no road covering the circuit of the island, only a path which, from the different routes starting and ending at Carloforte, explores the western side.

You start from **Carloforte**, following the road signs pointing to the beaches, riding along the old salt mines, where you can spot flamingos and herons. Shortly ahead, turn left, heading towards Punta Spalmatore, then left again for the Colonne, rocky formations emerging from the sea, which you can reach by covering a

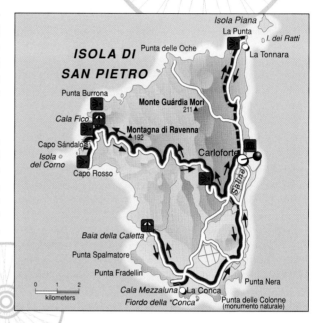

Technical info

Route
Approximately 45 Km:
Carloforte - Punta delle Colonne - La Conca - Baia della Caletta - Carloforte - Capo Sandalo - Carloforte. You can reach the island by ferry boat (Saremar, t. 0781854005) from Portovesme and Calasetta to Carloforte.

Difficulty
This is not a flat itinerary, but it has no difficulties, such as long climbs or too steep spurts. It's a varied route you must cover at ease, planning many stops at the most panoramic

places on the coast. We suggest covering the itinerary with a good touring bike equipped with 18-speed gear or with an MTB.

Cycling period
All year round.

Map
• *Atlante stradale d'Italia,* Central volume, 1:200,000, TCI.
• *Isola di San Pietro,* 1:30,000, Pro Loco Carloforte.

Bicycle rental
• Attilio Borghero, piazza Repubblica, Carloforte; t. 0781854123.
• Marinatour, via Porcile, Carloforte; t. 0781854110.

Tourist information
• Pro Loco, corso Repubblica 1, Carloforte; t. 0781854009.
• Agenzia Tabarka, corso Battellieri 24, Carloforte; t. 0781855055. Sea and air booking office, excursions, car rental, booking of hotels and houses.
• Dea, corso Tagliafico, Carloforte; t. 0781854331, 3383917132. Excursions and boat trips.
• Paradiso, Carloforte port; t. 0781854244.

POINTS OF INTEREST

In spring, you can watch the traditional **tuna fishing,** *which takes place using the old "tonnara" technique. The Isla Diving (via Cantieri, at Spalmadureddu, Carloforte; t. 0781855 634, cell. 335462502) organizes outings on fishermen's boats and spectacular diving inside the "tonnara". News, material and models of the "tonnara" are displayed at the Town Museum of Carloforte (via Cisterna del re 24, t. 0781 855880)*

short pathway across the fields. The itinerary continues by following the road signs for the La Conca restaurant and after taking a path ending just shortly after, near the amazing Conca inlet.

Once you're back at the crossroads, continue riding towards Punta Spalmatore, and after passing by the camping site, where the asphalt road ends, turn left for La Caletta, the most beautiful beach of the island. At this point, go back to Carloforte

on the direct road (at the crossroads for La Conca, Cala Mezzaluna and the Colonne), turn left, and after reaching the salt mines, turn left for Capo Sandalo, which you can reach by riding on a spectacular road approximately 8 km long. The road ends near a large square. You can continue on foot along small pathways that flank the upper edge of the sea cliffs and face the rocks below and the small island of the Corno. In this area (240 hectares),

ABOVE, San Pietro island, the coast at capo Sandalo.
BELOW, the Carloforte "tonnara".

stretching between Capo Rosso and Cala Vinagra, you meet the Oasis for the Fauna Protection of Eleonora's falcon, which finds the best nesting spots in the recesses high up on the sea. Another detour worth taking leads to Cala Fico. You can reach the locality by covering for a couple of kilometers the road that returns to Carloforte and then turns left on a dirt road. You arrive near the pebbly beach in the deepest and most sheltered area of the inlet. The itinerary ends by covering the same road that takes you back to **Carloforte**.

ALTERNATIVE

From Carloforte towards La Punta, up to the old facilities of the "tonnara" (11 km there and back).

Tuscany Umbria Marche

 ## From the Tyrrhenian to the Adriatic 540 Km
Crossing the heart of Italy

*Discovering the most genuine parts of Italy across three regions that connect the two seas. Along by-roads, you ride across villages, countryside and mountains, experiencing the slow speed of a trip to relish by stage. The Tirreno Adriatico is a classic bicycle race that professional cyclists know too well; in our case, this is no race, it's an in-*vitation to discover what it's like to travel on a bike, leaving with a small load and a big craving for cycling.*

From **Castagneto Carducci**, ride towards Sassetta (7 km), where a spectacular descent starts amid cork oaks towards the medieval village of Suvereto (13 km); continue by taking the road on your left and following the road signs pointing to Monterotondo Marittimo.

After about 3 km, turn right to Massa Marittima. After passing by Montioni, turn at the first crossroads on your left and take the road that passes by the Fattoria Marsiliana, and with a series of short uphill spurts, reaches (14 km) the alternative route

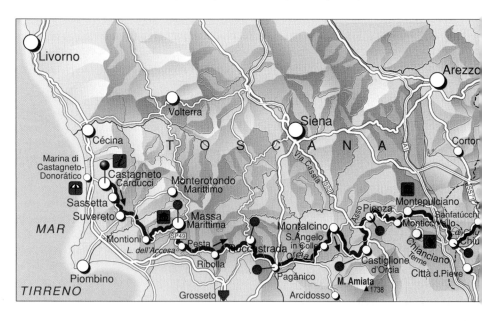

POINTS OF INTEREST

In brief: the road from Castagneto Carducci *to* Suvereto; *the square and Cathedral of* Massa Marittima; Montalcino *with its fortress and the Sant'Antimo Abbey;* Castiglione d'Orcia *with the Tentennano fortress;* Pienza *and the Orcia Valley;* Montepulciano *and its splendid wine cellars,* Solomeo *and the Brunello Cucinelli factory (see itinerary Colli Perugini Doc-The cashmere and wine path),* Spello *and the road reaching* Colfiorito *crossing Capodacqua, Rio and Annifo; the* Sant'Angelo *Valley;* Camerino *and its belvedere on the Apennines; the magic solitude of Elcito, a village perched on the slopes of Mount San Vicino; the Duomo of* Osimo; *the* Mount Conero *Nature Park and the Sirolo beaches.*

ABOVE, climbing up to Solomeo.

at the foot of the small town of Massa Marittima; to get to the town center, ride uphill for about 3 km.

From **Massa Marittima**, continue along the S.P. 49 provincial road to Lake Accesa, to Pesta up to an intersection (15 km), where you turn left towards **Ribolla** (10 km) and then towards Roccastrada (17 km, last 8 km uphill).

From Roccastrada, ride down to **Paganico** (14 km), where you take the road to Arcidosso-Castel del Piano; after 13.5 km, turn left towards Montalcino. Once you've crossed the bridge over the River Orcia, that's where the uphill ride in the vast vineyards starts towards

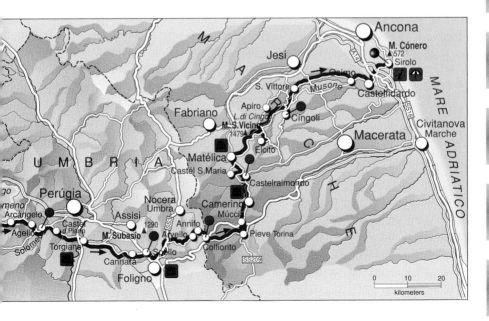

Technical info

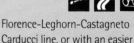

Route

Approximately 540 Km:
Castagneto Carducci -
Suvereto - Massa Marittima -
Ribolla - Paganico - Montalcino
- Castiglione d'Orcia -
Bagno Vignoni - Pienza -
Montepulciano - Chiusi - Lake
Trasimeno - Solomeo - Torgiano
- Spello - Annifo - Colfiorito -
Sant'Angelo Valley - Muccia -
Camerino - Castelraimondo -
Matelica – Mount San Vicino -
Elcito - Castel San Pietro -
Moscosi - Cingoli - Musone
Valley - Osimo - Sirolo.
This is an itinerary covered
mainly on lightly-trafficked
by-roads. There are also some
unsurfaced, though well-beaten
and cyclable stretches.

Difficulty

This is a real journey that
requires adequate preparation:
cyclists and bicycles must be
in good conditions. The most
challenging stretches are the
climbs up to Montalcino,
San Quirico d'Orcia
and the Colfiorito and Mount
San Vicino passes.

Cycling period

The ideal seasons to cross
Central Italy are spring and fall.
It may be hot in summer
and the art cities
over-crowded. Winter is out
of the question, because
of the chilly weather and
the snow-covered passes.

Cycling time

If you ride for an average
45 km per day, it'll take you two
weeks; with an average 60 km
per day, you can end the tour
in 9-10 days.

Bicycle + Car, Bicycle + Train

The trip back to the starting
point can be made by train on
the winding Ancona-Bologna-
Florence-Leghorn-Castagneto
Carducci line, or with an easier
ride by renting a car at Ancona.

Map

Atlante stradale d'Italia,
Central volume, 1:200,000, TCI.

Useful addresses

• Farm Holidays,
Casella Postale 84,
58100 Grosseto;
t. 0564417418.
All the information and
assistance to book the stage
points along the route.

Tourist information

• Azienda Promozione
Turistica, piazza Cavour 6;
Leghorn
t. 0586204611.
For the first stretch of
the itinerary from Marina
di Castagneto Carducci to
Massa Marittima (excluded).
• Municipal Tourist Office,
piazza Garibaldi;

Sant'Angelo in Colle (7 km), then to Montalcino (9 km), where you continue downhill to Sant'Antimo, with the beautiful Cistercian abbey and the Monte Amiata railroad station.

Now cross the bridge over the Asso and then start the ascent with hairpin bends to **Castiglione d'Orcia** (16.5 km), then taking the steep descent (4 km) towards the bottom of the valley where, after reaching the S.S. 2 Cassia main road, you turn left, reaching the nearby Bagno Vignoni. Once you're back on the Cassia, turn left, and after 600 m, turn right, following the road signs pointing to Monticchiello-Pienza up to the crossroads (1.5 km) on your left, just before a bridge, where the dirt road to **Pienza** starts. After 5.1 km, turn left and enter the asphalt road that reaches the quaint town (2.1 km) overlooking the Orcia Valley. The last 3 km towards Pienza are uphill. Now ride down towards the valley, taking the same road (always ride on the asphalt stretch) up to the bridge over the Tresa (5.4 km), after which, you turn left to Monticchiello: the uphill stretch starts after 1 km and ends after 3.7 km in the small village. From Monticchiello,

Massa Marittima,
t. 0566902289.
• Tourist Office,
Roccastrada;
t. 0564564086.
• Ufficio Turistico Val d'Orcia, ,
via Dante Alighieri 33,
San Quirico d'Orcia;
t. 0577897211.
• Municipal Tourist
Office,
costa del Municipio 8,
 Montalcino;
t. 0577849331.
• Tourist Information
Office, corso Rossellino 59,
Pienza;
t. 0578749071.
• Pro Loco of Pienza,
via Case Nuove 4;
t. 0578748072.
• Pro Loco of Spello,
piazza Matteotti 3;
t. 0742301009.
• Pro Loco, of Montepulciano,

via Di Gracciano nel Corso;
t. 0578757341.
• Strada del Vino Nobile
di Montepulciano,
piazza Grande 7;
t. 0578717484.
• Tourist Information
Office, piazza Cavour 2,
Camerino;
t. 0737632534.
• Tourist Information
Office, via Luigi Ferri 17,
Cingoli;
t. 0733602444.
• Comunità Montana
del San Vicino,
seat of Cingoli;
t. 0733602479-0733602823.
• Centro Visite Parco
del Conero,
via Peschiera 30/A, Sirolo;
t. 0719331879.
• Consorzio Parco del Conero,
via Vivaldi 1/3, Sirolo;
t. 0719331161/518.

ABOVE, the road for Colfiorito. TOP, the Sant'Antimo Abbey. PAGE OPPOSITE, the countryside near Chiusi.

continue towards Chianciano-Montepulciano: a short descent, then a 3.5 km uphill stretch, then 1.5 km up to an intersection, where you turn left towards Montepulciano. From this point, continue along the main road to Chiusi up to a crossroads on your left, at a clear curve on your right leading to Argiano; the road soon becomes unsurfaced and drops gently down amid extensive vineyards.

After 5 km, you reach a crossroads (on your left, down below, you can spot the large Fattoria del Cerro concern), where you keep right, riding downhill towards the hamlet of San

ORGANIZING YOUR TOUR: BY BICYCLE OR BICYCLE + CAR

There are mainly two alternatives to cover the Tirreno-Adriatico: 1) entirely and solely by bike with your baggage; 2) by car with your bike along. In the first case, you need to arrange your journey properly, planning the routes in advance and booking the various stage points depending on your own time requirements and traveling skills. It's not such a tough itinerary, but you will often encounter challenging stretches in the inner part of the Peninsula. This is a highly assorted itinerary from all sides: type of road, altitude, climate and environment crossed. You should therefore be physically and mentally ready and set at the starting point, with satisfactory practice in your legs and good knowledge of the maps. Since you don't have much time at hand, you can opt for a partial route, choosing, alternatively, the Tuscan, Umbria or Marche stretch.

As for the second case (car with bicycle along), you must plan a certain number of stages, stopping for two or three days at farm holidays and making daily excursions. This way, even the not too practiced cyclists can brave the journey by riding with an unloaded bike. The recommended base zones for bicycle outings are: in Tuscany, Castagneto Carducci and the Etruscan Coast, Massa Marittima and the upper Maremma, Pienza and the Orcia Valley. In Umbria, Spello with the Foligno plain and Mount Subasio, the Colfiorito plateau, the Apennine area of Mount San Vicino (for cyclists with trained legs). In Marche, the Cingoli countryside and the Mount Conero Nature Park.

Savino. After crossing the A1 Naples-Milan freeway, turn right on the S.P. 326 provincial road at Montallese, for **Chiusi** (7 km). From the town center of Chiusi, take the road that drops down to the homonymous lake, crossing the historical border between Tuscany and Umbria near the two towers known as "Beccati questo" and "Beccati quest'altro" ("Take this" and "Take that"!). After the bridge, the road starts climbing up to a crossroads, where you turn left (to Vaiano-Gioiella). Once you reach the next crossroads, continue on the dirt road to Sanfatucchio (5 km).

After crossing the town, take the S.S. 71 main road, turning right, and immediately after, turning left towards Macchie-Panicale, up to the junction (1.3 km) on the S.P. 699 provincial road that runs along the banks of Lake Trasimeno. Now cross Sant'Arcangelo, and after 3 km, turn right riding up towards Agello and, immediately after, towards **Solomeo**.

From this point, continue on up and downhill stretches crossing the towns of Capanne, Castel del Piano, Pila, San Martino in Colle and San Martino in Campo (about 15 km), and then continue towards Torgiano and its vineyards, Passaggio, Can-

nara and Spello, at the foot of Mount Subasio. At this point, get ready to cross the Apennine ridge.

From **Spello**, you reach San Giovanni Profiamma (passing by the Umbria camping site) and ride up the Topino Valley (avoiding the S.S. 3 main road to Nocera Umbra) towards Pontecentesimo: at this point, take the S.S. 3 main road for 1.4 km up to a crossroads on your right for Capodacqua, where you proceed on a clear uphill stretch that passes by Rio (5 km). You

now meet the crossroads on your left for Arvello (2.6 km) and the hill crossing near **Annifo** (2 km). From this moment, ride down towards the Annifo and Colfiorito plains. At **Colfiorito** (near the dairy), take the road for Taverne, which penetrates, after a short uphill stretch, the solitary Sant'Angelo Valley, on a constant descent across the small village of Fiume (10 km) and Pieve Torina (4.5 km), where you turn left on the n° 209 up to the Maddalena crossroads (4.2 km).

PAGE OPPOSITE, herd in the Sant'Angelo Valley. RIGHT, cycling towards Massa Marittima.

Now turn left up to Muccia (2 km), where you follow the road signs indicating Camerino (8.5 km: 2.5 uphill, 2.5 downhill and 3.5 uphill). From Camerino, ride steadily down to **Castelraimondo**: after crossing the town, turn left on the path that crosses Rustano and climbs up to Castel Santa Maria and Castel Sant'Angelo. From this point, passing by Castel Santa Maria again, ride down through the hamlet of Vasconi to Matelica (7 km), where the climb towards the Mount San Vicino pass starts: 12 km uphill, passing by Braccano, Vinano crossroads. Just before the hill crossing (1,177 m above sea level and the highest spot of the tour), turn right toward the spectacular village of El-

cito perched high up (5 km). Proceed downhill to Castel San Pietro, where you follow the signs for Apiro. Now ride on ups and downs to the crossroads on your right for Moscosi, continuing your ride skirting, from above, Lake Cingoli. After crossing the dam, turn right on the bridge that heralds the climb to **Cingoli** (8 km). From the

village, known as the "balcony of the Marche", continue downhill towards the hamlet of Villastrada, where you turn left on the dirt road that continues dropping down to the Rangore district and the small town of San Vittore. From here, ride across the Musone Valley following the left orographic side and passing by the hamlets of Casenuove and Campocavallo across the countryside surrounding Filottrano, Osimo and Castelfidardo. After reaching the Villa Musone crossroads (Q8 petrol station reference on your right), turn left riding on sharp up and downhill stretches towards Crocette, up to the entrance to the S.S. 17 Adriatica main road (very busy), which you cross. After crossing the railroad line and the A 14 freeway, turn right towards Coppo, then towards **Sirolo**, at the foot of Mount Conero, on the Adriatic coast.

ABOVE, Spello, the Ulivi Valley.
LEFT, Spello, "Le due Torri" farm holidays.

RECOMMENDED STAGE POINTS

- **Castagneto Carducci**
Residence Hotel & Bambolo restaurant
Il Bambolo;
t. 0565775206-0565775474:
hotel fitted for cyclists, with swimming pool, gym and sauna
Zi Martino Hotel
San Giusto;
t. 0565766000:
for cyclists, family-run
Podere Santa Maria
farm holidays
Grattamacco;
t. 0565763933:
the owners are expert cycle tourists.
- **Massa Marittima**
Il Cicalino
farm holidays
via Cicalino 3;
t. 0566902031:
magnificent position, 2 km from Massa Marittima.
Massa Vecchia
farm holidays
S.S. 439;
t. 0566903885:
specialized in cyclists' accommodation and assistance.
- **Roccastrada**
Poggio Oliveto
farm holidays
Venturi;
t. 0564 577257,
fax 0564577394:
at the start of the climb to Roccastrada, in an old village overlooking the Maremma.

- **Paganico**
Podere Piatina
Monte Antico
(8 km from Paganico);
t. 0564991037/991027:
a farming concern where you can breath the genuine Maremma atmosphere; excellent cuisine and 30 horses available for trekking.
- **Monte Amiata**
La Grossola
farm holidays
Grossola (a couple of km from the station towards Castiglione), 53023 Castiglione d'Orcia;
t./fax 0577887537:
at the foot of the Amiata, warm atmosphere and splendid position.
- **Pienza**
Santo Pietro
farm holidays
SS 146 main road (5 km from the town on the road to Montepulciano);
t./fax 0578748410:
in an old 18th century country house, with swimming pool.
Terrapille
farm holidays
Terrapille 80;
t. 0578749146:
at the heart of the Orcia Valley with a view on Pienza.
- **Chiusi/Città della Pieve**
Madonna delle Grazie
farm holidays
Madonna delle Grazie

6 (on the road from Ponticelli and Città della Pieve);
t. 0578299822:
family-run business with swimming pool and horses; oil, wine and vegetables from organic farming.
- **Solomeo**
Locanda Solomeo
piazza Alberto dalla Chiesa;
t. 0755293119 (www.solomeo.it):
country house with swimming pool immersed in the tranquility of the medieval village.
- **Spello**
"Le due Torri"
farm holidays
via Torre Quadrana 1, Limiti di Spello (on the Cannara-Spello station road);
t. 0742651249:
excellent stage point with swimming pool before challenging the Apennines.
- **Colfiorito**
Villa Fiorita Hotel
via del Lago 9;
t. 0742681125:
traditional hotel near the pass.
- **Castelraimondo-Matelica**
Il Giardino degli Ulivi
farm holidays
Castel Sant'Angelo (6 km from the crossroads on the road to Matelica);
t. 0737642121-

0737640441:
splendid position; romantic atmosphere, excellent cuisine.
- **Cingoli**
Gli Ulivi farm holidays
via Capovilla 41, haml. of Torre di Cingoli;
t. 0733603361:
family-run.
La Corte sul Lago
farm holidays
haml. of Moscosi 32 (before the town, overlooking the lake);
t. 0733612067:
typical products.
- **Sirolo–Mount Conero**
Il Girasole
farm holidays
via Loretana 277, Camerano;
t. 0717304033:
open countryside, a few minutes from the seaside; excellent cuisine and local products (oil, wine, fruit).
Il Ritorno
farm holidays
haml. of Coppo via Piani d'Aspio 12, Sirolo;
t. 0719331544:
in the Conero Nature Park; horse trekking.
Il Corbezzolo
farm holidays
via Piancarda 124, Massignano;
t. 0712139039:
traditional gastronomy and horse trekking.

Styria
The Mur cycle lane

355 Km

ABOVE, the Marktplatz at Tamsweg.
PAGE OPPOSITE, Weisspriachtal, the vast valley near Fannins.

Along the Murradweg, the path starting from the Alti Tauri mountains and crossing the length and breadth of Styria. From the majestic mountains to the "miraculous" thermal springs of Bad Radkersburg, you cross woods, countryside, small villages and the charming Graz. Due to the length of the itinerary, each stage has the progressive mileage in brackets.

You start your trip from the **Sticklerhutte refuge**, at an altitude of 1,752 m, a one and a half hour's ride from the sources of the River Mur.

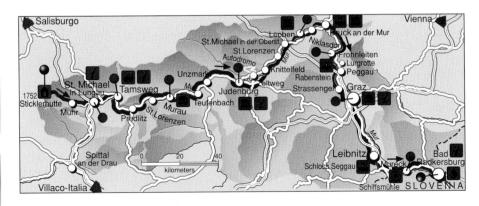

POINTS OF INTEREST

Graz: *the Schloßberg park, the Clock Tower, the Landhaus (Parliament), the Town Hall in the downtown Hautplatz; the Sackstraße, the antique shops street; the Hofgasse with the woodcarved portal of the Edegger-Tax court bakery; the Glockenspielplatz, famous for its carillon that chimes at 11 a.m., at 3 and 6 p.m.; the Cathedral and the Mausoleum which, together with the Burg (seat of the Styrian Government) and the Opera Theatre, form a monumental complex known as the "city crown of Graz".* **Bad Radkersburg:** *the old town center with the Town Hall Tower, the statue of Saint Mary, the Renaissance Herberstorff Palace and the Museum of History and Local Traditions.* **Mariahof,** *near Teufenbach: the Bird Museum.* **Knittelfeld:** *the Seckau Abbey (visits from 10 a.m. to 5 p.m.).*

You can reach the starting point of the cycle lane by taxi (passengers + bicycles) from St. Michael in Lungau. Only the more practiced cyclists can try to reach the refuge by bike: it's only 13 km away from Muhr, but you have to brave the 650 m rise, mostly squeezed in the final part of the road with gradients ranging from 10% to 19%.

After crossing the village of Muhr, you reach **St. Michael in Lungau** (26 km) along a mainly downhill route. St. Martin (hamlet next to St. Michael) is the ideal spot to leave your car (parking lot near the chairlift), organize the ride by taxi to the Sticklerhutte and the return trip from Bad Radkersburg (end of cycle lane), making your reservation at Bacher Reisen in Meixnergasse 30, t 0043 6477347, fax 004364777606.

The cycle lane reaches **Tamsweg** (41 km), capital of Lungau, brushing the villages of St. Margareten and Unternberg, ideal stages to stop and snack, on a level and very pleasant route. This charming town is worth a visit, especially to the wonderful market square and the St. Leonhard Church.

From Tamsweg, take the 95 main road that steadily drops towards Ramingstein, then take the nice cycle lane, partly unleveled, immersed in the green expanse that follows the hydrographical left side of the river and passes near Predlitz. Continue your ride far from motorized traffic through Stadl an der Mur and St. Lorenzen, until you reach **Murau** (80 km), one of the most beautiful medieval villages along the Murradweg. A sight worth seeing is the Beer Museum.

From Murau, you can either continue your ride on the R2, along the left hydrographical side of the Mur, following the Bundesstrasse B26, or you can take the alternative route along the hydrographical right side, on a more challenging and mainly dirt route, up to Frojach, where you get back on the R2 (in this second case, it would be wise for you to ask for the conditions of the route first), then you continue your ride to Teufenbach and St. Lorenzon, where you turn left. Cross the River Mur on a picturesque covered wooden bridge and ride down to the bottom of the valley that narrows at this point, then pass by Unzmarkt, and keeping left of the river, reach **Judenburg** (130 km). The cycle lane emerging

from Judenburg is really beautiful, crossing a park in the initial stretch, then the Fisching countryside. Now continue riding towards Zeltweg, famous for its F1 circuit, and Knittelfeld, where we suggest taking the southern alternative route (Südvariante) of the R2 reaching Leoben and passing by St. Margarethen, St. Lorenzen, St. Stefan and St. Michael in der Obersteiermark, where it reconnects to the main route of the R2. Cover a further 11 km with a few forest stretches, before you emerge at the quaint town of **Leoben** (183 km), an ideal spot to stop in the magnificent Hauptplatz. Exit the town center of Leoben, riding along the 116 main road; after reaching Niklasdorf, near a supermarket, turn left, crossing the river and taking the track that passes by Oberaich and continues up to Bruck an der Mur. Points of interest here are the castle and the town hall. Parallel to the railroad,

Technical info

Route
355 Km: Muhr-Bad Radkersburg. On cyclable tracks, by-roads (sometimes unleveled) and very short stretches on main roads.

Difficulty
The first stretch of the route has a varied altitude with lots of up and downhill sections (only a few tough). From Leoben to Graz, the route is slightly rolling, while in the final part, from Graz to Bad Radkersburg, the road is level.

Cycling period
From June to September.

Cycling time
7-12 stages in 8-15 days.

Bicycle + Car
Across the Tarvisio pass, with a further stretch to Villach, the Katschbergtunnel and St. Michael exit.

Bicycle + Train
You reach Salzburg by taking the Brennero-Innsbruck line and then continue towards Bischofshofen, Radstadt and Tamsweg (via Murau). Otherwise, you can reach the Bischofshofen station on the Udine, Tarvisio and Villach line and continue towards Radstadt and Tamsweg.

Bicycle + Airplane
The Salzburg airport is about 120 km away.

Map
Murradweg-entlang der Mur und der Mürz, published by Schubert & Franzke, 68 pages with 1:100,000 maps: detailed description of the route, up-to-date information and excellent readability of the maps. Available at Austria Turismo or on sale at local tourist offices.

Road signs
"Murradweg" or "R2" green boards designed exclusively for cycle tourists.

Bicycle rental
21-gear touring bikes, 24-gear mountain bikes, bicycles for children and bicycles equipped for child transport (baby chair) can be rented in almost all the main centers crossed by the cycle lane: just contact (better in advance) the local tourist office. Moreover, you can find a very efficient service at the Tamsweg, Murau, Judenburg, Leoben, Bruk an der Muhr, Frohnleiten, Graz, Leibnitz and Bad Radkersburg railroad stations.

Organized trips
Hik Bik, Via Bolzano 78/2, 39011 Lana; t. 0473550355. www.hikbik.com

Useful addresses
Austria Turismo, P.O. Box 1225, Milan; t. 0243990185, fax 0243990176 www.austria.info/ Austrian National Tourist Board Margaretenstrasse 1 A-1040 Vienna t. 00431588660.

ride along the cycle lane that offers one of the most spectacular and pleasant stretches up to the village of **Frohnleiten** (228 km), an ideal stage point. From Frohnleiten, take the alternative route at the R2 (towards Rabenstein) that constantly follows the hydrographical right side of the River Mur, passing by the Rabenstein Castle. Following the railroad, you reach the gates of **Graz** (264 km), passing by Gratwein and Juden-

PAGE OPPOSITE, Mureck, the floating mill on the River Mur.

dorf. Once you enter the town, the road signs aren't really perfect; in any case, ask for the way to the "haupt-bahnhof", then take, on your left, Annenstraße up to the center near the town hall (Rathaus). The town is worth at least a day's visit.

After reaching the Styria plains, ride smoothly towards Lebnitz, which is actually just brushed by the cycle lane, where you can take a detour towards the Seggau Castle (Schloss Seggau); the lane continues amid corn fields

and wooded stretches just a stone's throw away from the border with Slovenia up to **Mureck** (329 km), where an interesting point here is the floating mill (Schiffsmühle). The final kilometers of the Murradweg on level ground are really great. The lane ends in the splendid historical town of **Bad Radkersburg** (355 km), where you can have the chance to drink fine wine and spend a full day at the thermal park and enjoy the baths, the relax and the Jacuzzi.

---

www.austria.info/
Tourist guides and informational and illustrative material.
• St. Michael in Lungau
Tourist office,
Raikaplatz;
t. 00436477342.
Bicycle assistance
Sport Friedrich,
Markstraße 3;
t. 00436477246.
• Tamsweg
Tourist office;
t. 00436474416.
Bicycle assistance
Zweiradcenter Krug,
Gartengasse 184;
t. 00436474416.
• Murau
Tourist office,
Am Bahnhof;
t. 004335322720.
Bicycle assistance
Intersport Pintar,
Schwarzenbergstr. 7;
t. 004335322397-0.

• Judenburg
Tourist office,
Hauptplatz 1;
t. 0043357285000.
Bicycle assistance
OMV Tankstelle und Servicestation Kaltenbrunner,
Burgasse 85a;
t. 0043357282469.
• Leoben
Tourist office,
Hauptplatz 12;
t. 0043384244018.
Bicycle assistance
Fahrrad Klösch,
Josef Heißl Straße 33;
t. 0043384227555.
• Frohnleiten
Tourist office,
Brückenkopf 1;
t. 004331262374.
Bicycle assistance
Zweirad Baumschlager;
t. 004332162487.
• Graz
Tourist office,

Herrengasse 16;
t. 00433168075-0.
Bicycle assistance
Kastner Ohler-Das Spothaus,
Sackstraße;
t. 00433168700.
Fa. Bicycle,
Kaiser-Franz-Josef-Kai 56;
t. 00433169848-15.
• Mureck
Tourist office,
Hauptplatz;
t. 004334722105-12.
Bicycle assistance
Zentrasport,
Nikolaiplatz 1;
t. 004334723269.
• Bad Radkersburg
Tourist office,
Hauptplatz 14;
t. 004334762545.
Bicycle assistance
Radservice Zentrasport Kolletnigg,
Langasse 31;
t. 004334763766.

Switzerland

The Poschiavo Valley 70 Km
The Bernina Express

An extremely fascinating itinerary along the magnificent Poschiavo Valley, across the Bernina pass and up to Pontresina. The dominant theme of this high-peak tour is the spectacular red train known as the Bernina Express that links Tirano, in Valtellina, to St. Moritz, in Engadina. This is a combined bicycle+train route that allows you to ride at ease in high mountain settings, before eternal ices and rocky walls.

The route starts at **Poschiavo**. Take the red train and climb up the entire valley following daring trajectories that ascend to reach the Cavaglia station, then shortly after, the Alp Grüm scenic road in the presence of the imposing Piz Palü.

This is where the stretch towards the Bernina pass starts (2,300 m): after skirting Lake Bianco and Lake Nair, start the downhill stretch towards the Engadina. Ride down to Pon-

tresina, and from the forecourt opposite the station, start riding along the road to the Roseg Valley. After a short asphalt stretch, you ride on dirt road, rising gently for 7 km up to the Roseggletscher hotel, a possible refreshment spot (watch out for the prices!).

From here, continue cycling

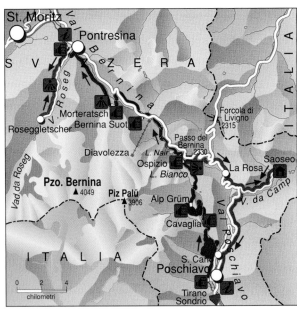

along the valley for a short stretch, then get off your bike when the path gets rougher and continue on foot for about one hour, up to the lake under the ices of the Vad da Roseg and Vad da la Sella. Opposite, you can admire the majestic frozen front of the Pizzo Bernina chain (4,049 m above sea level).

Return to Pontresina covering the same road and catch the train again to climb up to the Bernina pass, where you get off and continue by bike. From the forecourt of the Ospizio Bernina railroad station, you reach, after a short ascent, the pass situated at an altitude of 2,330 m. This is where the second part of the

BELOW, on the Bernina pass (2,330 m). PAGE OPPOSITE, the market square at Poschiavo.

POINTS OF INTEREST

In the Poschiavo Valley, there are numerous activities fostered by the local tourist board: a guided visit to the town, breakfast at the "casaro" (cheesemaker) on the Somdoss alp (2,259 m) in July and August, brunch at the "casaro" on the Palù alp, an excursion to the Cavaglia glacier garden, and a visit to the organic garden, tasting some fresh produce. Another point of interest is the market held in the Poschiavo square (July and August, Wednesday, from 1.00 p.m.) and the organic vegetables market (Friday, from 9 to 12 a.m.). Other sights to see at Brusio: the Bernina railroad viaduct.

At Poschiavo, the Collegiate Church of San Vittore, with its XVIII century portal, the XVIII century charnel-house, the XVII century Palazzo Albrici, with the Sibille hall; via dei Palazzi (Spanish block), the old Monastery (XVII century), a spiritual center for ecumenism and culture, the Baroque Church of Santa Maria Assunta and San Pietro, the XII century Romanesque church. Among the museums, we suggest the one in the Poschiavo Valley, palazzo Mengotti, t. 081-8441571, Tuesday and Friday from 2 to 5 p.m., July and August also on Wednesday.

Weaving in the Poschiavo Valley, palazzo Mengotti, via da Spultri, t. 0818440503, from Monday to Friday, 9 to 11.15 a.m. and 2 to 5.30 p.m.

cycle tour starts, a long fast ride on tarmac into the heart of the Poschiavo Valley.

After approximately 9 km, passing the Plan de Campasc and the hamlet of La Rosa, at the restaurant-hotel Sfazù (1,622 m above sea level), you can take a wonderful detour on the dirt road that enters the Da Camp Valley. After 4 km uphill, you reach the Saoseo refuge, a refreshment spot and starting point towards Lake Saoseo (15/20 minutes on foot).

The itinerary continues on asphalt road dropping gently down to the bottom of the valley. After crossing the hamlet of San Carlo, continue smoothly up to **Poschiavo**.

EXCURSIONS

The Poschiavo Valley offers lots of opportunities, like the

Technical info

Route
32 Km (40 with the detour in Da Camp Valley):
Poschiavo - Bernina pass - Pontresina (by train) - Roseg Valley (by bike) - Pontresina - Bernina pass (by train) - La Rosa - San Carlo - Poschiavo.

Difficulty
The route has no difficulties since the uphill stretches are covered by train. The road to the Roseg Valley is unleveled, although with a hard, cyclable

surface. The possible detour in the Da Camp Valley on dirt road has a 4 km uphill stretch that requires some effort. The way back is all downhill (18 km from the Bernina up to Poschiavo).

Cycling period
Given the high altitudes, ranging from 1,000 to 2,300 m, the best period to cover the itinerary is from June to September.

Bicycle + Train
You can easily reach the Poschiavo station

from Italy, precisely from Tirano, in Valtellina, where you catch the red Bernina Express train. Bicycle transport is regularly scheduled; on the main trains, you can also travel in open observation carriages.

Technical assistance
Claudio Bike,
via Resena 254 A,
CH-7742 Poschiavo;
t. 0041818441378
and 0041794689781;
claudio-bike@bluewin.ch
Repair, rental, sale of bicycles and accessories.

nice easy ride around Lake Poschiavo (you reach Le Prese, then complete the circle: a total of 11.5 km). We also suggest the pleasant excursion to San Romerio (by bike for very trained cyclists only). This is an extraordinary spot, from where you can enjoy a superb view on the valley and Lake Poschiavo. You can reach it on foot from Poschiavo (about 3 hours), the first stretch on a road, then along a track that passes by the Braghi alp, crossing the Terman Valley; or from Brusio, you can reach the village of Viano by bus (or by car), and then San Romerio on foot (2 hours);

by car, reach the parking lot of Piaz (half an hour on foot). On the alp, we suggest a visit to the small church (XII cen-

tury) and a comfort stop at the chalet owned by the Bongulielmi family, where you can rest for the night.

PAGE OPPOSITE, unloading bicycles at the Ospizio Bernina station. RIGHT, the Roseg Valley and the Bernina glaciers.

Map
• Excursion map, *Oberengadin*, 1:60,000, Kümmerly+Frey.
• Wanderkarte, *Valposchiavo*, 1:40,000, Kümmerly + Frey.
• Trekking guide - Bike guide, *Alta Rezia (Valtellina, Valposchiavo, Engadina)*, 1:100,000, APT Valtellina, Livigno, Bormio - ET Valposchiavo, Engadinferien.
Tourist information
• Ente Turistico Valposchiavo piazza Comunale, 7742 Poschiavo -

Grigioni - Switzerland; t. 0041818440571, fax 0041818441027; www.valposchiavo.ch, info@valposchiavo.ch Informational material and special offers.
• *Rhätische Bahn - Ferrovia Retica*, Tirano t. 0342701353 bahnhof. tirano@rail.ch
• Poschiavo; t. 0818440132, poschiavo@rhb.ch www.rhb.ch.
Bibliography
• G. Pedrana, L. Valli,

Il trenino rosso del Bernina, from Tirano to St. Moritz, the tour and the stops. Tourist guide, Lyasis Edizioni, Sondrio.
• Tourist guide, *Bernina Express*, Graubünden - Ticino, Ed. Rhëtische Bahn.
Useful information
Area codes: from Italy to Switzerland: 0041 + subscriber number without the 0 of the area code. From Switzerland to Italy: 0039 + subscriber number including the 0 of the area code.

INDEX OF PLACES

Notes

....
....
....
....
....
....
....
....
....
....
....
....
....
....
....
....
....
....
....
....
....
....
....
....
....
....
....

FANO

City of art and sea

City of Fano
Tourist Service

UBB
Public Relations Office

Marche Region
IAT Fano

FREE GUIDE-BOOK
OF FANO